THE
DROVERS

Evan McHugh is an award-winning author who has written for many of Australia's leading newspapers and magazines, and for television. He is the author of thirteen books including *Outback Heroes; Red Centre, Dark Heart; Outback Pioneers; Birdsville: My Year In The Back Of Beyond* and *Shipwrecks: Australia's Greatest Maritime Disasters*. His guide *National Geographic Sydney* won the PATA Award for Best Travel Guide in the Asia-Pacific, and *Red Centre, Dark Heart* won the Ned Kelly Award for Best Non-Fiction. Evan was born in Sydney and now lives in a vineyard in the Hunter Valley, at the northern end of one of Australia's oldest stock routes.

THE
DROVERS

Stories behind the heroes of our stock routes

Evan McHugh

VIKING
an imprint of
PENGUIN BOOKS

VIKING

Published by the Penguin Group
Penguin Group (Australia)
707 Collins St, Melbourne, Victoria 3008, Australia
(a division of Penguin Australia Pty Ltd)
Penguin Group (USA) Inc.
375 Hudson Street, New York, New York 10014, USA
Penguin Group (Canada)
90 Eglinton Avenue East, Suite 700, Toronto, Canada ON M4P 2Y3
(a division of Penguin Canada Books Inc.)
Penguin Books Ltd
80 Strand, London WC2R 0RL England
Penguin Ireland
25 St Stephen's Green, Dublin 2, Ireland
(a division of Penguin Books Ltd)
Penguin Books India Pvt Ltd
11 Community Centre, Panchsheel Park, New Delhi – 110 017, India
Penguin Group (NZ)
67 Apollo Drive, Rosedale, Auckland 0632, New Zealand
(a division of Penguin New Zealand Pty Ltd)
Penguin Books (South Africa) (Pty) Ltd
Rosebank Office Park, Block D, 181 Jan Smuts Avenue
Parktown North, Johannesburg 2196, South Africa
Penguin Books (Beiing)
7F, Tower B, Jiaming Center, 27 East Third Ring Road North,
Chaoyang District, Beiing 100020, China

Penguin Books Ltd, Registered Offices: 80 Strand, London, WC2R 0RL, England

First published by Penguin Group (Australia), 2010

10 9 8 7 6 5 4 3

Cover design by Cathy Larsen © Penguin Group (Australia)
Text design by Laura Thomas and Arielle Gamble © Penguin Group (Australia)
Cover photograph by Oliver Strewe, Lonely Planet Images
Map © Pamela Horsnell, Juno Creative Services
Typeset in 10/16pt Linotype Centennial by Post Prepress Group, Brisbane, Queensland
Printed and bound in Australia by McPherson's Printing Group, Maryborough, Victoria

National Library of Australia
Cataloguing-in-Publication data:

McHugh, Evan.
The Drovers / Evan McHugh.
9780670072507 (pbk.)
Drovers – Australia – History – Biography
Droving – Australia – History
Australia – History.

636.213092

penguin.com.au

To all the drovers who
gave generously of their knowledge,
and gently put me straight when I strayed.

Contents

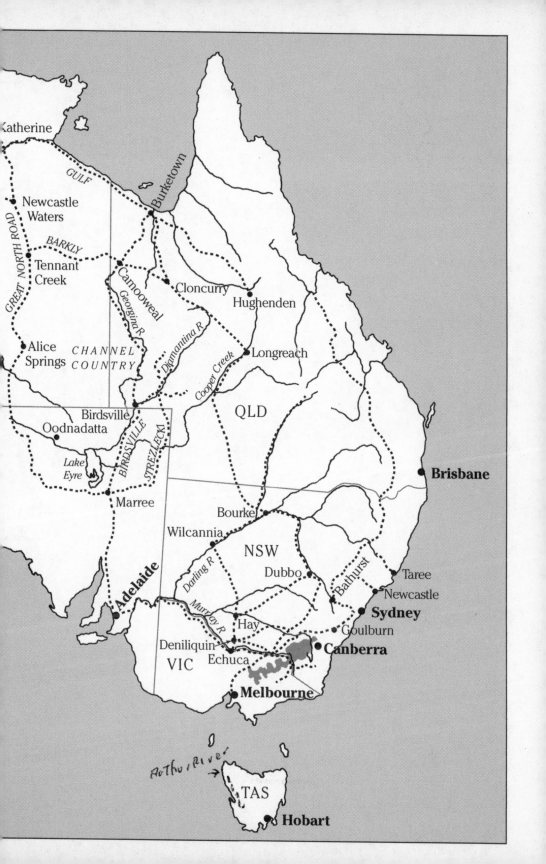

In my wild erratic fancy visions come to me of Clancy
Gone a-droving 'down the Cooper' where the western drovers go;
As the stock are slowly stringing, Clancy rides behind them singing,
For the drover's life has pleasures that the townsfolk never know.

— 'Clancy Of The Overflow', Banjo Paterson (1864–1941)

PROLOGUE

The meandering lines of livestock drifting through the shimmering heat of the outback have long since faded into the never-ending mirage. The road-worn wagons and battered old trucks that followed cattle, sheep and horses from camp to camp now rust and rot. Windmills that watered the stock routes no longer turn. Wells have fallen in. The stock camps, where men and women gathered around the warmth of the fire and human companionship, are scattered rings of stones. Even the graves that were all too common along many stock routes, silent memorials to the dangers of a hard and adventurous life, are disappearing. The wooden crosses have been eaten away. Floods have scattered the piles of stones that marked the passing of a drover whose name was forgotten long ago.

A legendary era of Australian history has all but disappeared. The image of the drover, a solitary figure etched against an unforgiving landscape, embodied qualities of resourcefulness and resilience. A cornerstone of Australia's character, the drover was a symbol of freedom that inspired generations. Whether real or imagined, a life where far horizons set no boundaries has been the envy of many a ruled and regulated clock-watcher.

The drovers who remain are growing old. With every passing year their numbers diminish, and each death marks the loss of living memory of how things used to be. Museums and libraries have become repositories of a way of life recorded in faded photographs, and written and spoken word. Dedicated volunteers, guardians of our national heritage, toil to restore and preserve the remnants of the droving days, from the mountain huts of the Victorian High Country to the wells of the Canning Stock Route. All the more reason to treasure the storytellers who can still recall the days when rivers of cattle, sheep and horses flowed from one end of the country to the other.

Australia was once covered by a network of stock routes. Among the oldest was the Colong Stock Route, in part pioneered by herds of escaped cattle through rugged, untamed wilderness as it crossed the Blue Mountains to the vast inland plains west of the Great Dividing Range. The Hume Highway follows another of the great old stock routes, the Sydney Road, once used to overland cattle from the stations of New South Wales to the new settlement that was to become Melbourne.

Perhaps the most evocative are the stock routes that wound up the slopes of the Great Dividing Range to the highest mountain peaks in the land. Droving in the High Country of Victoria and New South Wales carried many dangers – terrible precipices, weather that could bury stock in snow without warning – but it also took drovers into areas of raw beauty and demanded such daring and skilful horsemanship that, even in their lifetimes, poets were immortalising their extraordinary qualities.

Foremost among these legendary figures was Nat Buchanan, pioneer of many stock routes across the north of Australia. Among his many exploits he pioneered the Gulf Track, opening the way for cattle and sheep to stock the Top End and Kimberley. There, too, Buchanan was in the vanguard, making one of the most audacious droving trips in Australian history – 20 000 head taken from southern and central Queensland to the Top End of the Northern Territory.

Soon after, Buchanan found a shortcut to the eastern Kimberley that was to become one of the most famous, and most treacherous, stock routes in the country – the Murranji Track. Cattle didn't like it; drovers liked it less. Yet the Murranji was the final link in a chain of routes that soon saw vast numbers of cattle crossing Australia from the stations in the north-west to the markets in the south-east.

One of the last of the great routes to be pioneered was perhaps the most famous of them all. Cutting through one of the most unforgiving deserts on earth, the Canning Stock Route was one of the longest in the country and one of the most remote. In the event of an accident, the only help was at the start of the route, at Halls Creek, or at the end of it, at Wiluna, 1400 kilometres away.

The story of droving is also one of interactions with Australia's first inhabitants. For many Aboriginal people, their first contact with the world at large was with drovers. Some drovers treated Aboriginal people well; others responded to the least provocation with extreme violence. The Aboriginal response to the arrival of large numbers of outlandish-looking beasts and men who resembled ghosts was equally mixed. Some were hostile; others became guides for the drovers, sometimes to steer them away from sacred sites or to speed their passage through their lands. Dispossessed of their traditional lands and lifestyles, many eventually became drovers themselves, their knowledge of country an asset to any droving team.

Droving was not an exclusively male domain. Several women won fame among drovers, among them 'Red Jack' and Edna Zigenbine. When it came to the hard life of the stock routes, women such as these were the equal of the blokes. They had to be. There was little room for passengers on a droving trip, and women like Zigenbine

went on to become boss drovers, taking on the responsibility of getting mobs through.

To some extent, the decline of droving runs parallel to nation-
building in Australia over the last two centuries. As rail and road
transport developed, the need for droving diminished. A droving
trip that once took months is now a truck journey of just a few days
from stockyard to saleyard. The turning point came after World War
II, when surplus trucks from the war flooded the market. Trucks
became more affordable and thus more widely used, even in the outback, although the roads (or lack of them) remained a limitation.

In 1960 an estimated 80 per cent of Australian cattle travelled to
market on the hoof; the remaining 20 per cent went by rail. At the
time, the Federal Government was extremely active in constructing
the Beef Roads Network, the success of which can be measured by
the figures for 1961: 80 per cent of cattle were moved by truck and
rail, and only 20 per cent were moved by drovers.

At around the same time, government initiatives spelled the end
of droving in at least one area where the construction of roads has
required major feats of engineering – the Australian High Country
(country above the snow line, generally at least 1300 metres). Throughout the twentieth century, conservation concerns applied increasing
pressure to restrict stock grazing in the Snowy Mountains, Victorian
Alps and the High Country of the Australian Capital Territory. By the
1960s government policy excluded grazing in the Snowy Mountains
and the Australian Capital Territory. Today there are no 'snow leases'
anywhere in the High Country.

It may be good for the environment, but the uncompromising position of governments and environmentalists has led to the demise of
a social and cultural heritage that helped form Australia's unique
identity. Their actions may have also contributed to the extreme
fires that have devastated the High Country, in part due to increased
fuel loads caused by reduced grazing and the exclusion of a burning

regime the High Country drovers inherited from their Indigenous forebears.

As the realities of droving become increasingly distant, it's easy to romanticise the life of a drover. The positive aspects readily stand out – horsemanship, freedom and mateship among them. However, sit down for a yarn with an old drover and they'll recall the hardships – long, lonely journeys through dust, rain and cold in a job fraught with danger and sheer hard work. 'Droving isn't so glamorous after nineteen hours in the saddle,' they'll remind you. They may also point out that most droving trips are pretty routine. Most mobs are well behaved and if the stockmen are doing their job properly, there aren't any problems.

Of course, for a writer, there's not much of a story in cattle and sheep quietly plodding along. Fortunately, many droving tales are compelling. Drovers are revered as iconic pioneers who helped build the nation we enjoy today. While many were extraordinary men and women, most were ordinary people who faced good times and bad with quiet determination. They are unknown to history and their stories will never be told, yet their contribution to the legend of the Australian drover should never be forgotten or underestimated.

It's the unsung heroes, as much as the famous and infamous of droving history, who have left a legacy that will endure long after they've hung up their spurs.

They were re issued on a limited scale but the Greenies managed to get them stopped again - this happed again up to v bad fires about 2005

I dare not ride him for fear he'd fall,

But he does a journey to beat them all,

For though he scarcely a trot can raise,

He can take me back to the droving days.

— 'In the Droving Days', Banjo Paterson (1864–1941)

I

FOLLOW THE CATTLE

In late December 1789, in the icy waters of the Southern Ocean, Lieutenant Edward Riou, RN, in command of the English store ship HMS *Guardian*, was flirting with disaster. The former 44-gun Roebuck-class frigate was carrying 300 passengers and crew, including twenty-one convicts, bound for the newly established colony in New South Wales. She was nearly two weeks and 2100 kilometres out of Cape Town, where she'd supplemented her cargo with as many cattle and horses as the already crowded ship could carry, for the nascent colony was utterly dependent on England for supplies to feed nearly 1500 convicts and their guards.

Riou may not have regarded himself as a drover of the high seas, but he was learning first-hand that there's one thing livestock can't live without – fresh water. On the *Guardian*, the animals were consuming the precious liquid at such a rate that it was certain to run out long before the ship reached the colony in Sydney Cove. Near the desolate storm-swept rock of Prince Edward Island, the *Guardian* sighted a large iceberg, and Riou decided to risk approaching it to replenish his water barrels.

While the ship took up a position to windward, her boats shuttled back and forth, filling empty casks with ice. Throughout the afternoon of 24 December, the operation proceeded smoothly. Just after sunset the last of the boats returned and was hoisted aboard. Then, as darkness fell, a sea fog enveloped the *Guardian* and the crew lost sight of the berg. All Riou knew was that it was perilously close to leeward.

Riou set just enough sail to give the ship steerage. As the vessel got under way, he set a course that would carry the vessel around the potentially deadly ice. To be doubly sure, he posted lookouts in the bows. Tense minutes passed but the iceberg didn't appear.

It was starting to look like Riou had managed to avoid the danger. Then, at around 9 p.m., one of the lookouts cried out that there was a strange pale glow ahead. Riou ordered the helm hard to starboard and the ship swung around into the wind, trying to claw away from the mass that now emerged from the fog. A wall of ice loomed alongside, higher than the frigate's masts. The vessel crept along its face and all seemed well until, with a lurch and the deep groan of her solid timbers being torn asunder, the *Guardian* struck a submerged shelf of ice.

The rudder was all but destroyed and a large hole was ripped in the hull. As water poured in, the pumps were manned and Riou attempted to manoeuvre his stricken vessel away from the iceberg using just his sails. There was soon nearly two metres of water in the hold. A sail was hauled over the side of the ship in an attempt to slow the inflow, but it soon tore as a gale arose and the seas grew mountainous.

Riou and the crew fought until 26 December to save the *Guardian*, by which time the ship was starting to settle by the stern. Many of the crew were begging their commander to allow them to take to the five boats on board.

Riou now jettisoned cannon and the livestock that had been the cause of all his troubles. The ship continued to sink and eventually Riou relented and allowed 259 people to take to the boats and attempt to navigate their way back to South Africa. Riou stayed on board the *Guardian* with sixty-two others.

It was only when the water had risen to nearly five metres in the hold that Riou realised the empty barrels below decks were giving the vessel just enough buoyancy to stay afloat. With his skeleton crew, which included the twenty-one convicts, he set about sealing the gun-deck hatches to help keep more air inside what had effectively become a raft. His men improvised a rudder, then tried to sail the waterlogged ship back to Cape Town.

In one of the greatest feats of seamanship in maritime history, the *Guardian* reached Cape Town on 21 February 1790. In the meantime, all but one of her boats had been lost at sea. A launch with only fifteen people on board had been picked up by a French merchantman at the beginning of January.

In Table Bay, Riou ran the ship aground rather than risk her sinking in the busy harbour. His hopes of repairing the vessel were dashed when a storm lashed Cape Town on 12 April and huge seas completed the destruction the iceberg had begun.

The loss of the *Guardian* is perhaps the most vivid demonstration of the difficulties of transporting cattle and horses on long sea voyages in the age of sail. If you had a choice, you'd opt to drove them vast distances overland rather than put them on a boat.

In Sydney, the *Guardian*'s aborted voyage brought the threat of starvation to the fledgling colony. More than two years after the First Fleet had dropped anchor in Port Jackson, not a single ship had arrived to resupply the colonists. Their attempts at farming and raising stock had been largely unsuccessful, and the stores of food that had been brought from England were almost exhausted. Severe rationing had been imposed, and some convicts had died from conditions associated with malnutrition.

Like the *Guardian*, when the eleven ships of the First Fleet stopped at Cape Town they had taken on board livestock. On behalf of the British government, the governor of New South Wales, Arthur Phillip, purchased two bulls, three cows, three horses, forty-four sheep and thirty-two pigs, plus goats and poultry. He and other officers purchased livestock privately as well.

Unfortunately, few among the 1332 members of the First Fleet who disembarked at Port Jackson knew anything about agriculture. That much was soon apparent to Governor Phillip, who wrote in a report to Under-Secretary Nepean in July 1788:

> If fifty farmers were sent out with their families they would do more in one year in rendering this colony independent of the mother country as to provisions than a thousand convicts.

He could have done with a few stockmen as well, for in the same report he added:

> The greatest part of the stock brought from the Cape is dead, and from the inattention of the men who had the care of the cattle, those belonging to Government and two cows belonging to myself are lost. As they have been missing three weeks, it is probable they are killed by the natives. All my sheep are dead and a few only remain of those purchased for Government.

The cattle that escaped comprised one or two bulls, four or five cows, and perhaps a heifer calf (accounts vary). While Phillip thought the blame lay with the men who were tending the cattle, another convict, Edward Corbett, who had escaped from the settlement at about the same time, was suspected of driving the cattle off in an attempt to supply himself with food. A concerted effort was made to search for the cattle, whose value to the starving colonists couldn't be overestimated, but there was no sign of the beasts. None of the accounts of the time noted that the search was hampered by a lack of horses in the colony, and there were no skilled trackers who could follow what was almost certainly an easily discernible trail. The searchers may also have been reluctant to stray too far from a settlement surrounded by an Indigenous population resentful of the invasion of their traditional homeland.

The hapless convicts who'd been trying to tend the herd on foot may not have realised that the cattle were losing condition on the poor-quality grazing around Sydney Cove; it was probably bad fodder that had killed all the governor's sheep. It's likely that when the hungry cattle caught a scent of better pastures elsewhere, nothing was going to hold them.

A few weeks later, the starving Corbett returned to the settlement, denying any knowledge of the whereabouts of the cattle. It did him no good. He was put on 'proper restoratives' until he was well enough to stand trial for escaping and stealing a jacket. Then he was sentenced to death.

Remarkably, it wasn't until seven years later, in 1795, that the escaped cattle turned up safe and well. Aboriginal people returning from tribal ceremonies around Sydney reported seeing strange beasts to the south-west of the colony. Then two convicts claimed they'd seen the herd on the plains of the Nepean River, while on a hunting expedition. The then-governor, John Hunter, sent the seaman-turned-explorer Henry Hacking to investigate.

The area had been explored as early as 1790 by Watkin Tench, William Dawes and George Worgan, but they'd not seen any sign of the cattle. Nevertheless, Tench recognised the potential of the area when he wrote: 'Progress of cultivation will probably steal along to the southward in preference to the northward from the superior nature of the country in that direction.'

The progress of cultivation may have been creeping, but the cattle were leading the charge. Sure enough, Hacking found the livestock in an area of lush grazing country 60 kilometres from the colony, which was soon to be known as the Cowpastures and is now the city of Camden. However, the herd no longer comprised the original half-dozen or so animals. They'd truly gone forth and multiplied, and now numbered more than sixty.

After hearing Hacking's report, Governor Hunter decided that he had to see the herd for himself. Unfortunately, the cattle were completely wild and the governor's party was 'attacked most furiously by a large and very fierce Bull, which rendered it necessary for our own Safety, to fire at him. Such was his Violence and Strength that six Balls were fired through, before any Person dared approach him.'

This may have been the first recorded encounter with 'scrub cattle', and was certainly not the last. In western Queensland such beasts are known as Mulligan bulls, after the river that forms the frontier to the brooding emptiness of the Simpson Desert. In one celebrated incident on Adria Downs Station, a Mulligan bull charged a passing station vehicle. The impact pushed the four-wheel-drive onto its side, much to the surprise of the station manager at the wheel. When the bull retreated, the vehicle's door was torn off. The bull disappeared into the scrub with the door still impaled on its horns.

Back at the Cowpastures, Governor Hunter beat a hasty retreat, declaring that the cattle should be left alone so 'they may become hereafter a very great Advantage and Resource to this Colony'. The reality was that the cattle had staked a claim to the best pasture in the immediate vicinity of Sydney Town, and the governor lacked the horses and experienced stockmen to argue with them.

Meanwhile the livestock became a 'great advantage and resource' to escaped convicts and the Aboriginal population that was doing battle with the invading British settlers. Left to their own devices, the herd continued to grow. In 1796 there were estimated to be ninety-four cattle at the Cowpastures.

As the pressure of numbers grew, some cattle wandered further afield in search of pastures new. As Watkin Tench had foreseen, the tendency was to head south-west, where the country offered better pastures than to the west and north, where rugged mountain ranges clad in eucalypts afforded little in the way of fodder. In fact the cattle were pioneering the first of Australia's great stock routes – from Sydney to what would be, in years to follow, the city of Melbourne.

In 1798, evidence of how far the bovine pioneers had travelled was found by ex-convict John Wilson, Governor Hunter's servant John Price and a convict named Roe, on an expedition that qualified them as the first Europeans to cross the Blue Mountains. Price wrote that, after crossing the Nepean River:

> We had a fine open country for 7 or 8 miles. We saw the dung and marks of cattle feet all the way till we came to a rockey creek, then we had a nasty scrubby stone country for the remainder of the day.

The cattle had found the ramp that gently ascends into the Southern Highlands of New South Wales, leading to some of the finest grazing country in the world. The discoveries of Wilson and company were not widely publicised, mainly because they'd been sent to prove that escaping convicts weren't going to find a land of milk and honey beyond the fringes of the convict settlement. Travel or settlement beyond the Nepean River was subsequently prohibited, but as increasing numbers of free settlers arrived in the colony and cast about for good country for raising stock, it was inevitable that their eyes would fall on the Cowpastures and beyond.

The cattle, meanwhile, continued to proliferate in the prohibited area. By 1800 the new governor, Philip Gidley King, a career naval officer of limited financial means, was pleased to learn that the numbers of wild cattle had grown considerably. Although newly arrived he was legally the owner of a third of them, having been gifted them by the owner of two of the original escaped cattle, Governor Phillip.

However, just as a bird in the hand is worth two in the bush, so it is with cattle, and it required a resourceful explorer to count them. This came in the person of Francis Barrallier, who led the second European expedition to cross the Blue Mountains. Once again, the scene for the expedition was the country south-west of the Cowpastures, and the route Barrallier took was to become one of the preferred stock routes across the ranges.

In the company of four soldiers and five convicts, and with a bullock wagon carrying his supplies, Barrallier travelled beyond the Cowpastures, heading for the Nattai Gap – a break in the supposedly impassable line of cliffs of the Blue Mountains. On 7 November 1802 he wrote:

After half-an-hour's walk we entered a valley where there was a herd of wild cattle. I counted 162 of them peaceably pasturing; they only perceived my party when it was a short distance from them. The cattle advanced several times, as if they were going to attack us, and I had the greatest difficulty in making them leave the place and allow my party to pass. I had even to send my men to pursue them, uttering loud shouts . . . One can see a large number of well beaten tracks which the cattle have made for themselves in all directions, on the height and in the plain, to reach the hills, which seem to be their place of rendezvous during flood time . . . When I had succeeded in going over that ridge, I saw a second herd of about 130 cattle . . . At a short distance from that place I made my small troop halt, and went alone to the top of a hill to reconnoitre the surrounding country. After walking some 300 paces, on the summit I saw another herd, which I judged was mainly composed of cows and their calves. I was able to count 221 of them, but from the spot where I was it was impossible for me to see them all, and I could only surmise from the lowings, which I heard from various

distances, that the number of these cattle must have been very considerable. I still heard the lowing after I had gone down to join my party,
and for more than an hour whilst continuing my journey.

Tallying all the cattle Barrallier could count gives a figure of 513
head. Given there were only half a dozen cattle in 1788, and that on
his expedition he thought there were many more in the vicinity, the
herd appears to have been growing at close to 50 per cent every year
since the First Fleet arrived.

On 10 November Barrallier left his supply base in the Nattai Gap
and descended to the Nattai River, probably down the relatively easily negotiated Sheehy Creek. As he followed the river, steep slopes
on either side led to towering sandstone cliffs – the famed barrier
to a passage through the Blue Mountains. However, when Barrallier reached the Wollondilly River and turned south to follow it
upstream, within a few kilometres he was in a broad grassy valley,
part of which now lies beneath the waters of Warragamba Dam's
Lake Burragorang.

To the east the slopes were topped with cliffs, but to the west the
mountains rose more gently. After exploring the river for several kilometres south, Barrallier turned west and ascended the gentle slopes.
Various authorities have suggested that his route led up the Tonalli
River to the ridge between the river and Byrnes Creek.

Barrallier's chart of his exploration is difficult to interpret, while
his journal, handwritten in French, doesn't record daily courses and
distances. Nevertheless, he was clearly able to make progress westward and his way wasn't blocked by unscalable ramparts of stone.
After penetrating a short distance inland, and meeting with the chief
of the Gangangara, seemingly on good terms, he returned to the Nattai Gap to resupply.

On 22 November Barrallier set off once again, with five of his best
men, to further his explorations. This time he almost certainly took

old silver mineing Town

the easier route up the slopes south of the Tonalli River and pushed further inland, probably to the present-day locality of Yerranderie. On the 24th, he climbed a hill to survey the route ahead and saw what he described as three large openings in the hills to the west.

The next day Barrallier headed towards the gaps in the hills. During the afternoon, storm clouds built up in the hot and humid late-spring air. Towards evening the storm broke in a monumental deluge, accompanied by thunder and lightning. Despite the wild weather, Barrallier sent two of his men to scout further ahead.

They soon returned with the news that they had arrived at 'an immense plain; that from the height they were on the mountain they had caught sight of only a few hills standing here and there in this plain; and that the country in front of them had the appearance of a meadow'.

Barrallier pressed ahead, through what is now known as Barrallier's Gap, to see for himself. On what was most likely the eastern side of the Bindook Highlands, he and his men set up camp for the night. As far as Barrallier was concerned, the Blue Mountains had been conquered. He wrote that night:

> After everyone was sheltered they congratulated themselves with having succeeded in accomplishing the passage of the Blue Mountains without accident.

Barrallier was certainly on the right track, but late in the afternoon of the following day he found his way to the west checked by the deep ravine of what was probably Ruby Creek. The narrow ridge he was following turned south but he decided to continue in a westerly direction. He was soon back in very difficult country. As he wrote:

> The current of this river is very rapid, and flows between two chains of very high mountains, which give to only one part of its banks an

accessible space . . . Very often I could not find any passage at all, and
was obliged to walk on the slopes of the steep mountains at the risk of
falling from the precipices into the water.

In fact, if Barrallier had followed the ridge he'd been on, he would
have found himself on Mount Werong, only a few kilometres away,
astride the Great Dividing Range and overlooking the headwaters
of the Abercrombie River, which flows west into the Lachlan and
the Murray–Darling system. He'd actually strayed from the general
course of the Oberon–Colong Stock Route, which until 1962, when
Lake Burragorang was formed, could be driven from Oberon to the
Cowpastures.

Barrallier's supplies ran low and his expedition turned into something of a swimming party as he and his men retraced their route
and spent the hot afternoons refreshing themselves in the many
pools they encountered on the streams they were following.

There are some suggestions that Barrallier encountered cattle in
the Burragorang Valley, and that he was told by an Aboriginal guide
that the sound of livestock he'd heard at night was actually a frog.
There was no doubt about the encounters once they ascended the
Nattai Gap and found a wagon driver on 4 December. The man told
him the governor had sent three men to try to catch some of the wild
cattle. The men, on foot, were going to set traps for the cattle. Wrote
Barrallier: 'The Governor had promised these men great encourage-
ments if they succeeded.'

It would have been helpful if he'd given them some horses, but
Governor King was a naval man to whom the notion of mustering
must have been a complete mystery. It didn't go well for the governor's men. On 5 December, Barrallier wrote:

The men who had been set to try and catch the cattle, and who had
left here early in the morning, returned in the evening very tired and

unsuccessful. They told me they had met a bull which was very lame from a wound inflicted by a spear thrown at him by some native defending himself, and which it still had in its side. This spear came three or four feet out of the side of the poor animal, and formed an acute angle with its legs.

Barallier assumed the beast was speared in self-defence. However, in subsequent years many Europeans who discovered livestock killed or injured in a similar manner were more likely to accuse indigenous Australians of attacking the beasts, either for food or in reprisals for trespassing on their lands. A pattern soon emerged where starving Aborigines, who had traditionally hunted native animals, faced punitive raids when they killed the livestock that had replaced their quarry.

After Barallier's return to civilisation he delivered his report on his discoveries, but history failed to accord him credit for finding a route across the Blue Mountains. In fact, he himself recorded that after he thought he'd crossed the range, he'd encountered more precipitous ravines that barred his passage west. If only he'd turned left, instead of descending to Ruby Creek, he might have pioneered what became one of the first stock routes across the Blue Mountains.

The Colong Stock Route is not so much a stock route as the only way through an otherwise impenetrable wilderness. The Colong eventually became a road, which was cut by the flooding of Lake Burragorang in the 1960s. What remains threads through what is now a World Heritage Area, a region of soaring cliffs and thickly wooded gorges. Four deep valleys have been carved from the sandstone ranges by the Coxs, Kowmung and Jenolan rivers, and Kanangra Creek, and the plunging gorges remain the domain of kangaroos, lyrebirds and only the most resilient bushwalkers.

For those who venture into the region on foot or along a handful of four-wheel-drive trails, it is a wild landscape of compelling beauty that is protected by its inaccessibility, despite being on the doorstep of Sydney, the largest city in Australia. The modern visitor sees what the first Australians saw, what Barallier saw and what drovers on the Colong Stock Route saw.

It is possible to explore much of the Colong Stock Route, approaching from the township of Oberon and driving the route to Yerranderie, accessible to two-wheel-drive vehicles in dry conditions. The road follows the stock route simply because there's no other way in – at several points near Mount Werrong, the narrow ridge is only metres wide, with almost sheer drops of hundreds of metres on both sides.

It is also possible to trace another route through the mountains along the Coxs River, at the foot of the escarpment that explorers Blaxland, Wentworth and Lawson followed in 1813, when they became the first Europeans officially credited with crossing the Blue Mountains. Like the Colong Stock Route, the Coxs River route satisfied the two main requirements for stock – water and feed – while the explorers' route was parched and mostly barren. In fact, when Blaxland's party reached the far side of the Blue Mountains, they were forced to make the treacherous descent from Mount York in order to obtain sufficient feed in the valley below to enable their horses to make the return journey. Indeed, once the road over the Blue Mountains was completed in 1815 and settlement extended rapidly into the interior of New South Wales, drovers moving livestock preferred the easier going of the Coxs River and, in later years, the Colong.

It was a similar story with the terrain north of the settlement of Sydney Cove, where the mountainous country was almost as rugged as that to the west. Routes such as that now largely followed by the Putty Road, from Windsor heading north to Singleton in the Hunter Valley, were probably pioneered by cattle rustlers before being officially recognised in the 1820s. As with the Colong Stock Route, in places the route was forced to follow narrow ridges flanked by cliffs and deep ravines.

In the early years of settlement in New South Wales, the communities on the coast north and south of Sydney found it was easier to send cattle to market by sea. They were landed in Darling Harbour, where the slaughterhouses and tanneries were located. Nearby, the precinct known as the Haymarket provided feed for the landed livestock.

Meanwhile, the stock-route pioneers, the descendants of the First Fleet cattle, continued to spread to the south and west of the growing colony centred around Sydney. By 1811 it was thought there were between 4000 and 5000 cattle around the Cowpastures. They were prevalent in the Burragorang Valley in the 1830s, by which time they were considered good sport for hunters. They were still being sighted in the upper reaches of Coxs Valley as late as the 1930s. Given time, the cattle had followed their appetites and found their way across the Blue Mountains on their own.

It is a curious irony that the only area that offered straightforward access to the interior of the country, with good feed and water along its distance, was closed to the early settlers. The early governors of New South Wales, prison wardens in all but name, feared an exodus of convicts to the south-west's greener pastures and forbade any settlement beyond the Nepean River.

It wasn't until wealthy landowners sought to expand their interests that the pressure to extend settlement beyond the Nepean led to confrontations with the autocratic governors. Land grants were made to men such as John Macarthur at the Cowpastures as early as 1803, but their eyes were already looking further afield. Stockyards *were* may have been built at Picton, 15 kilometres south of the Nepean, as early as 1805. Within a few years, squatters were taking up land far beyond the gazetted settlements. By the mid-1820s they'd reached as far as present-day Canberra. Soon cattle and sheep in rapidly growing numbers were heading for market in Sydney from the south-west, following the stock route pioneered by the ex-convict explorer John

Wilson and the First Fleet cattle. Wilson and those cattle didn't get any credit for their achievement. Instead, the route carries the name of the explorer who followed the convict who followed the cattle. It's called the Hume Highway.

I loved the wide gold glitter of the plains
Spread out before us like a silent sea,
The lazy lapping of the loose-held reins,
The sense of motion and of mystery...

— 'The Overlander', Will Ogilvie (1869–1963)

2

THE OVERLANDERS

If there was one thing that could compete with cattle when it came to increasing in numbers, it was the European settlers. Between 1810 and 1825, the population around Sydney grew from around 10 000 to 25 000. The restraints on settlement imposed by the military governors had more than a touch of King Canute about them, as a growing tide of free settlers arrived with a voracious appetite for agricultural land.

After Governor William Bligh was overthrown in the Rum Rebellion of 1808, he was replaced by Lieutenant-Governor Lachlan Macquarie in 1810. Macquarie was a military man but his ambition was to lay the foundations of a nation, not just a penal settlement.

Under his administration, a route over the Blue Mountains was 'discovered' in 1813. His land grants and expansion of properties to the far side of the Blue Mountains soon led to grants being made in the south-west as well. In 1815, the same year the road to the golden west was opened, Surveyor-General John Oxley took up a cattle

station near Bargo, 35 kilometres south of the Cowpastures and the
Nepean River. Bong Bong Station, near Moss Vale on the northern
edge of the Southern Highlands, some 35 kilometres south of Bargo,
was officially settled by Dr Charles Throsby in 1819, although settlements are thought to have existed in the area from 1817.

The rich grazing and fine sheep country of the Highlands drew
explorers and settlers south and south-west. Goulburn, 200 kilometres
from Sydney, was soon well established, and for a time it was the base
for the expansion of settlement into the Monaro. Black Mountain, in
the centre of what is now Canberra, was reached in 1820 and Joshua
Moore settled a property called Canberry in 1823. Duntroon station
was settled by Sydney merchant Robert Campbell in 1825. By then
the Monaro Plains, east of the Snowy Mountains, had been discovered
and they were settled soon after. The Yass area, 300 kilometres from
Sydney, was explored by Hamilton Hume in 1821, and he eventually
took up land and settled in the region. Hume and William Hovell
pioneered the route from Yass to Port Phillip in 1825.

The pace of squatting on the rolling plains south-west of the Great
Dividing Range was often far in advance of official surveying and legislative processes. In some areas, runs could be leased for minimal
rents until the government offered them for sale. The run-hunters'
hope was that properties far from settlement wouldn't attract much
interest and could be acquired for almost nothing.

Willie Ploma Station at Gundagai, 400 kilometres south-west of
Sydney, was settled in 1826, and runs were settled along the Tumut
River in 1828. The first runs on the Murray River at Albury, another
200 kilometres further south, were taken up in 1834, the year before
the first settlers arrived by ship in Port Phillip and began settlement
of what would become Melbourne.

Not surprisingly, graziers were tempted to send livestock south
through 'no man's land' to this potential new market, which was 300
kilometres to the south of Albury. The practice became known as

overlanding and, while it had its perils, it was in many ways preferable to transporting livestock by sea. Overlanding was the forerunner to droving, but it differed in two ways. First, it followed no established stock route, although it might pioneer such routes. Second, it tended to take stock from established stations to new areas, whereas droving took stock from established stations to markets or to other stations.

The first of the overlanders was Joseph Hawdon, in company with a Hobart banker named John Gardiner and a sea captain called John Hepburn. Regrettably, Hawdon kept no account of his historic trip, and only briefly referred to it in the journal he kept while overlanding cattle from Melbourne to Adelaide in 1838. Wrote Hawdon:

Towards the close of the year 1836 I travelled overland from the Murrumbidgee River to the new Settlement of Port Phillip, taking with me a herd of upwards of three hundred head of cattle, being the first expedition of the kind ever performed between that Settlement and the parent Colony. The distance I travelled over that portion of the country which was uninhabited was rather more than three hundred miles [480 kilometres], which I accomplished in three weeks and five days, arriving with the stock in perfect safety.

Port Phillip was then of very recent formation, the first Commandant, Captain Lonsdale of the Fourth or Queen's Own Regiment, having proceeded from Sydney by sea about the time I performed this first journey by land. The example of my success led the way to so extensive an emigration from the elder districts of the Colony, that within the last eighteen months there have been taken overland about five thousand head of horned cattle and about one hundred and fifty thousand sheep. The value of land within the new Settlement has consequently risen at a rapid rate.

Hot on Hawdon's heels was Charles Bonney. Also late in 1836 he explored the possibility of taking sheep overland from Charles

Ebden's Mungabareena Station on the Murray River to Port Phillip, following the track Hawdon took with his cattle. Initially, Bonney and his small exploration party were forced to retreat due to flooding in the Ovens River. In December 1836 he attempted the journey a second time and reached Melbourne early in 1837. In March he took 10 000 head of sheep over the same route, the first person to do so.

South of the Murray, the route became known as the Sydney Road and followed the approximate route of what became the Hume Highway. In New South Wales, the Great South Road, now also called the Hume, follows much of the original stock route, in particular the stretch from the Murrumbidgee to the border.

It was another of the first overlanders, Alexander Fullerton Mollison, who wrote the earliest detailed account of the journey from New South Wales to Port Phillip. He set out on the journey in April 1837, leaving Uriara Station (now Uriarra), near Canberra, with approximately 5000 sheep, 600 or 634 cattle (accounts vary), twenty-eight or forty bullocks, twenty-two horses and thirty men (some accounts erroneously refer to forty-five men). In addition, he was accompanied by an overseer named Donald McLean, and three Aboriginal men referred to as 'native boys'. His 'plant' – the equipment and horses used for overlanding or droving – included four bullock and two horse drays.

Born in 1805, Mollison was the son of a London merchant. He arrived in Australia in 1834 to work as a surveyor, and spent time in the field experiencing the Australian bush first-hand. The energetic young man, wearing a full beard in the style of the times, soon saw a chance to better himself, as the settlement in Melbourne presented an opportunity for someone of limited capital such as himself to establish a substantial property holding.

Mollison formed a syndicate to buy the station at Uriara for use as a collection point for the livestock he intended to take to the Port Phillip region, where he would go run-hunting. Purchase of the station would mean he was eligible to be assigned convict labourers, but in the list of shepherds and watchmen he provides at the beginning of his journal he makes no reference to the legal status of his men.

By early 1837 Mollison had sufficient stock for the journey, although many of the animals were in poor condition, having been brought from as far as the Lake Macquarie area, some 150 kilometres north of Sydney. For a man like Mollison, the key advantage of overlanding rather than shipping cattle to Port Phillip was cost. Shipping livestock not only incurred freight charges, but the animals also had to be supplied with sufficient feed to sustain them on their journey. Overlanding meant the feed came free of charge from the land, assuming there was sufficient available.

Mollison's herds, flocks, mobs and sundry components of his diverse menagerie set out from Uriara on 11 April 1837. Mollison brought along netting to build temporary yards in which to pen the stock, but on his first night he chose instead to have fires lit around the herds and flocks. His men watched them throughout the hours of darkness.

The next day, five working bullocks were missing. Mollison pressed on without them but by the following morning fourteen more had disappeared. Having lost half the bullocks needed to pull his drays, he couldn't go on, and he forfeited two days while a search for the missing animals was made.

A hint at relationships with the Aboriginal people in the upper Murrumbidgee comes from an early entry in his journal: '[The fourteen bullocks] were found by some native blacks on the 15th and brought to the camp.' The five other missing animals were found by a stockman from one of the stations Mollison had passed through. He paid the man who returned them 40 shillings, but there was no mention of a reward for the 'native blacks' who'd returned the fourteen a few days before.

With several setbacks, and time spent searching for missing stock, it took the party eleven days to cover the 90 kilometres from Uriara to Yass, essentially following the course of the Murrumbidgee River.

Mollison noted that the cattle weren't travelling well. On 22 April, at the Yass River, he wrote:

> The cattle so very weak that several bogged, or stuck fast in the mud of the crossing place at Yass. 2 died and 2, I sold for 10/- each. These cattle had most of them been lately driven to Uriara from distant places, and then tailed [shepherded or droved] over very bad feed.

Mollison moved on to the vicinity of present-day Bowning, the boundary of the lands that were available to be purchased at the time. There he was delayed because he needed some running repairs to be done by the local blacksmith. The problem was that the blacksmith was drunk, and remained so for several days. Wrote Mollison, with increasing exasperation:

> 24th. Waiting for repair of drays and horse shoeing.
> 25th. The same, Blacksmith being drunk, did little work.
> 26th. Blacksmith still drunk.
> 27th. Still waiting for Blacksmith's work.
> 28th. Several horses still unshod, moved on to Connor's Creek.

By 1 May Mollison had reached Jugiong, where he was able to get his smithing done at the comparatively sober Burton's Forge. While he waited, overseer McLean went in search of 105 lambs 'lost by the neglect of Green and Crier, the shepherds'. McLean found all the lost lambs, including three that had died.

The weather turned cold and wet at Jugiong, where the late-autumn nights can be bitterly cold. Locals today talk of a 'lazy wind' that can't be bothered going around you; instead, it goes straight through. The bad weather was too much for many of the stock and in one night Mollison lost eight head of cattle and eleven sheep. Four other cattle were too weak to travel and were left behind.

With his shoeing done, Mollison pressed on past Bogaloro Station, then Muttana and Gundaguia (sic). It was at Gundagai that he found it necessary to cross the south-westward-flowing Murrumbidgee River. Today, the Hume Highway crosses the river at approximately the same point, but in Mollison's day there was no bridge, so he sought a ford shallow enough to enable his entourage and menagerie to cross.

The cattle could swim across the strongly flowing current, but things were not so easy for the 5000 sheep. Mollison found that even at Stuckey's Ford, named after the manager of Willie Ploma Station, the water was too deep, and he and his men were compelled to build a temporary bridge. After a couple of days spent finding a suitable location, on 10 May they got started.

This is a pontoon or flying bridge, the drays being drawn in a line across the river and the shafts and poles supported by stakes. Long poles are laid from one to the other, on these we have placed hurdles borrowed from [station owner] Mr Brodribb's overseer and, on the hurdles, green boughs. The tarpaulins are laid on the boughs and triced up at the sides to poles fixed to each side of the bridge, forming a hollow or covered way. Some earth is spread all along the bridge. It is strongly moored to a sunken tree.

The bridge was finished the following day and all the sheep crossed within a couple of hours. Mollison was on his way again, although beyond the Murrumbidgee he found that feed for stock was scarce and in the continuing cold conditions he was losing three sheep a night.

Nevertheless, he pressed on to Tarcutta Creek, where on 23 May he had another Aboriginal encounter. A man named Dapto, and his wife, referred to as his 'gin' by Mollison, visited the camp and informed Mollison that the Murray River was rising, which would make it more

difficult to cross. He also said that a war party was coming from the
river for a tribal fight with the Donmot people. Dapto didn't explain
the reason for the fight, but in this instance it appears the European
settlers were not the target of Aboriginal aggression. Shortly afterwards Dapto left the camp, once Mollison had stopped him throwing
hot coals at his wife and beating her.

The next day, Mollison was delayed once more while he sent two
men back to his previous camp to search for more missing stock.
This time it was two pigs that had been left behind, and the wayward
porkers were returned to the fold that afternoon.

Mollison had so far managed to lose bullocks, cattle, sheep, lambs,
horses and pigs. A week later, he lost one of his men. John Holmes
had been sent to Father John Terry's Billabong Station for milk, and
been told to wait there for Mollison so he could take a message back
to camp. Mollison then forgot about Holmes until someone mentioned
that the messenger had been absent all day, and that he hadn't been
seen at Billabong Station either. Mollison feared that Holmes had got
lost, even though there was a 'beaten cart road' from the camp to the
station, and he sent his men out into the 'severely cold' night to fire
guns and coo-ee. There was no sign of the missing man.

Searches were made over the next two days, with a severe frost
on the intervening night, but Holmes seemed to have vanished. On
2 June, Mollison moved on and camped at Ten Mile Creek, in the
vicinity of present-day Holbrook. It wasn't until 9 June that the missing Holmes was found by a station manager in the district where
he'd been lost. 'Holmes had not tasted food during ten days,' wrote
Mollison. 'He chewed some tobacco, which was consumed on the
third day. He carried the two bottles [for the milk] full of water, but
had no great coat, blankets or fire. When brought to the station he
was very weak and emaciated but recovered in a few days.'

Holmes was soon able to rejoin Mollison's camp, which by then
had reached the Murray River and was making arrangements for

the crossing. The river was a major obstacle on the southward journey and on 14 June Mollison made camp a kilometre from the usual
crossing point on Charles Ebden's Mungabareena Station, near
present-day Albury. He and his men set about constructing a conven-
tional boat and a punt using materials Mollison had brought in his
drays specifically for that purpose.

On 17 June the first 300 sheep were punted over the Murray, forty
at a time. The next day another 800 made the crossing. On the 19th,
wrote Mollison:

> Ferried over Ashton's flock of sheep and drove the herd of cattle across
> the river, swimming. All came out of the water but one cow died on the
> bank. A very strong current carried them 300 yards [275 metres] down
> the stream before they gained the eddy.

While continuing to move his sheep across the river, Mollison was
honoured with a visit from one of the great figures of Australian
exploration. On 22 June he wrote:

> Mr Hamilton Hume, accompanied by Mr George Barber and Dr. Mackie
> of Yass, came to the river this morning. Close to us stands a tree on
> which Mr Hume cut 'Hume River' 13 years ago, when with Captain
> Hovell, he travelled overland to Port Phillip or Western Port. He had
> planted clover and peach stones around the tree but we could not find
> any appearance of their having grown.

Hume had named the river after himself. Six years later, Charles
Sturt named the river that formed a junction with the Murrumbidgee
the Murray, unaware that it was the same river as Hume's. Over
time, the Murray became the preferred title. At Towong, 150 kilometres upstream from Albury, the upper Murray also went by another
name, the Indi, and to this day some locals still refer to it as such.

The Murray's headwaters form the north-eastern boundary of the Indi Wilderness Area.

While Mollison's men were involved in moving the sheep, they noticed three armed men with one horse between them crossing the river from the southern side. Mollison didn't know it but these were bushrangers, members of the Dignum and Commerford Gang. Outnumbered by ten to one, the bushrangers were unlikely to attempt anything untoward. Instead, they told the party that they had been sent by Mr Ebden to look for cattle.

By the 22nd, all the sheep were across the river, with the loss of only one lamb, which had been smothered in the punt. The continuing cold and almost constant rain during the week spent crossing the river took a much heavier toll, with several sheep dying each night. 'Occasionally, too,' wrote Mollison, 'a strong sheep is found dead in the morning without having shown signs of illness on the preceding day.'

Beyond the Murray the rain was turning the ground to mud and Mollison's party could only manage 4 kilometres a day. Mollison was still in the vicinity of the Murray on 30 June when Chief Constable Hooson, from the settlement at Port Phillip, arrived at his camp accompanied by two soldiers and an assigned convict. Hooson explained that he'd spent the last eight days on the trail of three men who had robbed Ebden and a second man, Arthur Burton, at gunpoint near another of Ebden's stations, Carlsruhe, on the Campaspe River near Melbourne. There was no doubt it was the men Mollison had encountered a week earlier.

The following day was again spent searching for missing bullocks, which one of Mollison's men, Bryan, had again allowed to stray. After nearly three months on the road, Mollison's patience was beginning to wear thin. On 1 July, he wrote:

Since we passed Billabung he [Bryan] has constantly neglected his duty of watching the bullocks at night and our men, with few exceptions, have been growing lazy, careless and insolent, causing much delay and injury.

If Mollison made any allowances for the fact that his men had endured cold, wet and extremely rough conditions for nearly three months, he didn't mention it in his journal. Instead, a mutual loathing seemed to be developing between the boss and his workers.

At least Mollison shared these hardships. It's often mentioned that the best boss drovers would never send a man to do a job they wouldn't do themselves. Mollison clearly shouldered his fair share of the work, particularly when it came to retracing his tracks to search for lost cattle, bullocks, sheep, lambs, horses or pigs. He was also responsible for keeping his considerable investment moving towards its uncertain final location. Nevertheless, the trip was taking much longer than Mollison had planned.

At the beginning of July Mollison set up camp on a tributary of the Murray, Indigo Creek, near present-day Chiltern on the route followed by the Hume Highway. He then set off with an Aboriginal guide, overseer McLean and one of his men to examine an area the Aboriginal said would make a good station.

This black, Jimmy, came to us at the Murray and has been daily pressing me to make my station on his ground. We kept Mr Ebden's track towards the Ovens the whole of this day. The first six miles [10 kilometres] over ground so very boggy and rotten that we proceeded but very slowly, leading our horses and wading up to our ankles in mud and water.

It's curious that Jimmy was encouraging Mollison to set up a station on his land. Clearly, he saw advantages in the arrangement – most likely handouts of food and gifts – without realising that it would ultimately result in the loss of his country. Nevertheless, it stands in stark contrast to the presumption that Aboriginal land was usually taken by force.

Mollison felt no danger from the Aboriginal people he encountered, unlike the attitude of three European men he encountered the same afternoon. They'd been returning from the Goulburn River, where they were setting up another station, when they'd met a tribe of Aboriginal men. Mollison noted that they had 'just been much frightened' and gave them powder for their guns.

The following day Jimmy reached his country. It was as good as he'd promised. Mollison found himself on a wide plain with young grass sprouting after being recently burned. There was a creek with plenty of large waterholes. 'We thought ourselves well repaid for our journey from the camp,' Mollison wrote. 'Jimmy was delighted to observe that we were pleased and repeatedly reminded me of it.'

'Cobawm bimble, Bunderambo,' Jimmy told him, meaning there was good country at Bunderambo (now Bontharambo, near Wangaratta). 'Tousand birribi [emu], tousand duck.'

Encouraged by what he found, Mollison returned to his base at Indigo Creek, where he decided he would make camp for a month or so while a thousand of his ewes lambed, and take the opportunity to travel to Melbourne for supplies.

Mollison set out on 12 July with eight men, two drays, twenty-five bullocks and two horses. The recent rains made it hard going for the drays, which frequently sank in quagmires. At the Ovens River, Mollison almost lost his horse. 'He sank suddenly into the mud,' Mollison wrote, 'and it was with much difficulty that we got him on firm ground.'

Four days later they were crossing low swampy ground and creeks when Mollison's problems got much worse. One of the dray drivers, James Byrnes, was leading his bullocks through the swamp. Before he knew it, the animals were in over their heads, thrashing to get free, with the dray full of bedding, clothing, provisions and guns following them into deeper water. They managed to get the bullocks out but the dray was 2 metres under.

In the middle of winter, nearly everything they had was soaked and what little food was left was ruined. Their situation was growing bleaker by the day, but they pressed on doggedly.

Four days later, Mollison came to a creek that comprised a chain of ponds. Most of the creeks in the area were running, but the winter rains were yet to fill the ponds on this creek. Mollison had access to the expedition notes of Major Thomas Mitchell and noticed that this was what he'd described as a 'chain of ponds, running'. In modern times, in his book *Back from the Brink*, Peter Andrews points to these descriptions as indicators of the original condition of Australia's inland waterways, which he believes used to capture much more of the water that passed through them and distribute it across the surrounding country. Overgrazing and logging along the waterways has since degraded the landscape.

Mollison was experiencing that distribution first hand as his drays slogged through the heavy mud and swampy conditions. They were now travelling with very little to eat, and on 25 July his men were so hungry they resorted to trying bush tucker. Wrote Mollison:

These plains abound with the root called by the natives at Port Phillip, 'Murnong'. It is about the size of the upper half of a small carrot. A milky juice exudes through the skin and, when roasted in the ashes, it is palatable and no doubt, wholesome and nutritious. The Port Phillip tribes bake these roots in a hole made in the ground where they half melt down into a sweet, dark-coloured juice. This they call 'Minni'. My men having exhausted their stock of provisions, roasted and ate some of these roots this evening. I ate some from curiosity.

The next day they reached the Campaspe River, where 'a few miles brought us to open forest hills, through which we were proceeding when we saw a horse in hobbles and presently, the sound of an axe directed us to [Barfold] the station newly taken up by Mr Coppock'.

Now that he was no longer in uninhabited country, things got easier for Mollison as he was able to obtain food for himself and his men. By the beginning of August they'd made their way down to the new settlement at Port Phillip, having taken three months and three weeks to get there, although his livestock were still languishing back at Indigo Creek. Mollison was relieved to find that his supplies had arrived by steamer, along with two more hired men in company with a seafarer named Ralph Snowdon.

The sight of overlanders was still a novelty in the fledgling town. A writer of the time described the picturesque attire many wore:

> The gentlemen Overlanders affected a banditti style of hair and costume. They rode blood or half-bred Arab horses, wore broad-brimmed sombreros trimmed with fur and eagle plumes, scarlet flannel shirts, broad belts filled with pistols, knives and tomahawks, tremendous beards and moustachios . . . The arrival of a band of these brown-bearded banditti-looking gentlemen created quite a sensation.

The beards can be explained by the difficulties of shaving in a droving camp. It's possible to shave using a cup of cold water and no mirror, but it isn't pleasant. And if you're out in the middle of nowhere, maintaining your appearance isn't such an issue.

When it came to choosing a place to camp, the New South Welshmen viewed the settlers of what was to become Victoria with mistrust, an attitude that endures to this day. Wrote Mollison:

> I encamped on the Yarra, in front of the settlement and drove the bullocks and horses across the river to prevent their being stolen or hidden, which is frequently done in order to obtain a reward for finding them. Distance from Indigo Creek to Port Phillip, 212 miles [340 kilometres].

The following day, Mollison started loading some of his supplies and storing the remainder. On 4 August he gave his men a day off, ordering them to be ready to set out on the return trip the following morning. Big mistake.

The next day, he lamented in his journal, 'My men drunk and unable to come to work.' On the 6th, 'Men drunk and refractory, refusing to come to their duty.' And on the 7th:

> Men still drunk and unable to work or travel.
>
> In the afternoon succeeded in getting out of town with the drays. Woods and Collins driving, both drunk. At a mile and a half [two kilometres] Collins broke the pole of his dray. Encamped them on the spot.

Mollison had earned himself the dubious honour of penning one of the earliest descriptions of drovers smashing their cheques at the first town they came to after a long trip. Typically, nothing could get them back to work until they'd spent every penny of their hard-earned money.

While the dray was being fixed, Mollison's horse, Captain, escaped. Mollison left Ralph Snowdon, who had decided to join the expedition, with the drays, then spent the rest of the week searching for Captain. He located the horse 'much strained and reduced by galloping in hobbles' on 13 August.

The return journey passed uneventfully until 24 August, by which time they'd reached the Winding Swamp or Broken River. Mollison was forging ahead in a lightly loaded dray while the others followed slowly with the bulk of the supplies.

At the base of Futters Range (now the Warbys), Mollison and his men were hit by a violent storm. It only lasted 90 minutes but the rain turned the ground to slush. Mollison's dray became stuck four times. Each time, the men had to unload the dray and carry the stores through the mud to where the ground became firm again.

'This was the only hard work which any of my men have had to do since leaving Uriara,' Mollison wrote, apparently dismissing night watches, bridge building, punting livestock and at times having to live off the land as having it easy. 'The ground was so rotten that when a man took a bag of flour, weighing 200lbs. [90 kilograms] on his shoulder, he frequently sank down to his knees and then remained fixed until the weight was lifted from him.'

That night Mollison made camp when the dray got stuck again. He left the vehicle in a bog until morning. They'd no sooner got it out, loaded it and set off than it became bogged again. When it happened a third time, within a kilometre of their original camp, Mollison had to admit the dray was too heavy for the soft ground.

I left about one half of the weight under charge of Robinson and the black native Jemmy [probably Jimmy, from Bunderambo], with directions not to move until the two drays came up. Robinson did not appear much pleased at being left alone for a day but consoled himself with the reflection and remark that, 'a man may as well be killed by the blackfellows as be hanged.'

The lightened dray travelled much more easily and within a couple of kilometres Mollison was on such firm ground that he unloaded it and went back for Robinson and the remaining supplies. That night he camped at the junction of the Ovens and King Rivers, the site of present-day Wangaratta. The next day he crossed the Ovens by means of a flying-fox arrangement that took only two hours to get the dray and supplies over the water.

Mollison left instructions for the following drays to wait on the other side of the Ovens because he intended to bring the livestock through to the Campaspe. On 2 September he arrived at his 'station', which overseer McLean had moved further up Indigo Creek, having found better feed for the stock.

Mollison estimated how far he'd travelled. 'Distance from Uriara to Indigo Creek, 191 miles [305 kilometres]. Distance from Indigo Creek to Port Phillip, 214 miles [340 kilometres].' He also noted:

> Thomas Livings, a man employed as a bullock driver, absconded from Indigo Creek soon after I set out for Port Phillip. Mr McLean had sent him to borrow some sugar. He was the most useless, incapable man I ever hired. The men always called him 'Lively' by way of antithesis.

As with his account of his men smashing their cheques, this is one of the earliest descriptions of members of a droving team walking off when they tire of a boss they perceive to be too demanding. In Mollison's case it didn't leave him short-handed, but the departure of a stockman often threw a greater workload onto the shoulders of those left behind.

For the next ten days preparations were made to move the stock on to their ultimate destination. Back with the bulk of the men and unable to be everywhere at once, Mollison was soon having further difficulties. On 6 September he accompanied overseer McLean and the sheep to their first camp, 6 kilometres from the 'station'. The supply dray that was supposed to be following them didn't turn up that night. Mollison wrote:

> Returned by the track to look for the dray with the nets and shepherds' supplies. Found it, as usual, sunk in a soft creek up to the axletree, entirely owing to bad driving and carelessness.

The next day:

> This morning Madden, the bullock driver, returned from the shepherds' camp to tell me that he had lost his bullocks. Before leaving them last night I had ordered this man and another to watch them by turns and

instructed Mr McLean to see that they did so. William Thomas, one of my stockmen, refused to gather in the outlying cattle and absconded in company with two men who I suspect of having absconded from Mr Ebden.

More worrying events developed on 13 September. News came from the camp at the Ovens River that there were 'a great many blacks about'. The men there were fearful that they were in danger of being attacked. Mollison thought otherwise:

I am convinced that their fears are groundless, because Mr Snowdon and the three men with him are armed. Collins [who brought the news] induced two of their boys to come with him and my companion, Jemmy, who belongs to the same tribe, is now quietly 'sitting down' with Mr McLean at Bunderambo, distant only six miles [10 kilometres] from Mr Snowdon. This tribe occupies the same ground between the Murray and the Ovens Rivers, sometimes crossing both rivers. They are inoffensive and docile and, I believe, perfectly trustworthy. I am quite persuaded that these natives and indeed, any of the Aborigines of this continent, might, in one generation, be taught habits of comparative industry if they were treated kindly by masters and protected from the insults of the convict and emancipist class.

As it turned out, Mollison didn't take up land at Bunderambo. The first squatter to do so promptly deserted it after his shepherds, of the convict and emancipist class, were killed by a group of local Aborigines. The land was then taken up by the Reverend Joseph Docker in 1838. Docker established better relations with the traditional owners, who are reputed to have held corroborees near his homestead. The property near Wangaratta, with its ornate towered homestead, remains in the Docker family to this day.

On 14 September, some of the missing bullocks were found by

Mollison's Aboriginal workers, who tracked them easily. There were more delays while enough bullocks were rounded up to be able to get the drays on the road again. The journey of a couple of days to the Ovens River became a matter of a couple of weeks of organisation and effort.

Mollison decided to leave McLean at Bunderambo with the weaker sheep, ewes and lambs. He then became occupied with building huts for the men.

On 5 October Mollison was at the Ovens, preparing to cross. That day he noted the loss of four strong sheep (three ewes and one wether), which seemed to have died without any signs of illness or injury. Mollison examined them closely but could find nothing wrong. One of his shepherds suggested that they might have been bitten by a snake that he'd seen among the flock the day before. It was now late spring and the warmer weather meant the reptiles were becoming more active.

The cattle were swum over the Ovens River on 6 October. The next day the men started moving the sheep over but after 500 had been punted across, the punt sank. When Mollison identified the man he considered responsible, he sacked him on the spot. There was one consolation: 'I was glad to observe that some of the most active men, without orders, swam over the river to assist us when the punt was sinking.'

On 9 October, Mollison had more trouble:

About five minutes after sunset, McGrath, a man receiving eighteen shillings a week, refused to set up a sheep net, although I told him that I would send other men to assist him and that there were two flocks of sheep not yet secured for the night. He said he did not care who took care of the sheep during the night, but that he would not work both night and day. McGrath's ordinary duty is to set up sheep nets and to take care of the sheep during the night, but at the crossing of rivers or in case of accident, to make himself generally useful. He had been working yesterday from nine o'clock until six, but on an average of the days since leaving Uriara, I suppose he has not worked one hour a day. He is another example of the general worthlessness of the emancipated convicts of this colony.

On 20 October, beyond the Ovens, the overlanders' camp was again visited by Aboriginal men. They camped close by but did not appear to be threatening. Then, on 24 October, it was noticed that one of the cows had a broken spear protruding from its rump. The cow was thought to be a stray, one of the cattle that had been left behind when Joseph Hawdon and his mob had passed through the area a year before. Once again, Mollison was diplomatic in his assessment of what might have happened. He reasoned:

This has been done by the tribe of blacks who were with us at the Ovens, but before the cow came into our herd. These blacks knew well that four head of cattle had escaped from Mr Hawdon's men and, that they were feeding at the junction of the Ovens and King Rivers and between the two. They also knew that Mr Hawdon's men had proceeded on their journey and that there was no person looking for the cattle. On the other hand, they saw that our cattle were mustered twice a day and that we were prepared to punish them for any aggression. These considerations no doubt induced them to cross the King River and to make an attempt on the four strays of Mr Hawdon's.

As they continued on their journey and crossed the Broken River, Mollison noted that many of the weaker animals were improving as the warmer spring conditions brought up good feed. The same couldn't be said for his opinion of his men. On 28 October he reported another instance of neglect. One of the dray drivers following the mob was instructed to pick up any young calves that became too tired to keep up with the stronger cattle, and tether them so they wouldn't stray. The driver decided to take a short cut and left all the calves behind. That evening someone had to go back and retrieve them.

Once again, Mollison offered the event as further evidence of the difficulties he faced. 'This is a fair instance of that continual indifference and neglect of duty among my men, which by causing such repeated delays, prevented me from reaching the Goulburn before winter set in.'

At this point in his journey, Mollison and his men had been on the road for six and a half months, long enough for resentments to build from irritations into utter loathing. And it wasn't over yet.

Mollison's trip had highlighted the challenges of overlanding. The route he chose often brought difficulties with the drays when they hit boggy ground. On a stock route, there was generally an established track for vehicles to follow, which deviated from the shortest route in order to skirt known problem areas. As an overlander, crossing rivers involved major earthworks or searches for fording places, whereas drovers often had the luxury of knowing where to go across and the crossings had to some extent been tailored to the needs of travelling stock.

For the overlanders, water and feed had to be scouted ahead of the mob, rather than risk taking them into an area where they could starve or die of thirst. Stock routes often had the benefit of wells, and other drovers could provide some indication of the condition of the feed along the way. Good stock-route inspectors could close a route if there was insufficient feed for a mob to travel through. Of course, there was no risk that the route overlanders took had already been flogged out by a mob that had preceded them. When travelling through lush, virgin country, the stock could have their pick.

As he headed towards the Campaspe, Mollison continued to experience small but vexing difficulties. One of his best bulls was injured in a fight with another bull that had been putting on condition rapidly as the stock found themselves on good spring feed. The prize bull's injuries left him too lame to travel. Mollison had his men rope the strong, young aggressor and branded him on the forehead to make fighting too painful. Within a couple of days, the original pecking order was restored.

Mollison noted that as the weather grew warmer, snakes were becoming increasingly numerous. Three of his dogs were bitten by the same snake. One dog died but the other two, including a puppy, suffered for a couple of days before recovering.

On 4 November Mollison reached the Goulburn River, where the mixed blessings of overlanding were once more in evidence. He wrote:

> Moved the sheep and drays to the Goulburn and encamped them close to the usual crossing place. Before they came up I rode about four miles [6 kilometres] along the river, above and below, but could not find any place more suitable for our operations. The grass on the banks of this river, near the intersection of the road, is at present young, sweet and abundant.

Once more the men built a punt in order to get the sheep across. While the work of punting the sheep went on, Mollison sent men ahead to scout for good water and feed. He was worried because in some of the places he'd camped on his way to and from Melbourne for supplies, he'd found the waterholes and creeks were dry. Fortunately, his men took a slightly different route and were able to find sufficient water and feed for the cattle and sheep to proceed in separate mobs and flocks.

Mollison managed to get all his sheep across the Goulburn by 13 November, after which it took the livestock just five more days to reach the settled areas around the Campaspe River. On 18 November 1837, Mollison set up camp in a deep glen on the Campaspe. His overlanding journey was now complete.

Mollison's journey had taken seven months and one week. It didn't compare well with Hawdon's expedition of just three weeks. However, Hawdon had a mob of just 300 cattle, which could swim across such obstacles as rivers and creeks. Mollison, with a mixed herd of some 6000 head including cattle and calves, bullocks, sheep and lambs, horses and pigs, was reduced to the speed of the slowest animals, and delayed when he had to build boats for some of them. Indeed, if Noah had decided to take Mollison's menagerie to Port Phillip by ship, he would have been well suited for the job.

Mollison was quick to criticise his men for their shortcomings, but nowhere in his journal does he concede that he was himself the architect of many of his problems. There were delays while stock crossed rivers, while they lambed and while he went to Port Phillip for supplies. With many stock cooling their hooves, it was no surprise when they strayed. He started out with stock that by his own admission were in poor condition, and many were clearly not up to a journey of some 500 kilometres.

While the stock that had survived the journey were camped on the Campaspe – tellingly, Mollison doesn't provide a head count of the number that arrived – Mollison went out with a handful of men to find an area where he could set up a station. They roamed west of the Campaspe, then doubled back and headed south-east, towards Port Phillip. The first land that Mollison considered suitable for a station was rejected because it was too close to Port Phillip and would 'invite competition for the purchase when it should be put up for sale'.

Mollison doubled back towards the Campaspe, where he decided that the land he'd seen west of the river was better than he'd originally thought, 'owing perhaps to having seen more barren and inferior ground than I had imagined could be found so near Port Phillip'.

The station he formed, near present-day Malmsbury, comprised 23725 hectares of pastoral leasehold and was called Colliban.

He soon took a leasehold on another 24 290 hectares that he named
Pyalong Station. Mollison bought out his partners in 1841 and sold
Colliban in 1848. He then bought Terrick Terrick Station (near
Bendigo), a 26 300-hectare lease. In 1850, he sold a third of Pyalong
to his brother, William Thomas Mollison, and returned to England.

Mollison returned to Australia in 1859 to sell the remainder of
Pyalong, then again sailed back to England. In 1873 he returned to
what was now Melbourne, dying there in 1885. The manuscript of
this pioneering drover was presented to the State Library of Victoria
by his sister in 1886.

Mollison made only this one epic overlanding journey. Despite
its hardships, frustrations and pressures, it laid the foundations of
a prosperity that he enjoyed for the rest of his life. As such, Mollison
was in the vanguard of an extraordinary expansion that within forty
years would see overlanders and drovers spearhead European settlement across the entire country.

3

THE HIGH COUNTRY

Nestled among twisted and stunted snow gums, the slab hut's windows cast a warm glow into the chilly spring night beyond. On the fading breeze, smoke curls from the chimney and wafts slowly away over the snow grass of the high plain. One more armful of wood should be enough to keep things cosy until morning. From a distance the rustic hut is like a beacon, a bead of light in the all-consuming darkness that promises sanctuary, comfort and companionship. In this, at least, nothing has changed since the first stockmen ventured into the Australian High Country as far back as the 1830s.

The first of them may have followed the Aboriginal people drawn each spring to the mountains to enjoy the protein bonanza offered by prolific numbers of bogong moths (*Agrotis infusa*). It's also possible that shepherds whose flocks were perishing during a drought around the Goulburn district were guided to the High Country by Aboriginal people who told them of lush pastures that were to be found even when the lowlands were parched.

True or not, we do know that in May 1823 an expedition led by
Captain Mark Currie and Major John Ovens was guided by a former
convict, Joseph Wild, to the present site of Canberra and on to an
immense treeless plain that local Aboriginal people called Monaroo
or Maneroo. The fact that Joseph Wild was acting as a guide suggests he was showing Currie and Ovens country he'd already visited,
so the gentlemen could 'discover' it. The expedition continued on to
the present-day town of Bredbo. From a nearby hilltop they sighted
a snow-capped mountain, possibly Mount Jagungal, well to the west.

No sooner had the explorers reported their discoveries than the
squatters swooped, with the first sheep appearing in what would
become known as the Monaro in 1825. In fact, the Pendergast family claimed they'd settled a run near Jindabyne before the Currie and
Ovens expedition. While it may be more folklore than fact, this tallies
with Joseph Wild acting as a guide and Aboriginal people introduc-
ing settlers to the country before that time. The Pendergasts were
certainly on Victoria's Omeo High Plains by the late 1830s. James
Pendergast and three other Monaro squatters are recorded as having located there in around 1839, and the Pendergast family remain
synonymous with the region to this day.

When a physician named John Lhotsky travelled to the High Country from Sydney in 1834, he found himself in a frontier society – hard
people living in squalid conditions. In *A Journey from Sydney to the
Australian Alps,* he wrote: 'I have lived before under absolute mon-
archies and under commonwealths; here I found myself surrounded
by absolute anarchy and lawlessness'.

Some grazing in the area around Kiandra is thought to have
occurred around this time, and stock routes and droving through
the high plains may have begun not long after. One of the features in
what is now northern Kosciuszko National Park is called Port Phillip Gap, indicating that it was a key point for drovers taking stock
to the newly established Port Phillip settlement that would shortly

become Melbourne. This was a tempting new market, but the handful of routes to the western side of the mountains were not for the faint-hearted. Snow and freezing conditions had already discouraged permanent settlement of the High Country, and the elements challenged anyone who risked a crossing.

The dangers of the mountains were documented in *Recollections of an Australian Squatter* by William Brodribb, station manager at Coolringdon, between Cooma and the Alps. Brodribb was the mercurial son of a lawyer who'd been transported to Australia in 1816 for administering unlawful oaths, when Brodribb was aged seven. The young William soon developed a preference for agricultural pursuits around southern New South Wales, but his early ventures proved unsuccessful. In 1843, deeply in debt, he went to work for William Bradley, owner of Coolringdon and other Monaro properties. The association proved fruitful for both employer and employee.

In 1848 Brodribb attempted to take some of his own sheep across the mountains, possibly to a property of his own near Gundagai; as detailed in the previous chapter, Alexander Mollison mentioned receiving assistance from Brodribb's overseer when he was crossing the Murrumbidgee in 1837. Brodribb knew he was taking a risk in crossing the mountains in late autumn, but he decided to chance it anyway. Brodribb wrote: 'I started in May with 1000 maiden ewes and three men, one an old man acting as guide (who professed to know the route), and three horses to carry our supplies, cooking utensils and blankets.'

They travelled for several days, covering a respectable 10 or 12 kilometres per day and crossing several tributaries of the Murrumbidgee River, which in the vicinity of Cooma loops south then north to skirt evocatively named peaks like Yarrangobilly, Nungar, Honeysuckle and Black Cow. Near the 1630-metre Yarrangobilly Mountain, 75 kilometres north-east of Cooma, Brodribb's luck ran out. He wrote:

We reached what is called the 'Port Phillip Gap', about the centre of the tableland on the summit of the Alps. We were overtaken by a tremendous snowstorm; it commenced about 12 o'clock at night, and by daylight the ground was covered with snow six inches [15 centimetres] deep.

Brodribb's guide suggested they get moving early and push hard to reach the western edge of the so-called tableland, most likely Long Plain. Once they started descending, the guide reasoned, they'd drop below the snowline and out of danger. Unfortunately, as the day progressed the storm got worse. The sheep were struggling to make any progress in the blizzard conditions and deepening snow. Even with the help of sheepdogs, keeping the ewes moving along became almost impossible. Brodribb wrote:

The snow became deeper and deeper every hour and it fell so thickly we could scarcely see 100 yards before us, and the guide lost his way. The weather was intensely cold, and as the night closed in we came to a final stand still under the side of a high and woody mountain.

Man and beast were exhausted. The sheep may have had the benefit of their wool, but for the men the risk of hyperthermia loomed large. Brodribb noted he was so tired and 'worn out with anxiety' that he fell fast asleep while standing up. He woke with his head resting on the saddle of his horse.

With their camp blasted by wind and any kindling dampened by the snow, it took a major effort just to get a fire going. The beleaguered men used a couple of blankets to rig up a screen to block some of the wind and snow, and tried as best they could to get some sleep. Huddled for hour after hour, trying to gain some warmth from the flames, it must have been one of the hardest nights of their lives.

The snow fell all that night and throughout the next day, making it impossible to move. Brodribb was starting to doubt whether they were going to survive. As night fell, he wrote:

> Our position became very dangerous; if it continued many hours longer nothing could save us from perishing. At daylight the snow was nearly two feet [60 centimetres] deep, consequently it was impossible to move the sheep, and as our supplies were getting short, it was necessary to determine what had better be done. I made up my mind to leave the sheep where they were with two men, and make a search with the guide to make out 'Yarrangobilly Gap', from thence to a small cattle station down the western side of the mountains, and there procure some additional supplies. Fortunately I had a compass and watch with me, or, in all probability, we should have been lost altogether.
>
> I knew our course ought to be due west, and my guide was taking me north; we rode in this direction for more than an hour, across the spurs of the main range. I requested him to alter our course to west; in half an hour we found ourselves on the water shed to the Tumut River.

'We are all right, sir!' Brodribb's guide exclaimed, perhaps with new-found admiration for the navigational skills of his boss. 'Any of these watercourses will take us to the stock station.'

Brodribb estimated they were no more than 12 kilometres from the cattle station, but struggling through snow and fallen timber, it took most of the day to get there. The station was just a hut, but Brodribb wasn't complaining. 'We enjoyed a quart-pot of tea, damper, and salt beef, with a great deal of relish', he wrote.

Brodribb had been lucky to find the place he identified as Yarrangobilly. The stockman turned out to be on his own, his nearest neighbour some 30 kilometres down the mountain on the Tumut River. There may have been other huts in the area, since stock had been visiting the high plains since the mid-1830s, but so close to winter the shelters that were used for summer grazing would have been abandoned.

It would certainly not be the last time that a High Country drover would be glad at the sight of one of these huts, and Brodribb may have recorded one of the earliest instances of a High Country hut saving a life. He hadn't been there long when another traveller appeared:

> The poor fellow had been five days without any food. He lost his way in the mountains, and he had to abandon his horse, and for two days he carried his bridle and saddle; he became so tired and weak that he had to leave these articles behind. It was merely accident he made the hut.

The following day the weather started to clear, although the snow still lay deep on the ground. Armed with what food the stockman could spare, Brodribb and his guide set out on the return journey. In some places the snow was up to their shoulders and several times Brodribb suggested they retreat to the stockman's hut, reasoning that his shepherds weren't about to starve, having a ready supply of mutton to hand. Once again it took them an entire day to reach the camp, where the shepherds were extremely glad to see him.

The sheep hadn't suffered at all in the harsh conditions, and the next day Brodribb attempted to move them on. He and the other men made paths by using their horses to trample down the snow. 'The sheep followed in the tracks, two or three abreast, and they extended in file for nearly 2 miles [3 kilometres].'

It was a slow and laborious process. The weather was fine but it remained bitterly cold as winter tightened its grip in the Alps. By the end of the day, the flock had only covered a little over 3 kilometres. They had, however, reached the western slopes of the Alps. The next day, when they started to descend, the snow grew shallower and the sheep made good progress. The following day they arrived back at the stockman's hut, 'all safe'.

A few days later, at the township of Tumut, Brodribb delivered the sheep to his brother-in-law James Kennedy, who had married Brodribb's sister Lavinia, while Brodribb had married James's sister Eliza. He then started on the return journey to the Monaro with his men. Back in the Alps, the snow remained but wasn't as deep as before. Approaching Coolringdon, Brodribb's horse became exhausted but he happened to find one of the station's stockhorses. Brodribb mounted up and rode to the homestead, where Eliza and their children were overjoyed to see him.

By 1854 Brodribb had prospered so much from fattening sheep for the Melbourne market that he was able to purchase his own 600-square-kilometre property, Wanganella Station, near Deniliquin. His employer, William Bradley, was sorry to see him go.

'Well, my dear Brodribb,' Bradley wrote to him. 'We part perhaps never to meet again. I need not tell you I regret our separation very much, not because I am losing a valuable manager, but I feel I am parting with an old and valuable friend.'

As a parting gift, Bradley cancelled a debt of £900 that Brodribb owed him, then lent him an additional £2000. It was an extremely generous gesture, but as Brodribb noted, 'I joined him with 18 000 sheep, and 2000 cattle, in August, 1843, and left him December 31, 1854, on Maneroo, with 65 000 sheep, and over 5000 cattle, divided into four separate establishments, with an overseer on each, all under my management and control.'

As he prepared to leave, Brodribb was honoured at farewell dinners attended by many of the leading citizens of the now increasingly respectable Monaro district. Old shepherds travelled great distances to shake his hand and say goodbye. 'On one or two occasions I saw tears in their eyes,' wrote Brodribb. However, the High Country still stood between Brodribb and his property at Wanganella, 400 kilometres to the west.

Having sent his family and much of their belongings the long way around, via Yass, 200 kilometres north, Brodribb set off with twenty saddle horses, five pack horses and sixty-five unbroken mares, fillies and colts. He picked up a mob of cattle and sheep from the station of a man named Brooks, and a guide to show him a route that to Brodribb's knowledge had only been used once before. He referred to the route as 'the way over the Snowy Mountains by the Murray Bogong to the head of the Murray', and believed that it had been used just once to drove cattle, possibly by the Ryrie brothers – William, Donald and James – overlanding 250 cattle to Port Phillip in 1837.

Setting out in early January 1855, Brodribb had no idea what he was getting himself into. Afterwards, he was to reflect 'a dreadful route it is'. From Stewart Ryrie Jnr's station at Jindabyne, it tracked through the heart of the Alps, past 2068-metre Gungarton Mountain and 2061-metre Mount Jagungal (also known as Big Bogong) to the Tooma River, then down to its junction with the Murray Valley at another station, Walaragong (Welaregang), owned by John (later Sir John) Hay. In a straight line it was 75 kilometres, but Brodribb esti-mated the journey to be more like 250 kilometres.

His drovers consisted of six men to help him with the cattle, plus an overseer named Nicholls and two men to take care of the sheep. The number of livestock isn't clear.

The first two days were relatively easy, but in the rough terrain Brodribb found it increasingly difficult to keep the stock together. In addition, he wrote:

My men were young, and greenhorns for driving cattle. I had to be doubly active day and night. I had a magnificently strong little horse under me; he was wire itself, and he stood well to me all through the journey. After crossing the main Snowy Ridge (at this period of the year very little snow is on the mountains), we had to cross a table land, mountainous, and in many places very slushy for about 30 miles [48 kilometres], and very boggy; and in every valley a running stream. Some portion of this country is heavily timbered, other portions open country and rocky; but all well grassed. None of it is occupied; the squatters are afraid of the snow in the winter.

Brodribb's description of his 'strong little horse' suggests that in his time the qualities of the mountain horse that Banjo Paterson would describe in *The Man from Snowy River* were already being appreciated. Paterson described the animal as:

. . . a small and weedy beast,
He was something like a racehorse undersized,
With a touch of Timor pony – three parts thoroughbred at least –
And such as are by mountain horsemen prized.
He was hard and tough and wiry – just the sort that won't say die –
There was courage in his quick, impatient tread;
And he bore the badge of gameness in his bright and fiery eye,
And the proud and lofty carriage of his head.

Paterson was certainly right in suggesting that a mountain horse is not much to look at, particularly to anyone unschooled in the finer points of equestrian confirmation, but ride one up a steep mountain and it will have made a lasting impression long before you arrive at the summit. A mountain horse is the four-wheel-drive of the equine world, and can climb just about anything. They can certainly negotiate terrain that would thwart a trail bike, which is why horses are still the dominant mode of transport in the High Country today.

Brodribb's high regard for his own mount, Hector, may have been due to the constant work both horse and rider put in while crossing the High Country. Nearly every day, Brodribb needed to ride back to guide and help the shepherds, whose flock was struggling to keep up with the faster-moving cattle.

There were one or two nights when the sheep didn't reach camp and had to be camped separately. After the sheep were settled,

Brodribb and Hector still had to ride on to the cattle and horse camp, for, as Brodribb put it, 'they required my personal attention by night'.

After 'many difficulties' in what is some of the most rugged mountain wilderness in Australia, Brodribb reached the western slopes of the High Country. There he was presented with the extraordinary view of the lowlands stretching for close to 100 kilometres out to the western plains. Closer at hand, he wrote: 'I could see the valley of the Hume [the Murray] meandering down 30 miles [40 kilometres] off – it appeared a deep abyss.' Getting down there proved to be a major challenge:

> On coming to the falls of the Hume, the mountains I had to descend were very precipitous and rocky, and the first mountain more than one mile [1600 metres] to its base; and it was impossible to drive down the whole lot at once. We had to cut off about 25 or 30 at first. I forced them down some 300 or 400 yards [275 or 365 metres], to the first ledge of the mountain; leave [sic] two men on horseback with these, while I and the others went back for some more; and so continued until we had the cattle forming a long line to the bottom. All this was attended with much trouble and difficulty, and many of the cattle injured their shoulders, particularly the large bullocks, and some never recovered. Well, at last we reached the bottom of the mountain, a deep valley, thickly timbered, with plenty of grass. The men, cattle, horses, and myself were very much tired; in fact, I was nearly knocked up. Notwithstanding, I had to walk up this steep mountain, leading my horse, for the purpose of assisting the sheep down, and before we got these down to the cattle I was fairly done up, and yet I must, as leader of the party, take my watch during the night. I was truly tired of the journey.

It's not hard to see why Brodribb's men and colleagues thought so highly of him. Not only would he never send a drover to do a job he wouldn't do himself, he evidently did more than his fair share. From start to finish, the trip from the eastern side of the High Country to his new property took nearly a year, during which he never saw his wife or children. He wrote of their first seeing each other:

> O, what pleasure it is to meet those you dearly love! who have been parted from you for months, and after all the trials and difficulties and dangers of a stock expedition of some hundred miles [160 kilometres] across those Australian Alps.

For Brodribb, once (or twice) was enough, but by the mid-1850s other graziers were sending cattle to the High Country every year. As Brodribb noted, the fear of winter snows prevented permanent settlement, but from October to May the mountain pastures offered relief grazing during drought periods. They were soon seen as a supplement to the home station's available feed supply, allowing increased stocking rates.

In 1865 William Bradley's new station manager, W. Davis Wright, commented that the idea had been new when Brodribb had first tried it, but 'now it is one of the commonplace incidents of every station'. Until the late 1880s the practice was largely unregulated. However, in 1889 the New South Wales government amended its land act to allow the first snow leases to be issued.

At the end of summer much of the High Country was set alight to burn off the grasses left uneaten by the cattle, promoting new growth for the season that was to come. In some cases it was Aboriginal people who continued the practice, some of them having swapped their spears for spurs to join the drovers. They were maintaining the burning regime they'd been following for thousands of years, and passing it on to their European colleagues.

Other Aboriginal people came to the High Country from further afield. Around the turn of the last century, a Queensland Aboriginal named Skerry was horse-tailer (the man responsible for taking care of the drovers' horses) for a mob of store bullocks that were driven to Bringenbrong Station. After they were delivered, Skerry stayed. According to stock agent Harry Peck, 'Skerry was a wonderful rider. Mustering in bush country no one could pace him through timber and scrub.' One of the owners of Bringenbrong, Peter Mitchell, held Skerry in such high regard that he made provision in his will for Skerry's upkeep for life.

Photographs taken in the 1920s, when grazing was at its height, reveal hundreds of cattle watering at the lakes around Mount Kosciuszko. In earlier times sheep had grazed the High Country as well, but predation by dingoes, especially on sheep left unattended, took such a toll that cattle were generally preferred. By the 1930s most of the High Country was covered by snow leases, and mountain huts were to be found from west of the newly established Canberra, at the northern end of the Alps, to Omeo in Victoria.

Getting to and from the High Country hadn't become any easier since Brodribb's day. Routes climbed steep ridges from Corryong, Tumbarumba and Talbingo in the west; Omeo and Benambra in the south; Adaminaby, Jindabyne and Dalgety in the east; Tharwa, Brinda-bella and Tumut in the north. In many places, stock ascended more than 1000 metres to the summer pastures. Many of the routes were evocatively named – Jacob's Ladder, the Devil's Staircase – as were the peaks that surrounded them: Mount Terrible, the Fainter and the Pilot.

Some cattle only used the High Country as a route to stations in Gippsland. In the 1880s and 1890s stock belonging to the first 'cattle king', James Tyson, were brought from his Queensland breeding prop-erties to his fattening property, Heyfield Station in Gippsland. When they reached the Murray River, they'd follow it upstream to Tintaldra. There they turned south, and climbed a mountain range called the Gib. In places the track was only wide enough for the bullocks to walk in single file. The track climbed to a saddle 1800 metres high and it often took a day or more to get the mob over. If it took more than a day, the drovers were forced to overnight above the snowline, sometimes in blizzard conditions.

Once over the saddle, the drovers sought a spur that would take them down to the Dargo River. The river was then followed through the mountains until it came out onto the plains, after which it was an easy journey over open country to Heyfield.

In *Droving Days,* first published in 1966, Hector Barker explained that it was only possible for stock to travel the route when the country had been burned off.

> The way they managed was to burn off large areas of the undergrowth, leaving only the big trees standing. Then for the next two years it would be possible to drive the cattle through. *(Reproduced by kind permission of Hesperian Press)*

Perhaps the toughest stock route of all was Hannell's Spur. It was a true 'one miler', a vertical ascent of more than 1600 metres, from the Geehi Flats on a tributary of the Murray River at 500 metres to the pasturage around Mount Kosciuszko at 2200 metres. The route had been travelled by the explorer Paul Strzelecki as early as 12 March 1840, when he became the first to climb Kosciuszko, which he named and declared to be Australia's highest peak. Of the climb he wrote: 'The steepness of the numberless ridges intersected by gullies and torrents rendered this ascent a matter of no small difficulty.'

Taking cattle up the spur was even harder. Originally, it was impossible and livestock were taken by a circuitous route through the Tom Groggin flats, then up to Dead Horse Gap and onto the Rams Head Range, a loop of about 20 kilometres. The direct route, almost straight up, was only 10 kilometres. First, though, a track had to be cut. In the 1920s Kerry Pierce, who owned or partly owned North Greg Greg and Bringenbrong stations, joined up with Alf Hannell, another partner in Bringenbrong, to get the work done. The route was chosen by a local stockman, Leo Byatt.

In a collection of oral histories of the Snowy Mountains, another stockman, Errol Scammell, recalled the track's construction and use:

Hannel and Pierce owned part of Bringenbrong. They called it Hannels Spur because they paid for it. This old chap, he paid a lot of the local fellows – a pound a day, I remember at the time, which is big money – to go up there and cut that. Quite a lot of the young fellows around the district. They cut this track about eight foot [2.4 metres] wide through the scrub, just cut it straight up Hannels Spur. Then when they got up out of the snowgum, they got on the clear country, they made a camp and called it Byatts Camp. They had tents there all summer, they used to live there all the summer.

They'd take their cattle up and instead of going right around by Geehi and Groggin and coming back there, they cut this track up there. They used it then for tourists and hikers and everything. It was a terrible job taking cattle up because you'd just have to cut out what one man could handle, about twenty head. You'd force them up and the others would be a bit inclined to follow you then. Then another bloke would cut out another lot and push them on. You might even leave that lot when they start to knock up a bit and go back and get another lot. Somebody at the tail end would have the big mob you see. It was a pretty tough job. *(Reproduced by kind permission of Klaus Hueneke)*

Visitors to the mountain huts and cattle camps soon discovered a remarkable breed of stockmen. Many of them spent from October to May living in the High Country, far from the comforts of civilisation. They endured almost complete isolation during those months, and whatever the elements threw at them. Yet they also had some of the most ruggedly beautiful scenery in the country literally at their feet. Over summer, the pastures where the cattle grazed became meadows covered in wild flowers. The names they gave the high plains reflect the beauty that surrounded them – Town of Roses, Plains of Heaven, Ryrie's Parlour.

The drovers woke to mists shrouding the valleys far below, while they gazed down from cool, crystal-clear heights. Then there were the mountains, piercing the blue skies and scudding clouds with towering buttresses of stone. Ridges and ranges marched rank upon rank into the distant blue haze. The mountains could create their own weather – idyllic sunshine one moment, howling blizzard the next. The High Country drovers may have feared the snows of winter but the reality was, it could snow there any time of year.

It was little wonder that the exploits of the High Country drovers became the stuff of legend. This, after all, was the home of the man from Snowy River, a composite of people Banjo Paterson met during his travels in the High Country and the Monaro. Paterson met one of the men specifically credited with being the inspiration for the poem, Jack Riley, on a visit to the Australian Alps in 1890, just weeks before the poem was first published in *The Bulletin*.

Riley had worked on stations on the Monaro and western side of the Alps and was approaching the age of fifty when the poet visited him in his remote bark hut at the foot of Mount Kosciuszko at Tom Groggin. In the days before Hannell's Spur was cut, Groggin was the staging post on the stock route to the High Country via Leatherbarrel Mountain and Dead Horse Gap (the approximate route of the road now called the Alpine Way). In *Early Days of the Upper Murray*, Jean Carmody wrote of the meeting:

Walter Mitchell, then living at Bringenbrong, was the man instrumental in bringing together the stockman Jack Riley, and the poet Banjo Paterson, when Mitchell and Paterson went out into the mountains on a camping trip. The two men spent a night at Jack Riley's hut at Groggin, and during the evening Jack entertained the visitors with tales of his adventures in some of the wildest country in Australia. Next day, Jack guided the visitors up to the top of Kosciuszko, then around the Great Divide towards the Tin Mine and on to The Pilot. It was at this time that Jack mentioned to his companions the days he had spent on the banks of the Snowy River, not very far ahead of where they were. *(Reproduced by kind permission of Jean Carmody's estate)*

There are many stories of Riley's expertise as a rider and a guide to the High Country, where he spent his entire adult life. Greg Greg stockman Tom Evans recalled mustering stray bullocks with him on Leatherbarrel Mountain:

Old Jack says to me, he says, 'See 'ere now, young feller. Youse goes that away and wees goes this way.' And off they went leaving me to look for the bullocks on my own. I was only a bit of a kid and I did not know the country and I was scared I'd get bushed, and I had a hell of a job getting through the big snow-drifts in the gullies, and I was having a hell of a time when I walked right onto the missing bullocks camped right against a big snow-drift. They were wild as hawks and my horse was a bit knocked up and had a shoe loose by this time, and it was a good time after dark before I got the brutes down to the mustering paddock at Groggin. Old Jack and the others won't believe that I have got the bullocks all on my own, but the next morning when they wake up here they are, and old Jack says, 'Looka here now, they needs a boostin'.' And with that he after them and into them with his whip, and there were no two ways about it, he could ride like the very devil, and he stayed with those bullocks no matter what they turned and did, and the whole time he was cussing them and taking pieces off them with his whip. They got boosted all right.

While highlighting the horsemanship of High Country stockmen, Paterson's poem also drew attention to the grandeur of the region, 'where the rugged mountain ranges raise their torn and rugged battlements on high, and the night stars fairly blaze at midnight in a cold and frosty sky'. Increasing numbers of visitors were drawn to admire the scenery, hike its giant hills or ski its winter slopes. However, those who came expecting wilderness found herds of cattle grazing the summer pastures or autumn fires lit by the drovers to burn off the dying snow grass and promote new growth in the spring.

By the 1930s concerns were growing that the amount of grazing and burning on the summer pastures was damaging a fragile environment that was unique in Australia. In 1931–32 the Commonwealth Forestry Bureau commissioned forestry scientist Baldur Unwin Byles to conduct a study of the condition of the upper Murray catchment. Byles investigated timber resources and the progress of soil erosion, and reported: 'The efficiency of the catchment as it existed in 1928 has not been maintained, and, moreover, that it is decreasing slowly but surely'.

Byles believed the culprit was fire, and that 99 per cent of fires were lit by stockmen. He recommended that stock be kept off the steeper slopes but stopped short of suggesting that grazing in the High Country should be eradicated altogether. He believed such a measure wouldn't stop fires, as they would still occur naturally and would probably be much harder to control, in part because without High Country grazing, access roads would be closed or neglected.

Byles arrived at a somewhat startling conclusion: 'Contrary to the idea held by many people who have not lived in the mountains, the mountain pastures are not overstocked; they are actually understocked.' Byles argued that the reason stockmen were setting the mountain pastures alight was to burn off dead grass that their cattle hadn't eaten, and would find unpalatable when they returned for the next season. If there were more cattle grazing the High Country grasses, the stockmen wouldn't need to light the fires.

While Byles attempted to balance the interests of the High Country graziers with the need to protect catchment areas, the issue tended to polarise almost everyone else. Many stockmen appreciated the need to keep stock off fragile areas, but didn't believe they should be excluded from the High Country altogether. Nevertheless, in 1944 the New South Wales government created the Kosciuszko State Park and excluded grazing from the main range, essentially the area around Kosciuszko. Grazing was permitted elsewhere but the practice of burning was discouraged.

Conservationists such as Miles Dunphy and the National Parks and Primitive Areas Council had been advocating a Snowy-Indi Primitive Area since 1933 but, when it came to preserving the High Country, government agendas followed different lines. At the end of World War II Australia turned its mind to nation-building, and for the Snowy River and upper Murray that translated into a hydro-electric scheme, one of the biggest infrastructure projects the country had ever seen.

From 1949 onwards, work began on the creation of enormous dams that would soon flood large areas of the High Country. Tunnels were drilled, roads were built and bushland was cleared for the construction of massive pipelines, electrical towers and service towns. Yet even as the massive infrastructure was being carved out of the landscape, the Snowy Mountains Hydro-Electric Authority was concerned about the livestock eating the High Country pastures around its dams, and that grazing, erosion and fires would affect the run-off and water quality of the channels and storages of the scheme. In 1957 the Australian Academy of Science reported on the condition of the High Country catchment in New South Wales. On the recommendation of the Catchment Areas Protection Board, snow leases above 4500 feet (1370 metres) were terminated.

It should have meant the end of grazing in the New South Wales High Country. However, the annual tradition of droving stock up into the mountains continued – the ban was ignored. For many of the stockmen, each year's ascent meant a return to a landscape, lifestyle and freedom ingrained in their very being. For many, it was where they felt they truly belonged.

Their defiance was assisted by the ineffectual efforts of the authorities to enforce the bans. They lacked the resources and skills to evict the drovers from wild country they knew better than anyone else. Finally, in 1969, an examination of grazing and other leases in what was now the Kosciuszko National Park recommended a total ban on all grazing in the park. The move was backed by increased enforcement efforts. Finally, a practice that had operated under snow leases for eighty-five years, and on an informal basis for fifty years before that, was over.

The Australian Capital Territory had been following developments in New South Wales, and in 1963 a campaign by conservationists and bushwalkers sought to have the mountainous southern region of the Territory declared a national park. In 1964, Orroral Station was closed down by the government and turned into a space tracking station. In 1968 twenty-nine Tharwa graziers were given three months to negotiate their removal from the Tharwa Valley. Namadgi National Park was declared in 1979.

While the exclusion of stock from the High Country north of the Victorian border was seen as a great victory by environmentalists, a fundamental philosophical problem remained in the continued existence of the High Country huts. Most of these buildings were slab constructions built by drovers. Some were built by miners prospecting for gold. They numbered in their hundreds and they posed a difficult question: did a large number of buildings scattered across what was supposed to be wilderness have any place in a national park?

Many conservationists thought the answer was no; only the natural environment should be preserved. Wrote one wilderness advocate: 'Huts are alien to wilderness, the argument of huts for safety is spurious and if they are removed then those that enter either survive or perish, which is what wilderness is all about'. (*Reproduced by kind permission of the Kosciuszko Huts Association.*)

Of course, it took a good deal of self-delusion to ignore the large power-generating industry that had been erected in said wilderness. Nevertheless, during the 1970s while the New South Wales National Parks and Wildlife Service contemplated what to do with the huts in its care, some park rangers took matters into their own hands and burned at least two of the historic buildings to the ground.

Other conservationists took a different view. In 1970 the Kosciuszko Huts Association was formed by volunteers, park users and other interest groups to protect, preserve and document the High Country huts. The organisation lobbied the New South Wales National Parks and Wildlife Service to recognise the value of the human heritage of the huts, while actively recording the oral histories of the people who had built and utilised them.

At the same time, the New South Wales National Parks and Wildlife Service was also grappling with the fact that it had responsibility for a park that encompassed 649000 hectares and was 150 kilometres long. Theoretically, protecting the wilderness areas was simply a matter of letting nature take its course – the 'lock it up and leave it' approach.

Unfortunately, the areas in question hadn't been wilderness for an extraordinarily long time. Most of the country had been grazed and burned for more than 130 years by stockmen and drovers. Before that it had been subjected to the fire regime of Indigenous people for thousands of years. While most scientists were sure that droving and burning in the High Country was having a negative effect, few realised that they'd embarked on a 649000-hectare lab experiment to find out what would happen when it stopped.

Meanwhile, south of the Murray, Victoria had been chipping away at its snow leases since the 1940s, with a piecemeal declaration of parks and reserves as a result of recommendations by lobbyists and government authorities. A more encompassing Alpine National Park had been a long-held dream since the Town and Country Planning Association recommended it as early as 1949. However, when the park was finally declared in 1989, sixty-one snow leases allowing the grazing of 8000 cattle were allowed to remain.

It was just one of a great number of compromises, most of which can easily be guessed at after a cursory glance at the park's boundaries. It covers an area of 646 000 hectares but is shaped like a constricted bowel – bulging in some places and barely a kilometre wide in others. The misshapen intestine stretches 200 kilometres across north-east Victoria, and is so grotesquely distorted by attempts to accommodate the vested interests of various 'stakeholders' that the result is something only a politician hoping to win a few environmentalist votes could love.

It didn't take long to discover that giant parks weren't necessarily good for the environment. In 2002 and 2003, the High Country in Victoria and New South Wales was swept by the most severe fires they'd ever experienced. The Kosciuszko Huts Association referred to it as Kosciuszko National Park's 'worst disaster, with 45 bushfires burning across the Park destroying areas that had not been burnt in living memory, and 24 huts as well'. (*Reproduced by kind permission of the Kosciuszko Huts Association.*)

The Member for Burrinjuck, Katrina Hodgkinson, said in the parliament of New South Wales: 'I have seen at first hand and photographed some areas of the park where the fire was so fierce that the ground has been virtually sterilised and no regrowth has occurred. This happened only because of the heavy fuel loads that the [New South Wales] NPWS allowed to build up over many years of neglecting hazard reduction.'

For the Snowy Mountains Hydro-Electric Scheme it was their worst nightmare. Burning with extraordinary ferocity at the height of summer, vast areas of the hydro catchment were turned to ash in a disaster far worse than anything the drovers of the High Country could have initiated. Who could have known? As it happens, Baldur Unwin Byles, as far back as 1932.

In the Australian Capital Territory, the fires were just as bad. A firestorm tore out of Namadgi National Park, fell upon the virtually unprotected western flank of Canberra and destroyed more than 500 homes. In Victoria, the fires provoked a re-examination of the snow leases for grazing in the Alpine National Park. In 2005 the state government convened a task force, composed of four members of parliament, to take submissions and make recommendations on the future of the leases.

Despite the fact that grazing in the park had been restricted after fires burned through in 1998, the task force found that cattle damaged water catchments, affected water quality, modified and damaged vegetation, threatened endangered plants and animals, and spread weeds. Native plants hadn't evolved to cope with heavy, hard-hoofed herbivores, and cattle urine was capable of scorching the vegetation. Cattle were, in effect, the beasts from hell. The task force concluded that they didn't even help control fire.

Given that cattle and other livestock had been grazing the area since the 1830s, at times with stocking rates much higher than they'd been in the second half of the twentieth century, it was a wonder there was anything left. However, the report cited research into the long-term impact of grazing:

> The detailed analysis published in 1994 of vegetation records collected over a period of 50 years at the exclusion plots on the Bogong High Plains concluded that the grazed grasslands there may be described as 'stable, but in terms of soil and nature conservation values they are degraded'.

A High Country stockman will draw your attention to the word 'stable'. An environmentalist will seize upon the word 'degraded'.

Someone who is neither one nor the other might wonder how something can be both. Perhaps it's the scientific explanation for being able to see where cattle have been grazing, though the grass has grown back.

As for the 170-year history, heritage, skills and knowledge of High Country drovers and stockmen, the task force concluded: 'The mountain cattlemen's tradition is maintained and celebrated in a variety of ways outside the park, including through books, poetry, films and festivals'. And as for the mountain huts, 'Their significance and protection does not depend on ongoing grazing in the park.'

This, of course, is wrong. Culture isn't what you read in books. It's a way of life and a set of values experienced first-hand, which Banjo Paterson captured in his poem 'The Daylight is Dying':

Beyond all denials
The stars in their glories
The breeze in the myalls
Are part of these stories.
The waving of grasses,
The song of the river
That sings as it passes
For ever and ever;
The hobble-chains' rattle,
The calling of birds,
The lowing of cattle
Must blend with the words.

Ultimately, the Victorian government decided to terminate all snow leases in the Alpine National Park, but continued issuing leases in High Country state forests, where presumably cattle are less evil. After justifying its decision that the snow leases were costing the government money, it allocated $7 million (enough to cover its losses for twenty-eight years) to soften the blow. Some of the money was used to compensate the holders of the snow leases; some of it was spent on upgrading a road through the park, apparently without recognising that a kilometre of sealed road sterilises approximately 6000 square metres of the environment and increases impacts on wildlife through collisions with faster moving cars. Money was also set aside for signs that would explain what has been lost. The Man from Snowy River Festival, held each year in Corryong, received a grant.

In 2009 the Alpine National Park burned again. Across Victoria, a chain of fires claimed the lives of more than 170 people, the worst bushfire tragedy in the state's history. In a submission to the 2009 Victorian Bushfires Royal Commission, the Mountain Cattlemen's Association of Victoria engaged in a degree of 'We told you so' when it quoted a prediction it had made back in 1987:

> The Mountain Cattlemen warn that the eventual result of the lack of protective burning management will result in a holocaust on a scale never seen before. Fuel reduction burning has not taken place in many parts of the Eastern Ranges for 30 or 40 years and now dry matter lies on the forest floor 20cms or more thick. Before European settlement much of the area was burnt naturally every few years. Any good farmer will make sure that sheep and cattle are concentrated in the paddocks near his home and buildings to remove excess pasture growth before the onset of summer. The same fire-retardant effect is obtained in forested and alpine areas at no cost to the taxpayer. *(Reproduced by kind permission of the MCAV)*

The submission quoted a recommendation from the Victorian Premier's Department, which was undergoing a sea change in its approach to mosaic burning – patch-burning selected areas of country using small, manageable fires that nevertheless consume much of the fuel load: 'Mosaic burning provides positive fire protection and a better ecological result by breaking up age classes of vegetation and retaining more habitat across a broad area. It complements existing asset protection burning which aims for more complete coverage.'

The cattlemen noted: 'Mosaic burning is exactly what cattlemen were doing from the early days of taking cattle to the high country'.

On the Kosciuszko National Park website, the description of 'cultural heritage' at Currango Homestead, near where William Brodribb sheltered with his sheep more than 150 years ago, runs as follows:

> The complex of buildings, including homestead, cottages, sheds and out buildings, is one of the most intact examples of a High Country station in Kosciuszko National Park. The main homestead was built around 1895 and is the centre of Currango Station and the residence of the caretakers. The Homestead, 'Pines' and 'Daffodil Cottage' are part of an intact complex of buildings representing station life during the late 1800s and early 1900s. These three buildings offer rustic accommodation and an experience of life in the High Country over 100 years ago. *(Reproduced by kind permission of the NSW Department of Environment, Climate Change and Water)*

Except, of course, you won't see any cattle. You will see where the hydro scheme's Talbingo Reservoir regularly floods what's left of the High Country pasture the cattle once grazed. But you won't wake before dawn as the horses are saddled in preparation for a day spent mustering. You won't meet stockmen skilled in leathercraft, horsemanship, and survival in the bush. You won't see cattle driven down mountainsides that trail bikes would find impassable. You won't meet people whose cultural heritage reaches back in an unbroken chain to the first settlements in and around the High Country, people who for months of the year lived in such splendid isolation that they regarded themselves as being truly free. For that you'll have to get *The Man From Snowy River* on DVD.

The decision to exclude droving from the High Country of Australia is probably irreversible. The decision to exclude droving from national parks is probably correct. Yet there are many Australians who are as passionate about preserving our human heritage as they are about preserving our natural heritage. Both have value: the loss of either leaves us all a little poorer. What is more worrying are the consequences when you break the link between a social and natural heritage that has existed for hundreds, if not thousands, of years. No scientists, conservationists, politicians or drovers can tell us what the terrible costs of that might be. There are some clues, however.

The wilderness values of the High Country are under extreme pressure as a consequence of a succession of unprecedented fires. The resources of the authorities charged with managing the national parks are increasingly seen as woefully inadequate for the enormous areas involved. Weeds, wild dogs, brumbies, deer, goats, pigs, rabbits, cats and foxes are wreaking havoc.

As for the catchment, the entire Murray-Darling river system is considered to be on the brink of collapse, with much of the blame directed at global warming rather than the now long-banned grazing.

The total exclusion of droving in Australia's High Country has unquestionably cost us one of the revered pillars of our national character: the High Country drover. The failure to recognise that national parks can preserve more than just the natural heritage of the nation may yet cost far more than we could imagine. There is still a great deal at stake. Ultimately, history will decide whether dismissing the accumulated wisdom and experience of High Country drovers and stockmen was the right or wrong thing to do.

On all the earth there is no sadder sound
Than moan of cattle when their thirst is great;
It quivers in the trees, and sky and ground
With all its hopelessness reverberate

— 'The Overlander', Will Ogilvie (1869–1963)

4

THE ROAD LESS TRAVELLED

In September 1840, overlander-turned-explorer Edward Eyre stood upon the hill he had named Mount Hopeless. He was at the southern end of what would become the Strzelecki Track, and utterly unimpressed by what he saw.

'Cheerless and hopeless indeed was the prospect that lay before us,' he wrote of the salt lakes and saltbush that surrounded him. 'I had before me now a view that would damp the ardour of the most enthusiastic, or dissipate the doubts of the most sceptical.'

Eyre was on his second expedition on behalf of the newly formed government of South Australia. In 1839 he'd struck north from the township of Adelaide, skirting Spencer Gulf until he reached Mount Arden in the Flinders Ranges, still within sight of the sea. When he set out again, in May 1840, he explored north of the Flinders Ranges and discovered a chain of salt lakes – Lake Torrens, Lake Eyre, Lake Blanche, Lake Callabonna and Lake Frome. Finding salt lakes in every direction, Eyre believed they formed a single continuous barrier of salt, not unlike the supposedly impassable barrier of the Blue Mountains, west of Sydney.

Five years later, Charles Sturt managed to skirt the lakes on his expedition that was attempting to reach the centre of the continent. In 1844 he travelled up the Murray, then the Darling River, before striking north-west from the Menindee Lakes, heading for the centre of Australia. His route took him to the east of the salt lakes and he soon found himself on another creek that trended north by north-east. He named it Strzelecki Creek, after his exploring colleague of Mount Kosciuszko fame. Some deep pools persisted, despite the fact that Sturt was travelling through the country in the midst of drought, but the creek was dry for most of its length. It was a similar story when he discovered and crossed Cooper Creek. The further he went, the drier it got.

Despite experiencing extraordinary hardships along the way, when Sturt crossed Eyre Creek he was closing in on Australia's geographical centre. The only thing that could stop him was the Simpson Desert. He'd been through some hard country already, including the terrible red gibbers of what became known as Sturt's Stony Desert, but nothing could prepare him for this. Aboriginal people called the Simpson 'Munga-thirri', the land of sandhills. In waterless country almost bereft of vegetation, Sturt wrote:

> From the summit of a sandy undulation close upon our right, we saw that the ridges extended northwards in parallel lines beyond the range of vision and appeared as if interminable. To the eastward and westward they succeeded each other like the waves of the sea . . . My companion involuntarily uttered an exclamation of amazement when he first glanced his eye over it. 'Good heavens,' said he, 'did ever man see such country!'

Hundreds of kilometres short of his goal, Sturt was forced to turn back. His negative impression of the country he had travelled through appeared to confirm the findings of Edward Eyre. Neither of them realised that they'd seen the country at its worst. They had no way of understanding what could happen to the same country after rain or, better yet, a flood.

The idea that central Australia was a terrible wasteland was reinforced in 1848. In that year, Ludwig Leichhardt attempted to cross Australia from east to west. After leaving the Darling Downs in April, he and the six men with him disappeared without a trace. One theory regarding their fate is that they perished while attempting to traverse the Simpson Desert.

The fate of the explorers didn't entirely discourage the land-hungry pastoralists. Every year, they ventured a little further north from Adelaide. Initially, the pace of settlement was slowed by the more orderly management of land by the South Australian government, which didn't allow settlement until land had been properly surveyed. By 1841 settlement north of Adelaide extended only 130 kilometres, to the Clare Valley.

However, in 1842, in part to thwart the predatory squatters, the government legislated to allow annual tenure of land that was only defined by reference to available landmarks. In essence, it meant squatting was allowed, but only on a temporary basis. It effectively gave the government the option to evict the squatters whenever it wanted, or at least within twelve months, while collecting licence fees until it did. The consequence was that, despite the negative reports of Eyre and Sturt, the squatters weren't far behind. By 1846 they'd reached the Flinders Ranges.

Of course, the further north they went, the drier it got. Over time, the South Australians, whose state is the driest on the island continent, would become some of the best dry-country farmers and graziers in the world. Back in 1846, they still had much to learn, much of it through terribly bitter experience.

Nevertheless, the squatters were starting to realise that the country immediately north of the Flinders Ranges wasn't as bad as the explorers thought. Saltbush in particular was good fodder for stock, especially sheep, and it was remarkably resilient. And in good seasons, rain brought up additional feed that was extremely nourishing. The main problem, once again, was water.

To preserve what little water they had, the northern runs needed dams and wells. However, it was becoming clear that the system of annual tenure discouraged squatters from investing in such costly infrastructure. To address the situation, in 1851 the South Australian government introduced a pastoral lease arrangement that extended land tenure to fourteen years. The decision came at the beginning of a run of good seasons, and by 1854 settlement had reached Eyre's 'dreary waste', 400 kilometres north of Adelaide.

Only two years later, the notion that a barrier of salt hemmed in settlement not far to the north got its first dent. In 1856 a prospector, Benjamin Babbage, was searching for gold north of the Flinders Ranges. What had been a dustbowl when Eyre crossed it was now a grassy plain. Beyond that, near Mount Hopeless, Babbage found the MacDonnell River, 600 kilometres north of Adelaide. On it he located two large waterholes – Blanchewater and Saint Mary's Pool – just a few kilometres from Eyre's Mount Hopeless.

Babbage never found any gold, but the combination of good grass and a permanent water supply led to the formation of Blanchewater Station by a pastoralist and politician named John Baker, in February 1858.

Later that year, Babbage discovered what turned out to be liquid gold. Near Lake Eyre South, in the middle of a salt pan, he saw what looked like a bright green mound. It was a freshwater spring. At around the same time, Police Commissioner Peter Warburton discovered more of what soon became known as the Mound Springs, which formed an arc around the southern edge of the Great Artesian Basin. Explorers like Sturt had spent much of their lives searching for an inland sea, little knowing that it lay hundreds of metres beneath their feet. Babbage had all but shattered the notion of an impenetrable barrier of salt.

The final proof came that same year, when one of the great (and greatly underrated) explorers of Central Australia, Augustus Gregory, was commissioned to conduct a search for Ludwig Leichhardt. At the time, Gregory had more than matched Leichhardt's 1844 feat of travelling from Brisbane to Port Essington, in the Northern Territory's Top End. In 1856 he'd travelled from the Victoria River on the western side of the Northern Territory to Brisbane, while droving what started out as a flock of 200 sheep, which supplemented the supplies for his expedition of nineteen men. He explored 500 kilometres south into the interior along Sturt Creek, then turned east and travelled down the Elsey River, named after one of the expedition's members, from which point he followed Leichhardt's approximate route along what was to become the Gulf Track stock route (described in Chapter 6).

Following that remarkable feat, the New South Wales government asked Gregory to mount an expedition to discover whatever could be found of the long-missing Leichhardt. Early in 1858, Gregory left the Darling Downs and headed west. On 21 April he found a tree blazed with an 'L' near present-day Blackall. From there, he followed the Barcoo River across to its junction with the Thomson, just north of Windorah.

The Barcoo had first been encountered in 1846 by Major Thomas Mitchell. He'd mistakenly thought its north-western course meant it was a much-sought waterway to the northern coast of Australia, effectively providing a route across the continent from north to south. However, the following year Mitchell's assistant, Edmund Kennedy, led another expedition to follow up the discovery and travel down the river, which Mitchell had called the Victoria, to its mouth. The river soon turned west, then south-west, and joined a river Kennedy named the Thomson. As he got closer to the South Australian border, Kennedy realised he was now on the watercourse Charles Sturt had named Cooper Creek, and that he was headed for the supposedly dead heart of Australia. Kennedy renamed Mitchell's Victoria River the Barcoo, the local Aboriginal name for the waterway, and turned back rather than face the desolate country ahead.

Up to this point, Augustus Gregory had been following in Edmund Kennedy's footsteps, but when he reached the Cooper he found the conditions were so dry that he couldn't continue his westward search for signs of Leichhardt. Instead of turning back, he decided to head for Adelaide: if Edmund Kennedy was right, it would simply be a matter of travelling down the westward-flowing Cooper to Strzelecki Creek, which would take him south.

Edmund Kennedy had been right. Not only that, while it hadn't rained on the Barcoo, Strzelecki Creek was punctuated by a chain of freshly filled waterholes and pools along its length. Feed for Gregory's horses was also plentiful.

On 26 June, Gregory rode into Blanchewater Station, whose stockmen were more than a little surprised to learn where he'd come from. Gregory had destroyed the myth of impassable salt lakes north-east of Adelaide, as Benjamin Babbage had done to the north.

The significance of Augustus Gregory's expedition wasn't realised at the time. He hadn't discovered the fate of Ludwig Leichhardt but his journey down the Cooper and Strzelecki creeks established the route of what would become the first of the great stock routes that would soon cross Australia from north to south – the Strzelecki Track.

He'd also been very lucky. When Sturt had found Strzelecki Creek, it had been bone-dry. If it had been in the same condition when Gregory travelled it, he probably wouldn't have lived to tell the tale. He recognised as much when he wrote:

No permanent water was seen in the bed of the creek, though there were many deep hollows which, when once filled, retain water for several months, and this, combined with the existence of a fine reach of water in Cooper's Creek immediately above the point where Streletzki Creek branches off, renders it far the best line of route into the interior which has yet been discovered.

Even today, the significance of Augustus Gregory's achievement is barely realised. When combined, his 1856 journey from the Victoria River to Brisbane and his 1858 journey from Brisbane to Adelaide amounted to the first crossing of Australia from north to south. Both expeditions, though unquestionably perilous, were conducted with such professionalism that there was none of the high drama that would have ensured their enduring fame.

As it turned out, credit for the first north–south crossing, or in this case south–north, went to the explorer whose incompetence led to his death, and whose expedition would have achieved nothing but for the discoveries of those that searched for it.

In 1860, approaching the height of summer, Robert O'Hara Burke left the depot he'd established near the junction of Strzelecki and Cooper creeks, and struck north with a flying squad that comprised three other men, six camels, a horse and enough food for three months. He headed north to the Gulf of Carpentaria, passing through country that had already been explored by Sturt, Leichhardt and Gregory.

Burke succeeded in reaching the gulf, but it took him two months to get there and he had only enough food for half of the return journey. Three of the four men survived the return journey to the depot on Cooper Creek, where events ensued that would make headlines around the world.

The rest of Burke's expedition had abandoned the depot earlier on the day that Burke, his third-in-command William Wills and nineteen-year-old camel handler John King arrived, having stayed there a month longer than ordered. However, having reached the Cooper, the sick, starved and exhausted explorers now had as good a chance of survival as if they'd made it to Melbourne's Yarra River. The idyllic waterholes were brimming with water filled with fish. The mighty river red gums that shaded the grassy banks were teeming with corellas, parrots and finches. One hundred metres from the river the fields of red gibber rocks and dry white dust may have been a shimmering hell, but along the river it was paradise.

The only thing that wasn't working in Burke's favour was that the Cooper hadn't risen high enough to flood down Strzelecki Creek. Just as Augustus Gregory had noted, the Strzelecki's waterholes were ephemeral. When Burke and his men tried to travel down the creek to Blanchewater Station, they found it too dry and had to turn back. They were effectively trapped.

Still, they should have been able to survive on Cooper Creek until a rescue party arrived. Burke and Wills underlined their incompetence and ensured their fame by surviving the desert, only to perish at the oasis. The Aboriginal people whose offers of assistance were spurned could only watch as two of the stupidest white men they'd ever met starved to death in what to them was a grocery store. After Burke and Wills died, King accepted help from the local people and survived.

When word of the disappearance of Burke and Wills reached the settled areas of Australia, a number of 'rescue missions' were sent out. While the men had disappeared north of the depot on Cooper Creek, much of the 'searching' was conducted in western Queensland. In most cases the searchers, uniformly better bushmen than Burke, used the search to disguise their real purpose – run hunting.

In the year after Burke and his men disappeared, John McKinlay set out from South Australia and discovered the Diamantina River, which Sturt had missed because he'd encountered it at the point where, along with the waters of Eyre Creek, the Georgina and the Mulligan rivers, it spreads over the vast flood plain of Goyder Lagoon. In dry times, it's a dust bowl. After a flood, it transforms into hundreds of square kilometres of 250 species of native grasses and herbs, almost all of which fatten cattle.

William Landsborough and Frederick Walker from Queensland carried out no fewer than four 'searches', during which they journeyed to the gulf and back without loss of life, discovering much of the grazing potential of central and western Queensland, and the Gulf Country.

Alfred Howitt discovered excellent grazing between the Darling River and the Cooper, plus the remains of Burke and Wills and the emaciated but still alive John King, who was almost deranged after months of not knowing if he would ever see another European again.

In 1862 the rescuers' discoveries prompted Queensland to successfully lobby to move its boundary at the north-eastern corner of South Australia west another three degrees of longitude (from 141° to 138°), in order to include the rich grazing lands of what was to become known as the Channel Country. South Australia succeeded in having the entire Northern Territory placed under its jurisdiction in 1863. Victoria, which had sent Burke north hoping to promote its interests in the vast tracts of northern Australia, got nothing.

Pioneering settlers were soon taking up large areas of Queensland and spreading north across New South Wales and South Australia. However, Augustus Gregory's expectations that the Strzelecki Track would become the preferred route to central Australia didn't immediately materialise. In the 1860s, while far-western Queensland remained unsettled, the Strzelecki remained a road to nowhere.

In South Australia, settlement along the Strzelecki was also gradual. Beyond Blanchewater, first Monte Collina was taken up, then Carraweena Station and Wallelderdine. In 1867 the South Australian government allocated a parcel of land, Cullamurra, on Cooper Creek to express its gratitude to the Aboriginal people who had helped the stricken members of Burke's expedition. Lutheran missionaries may have travelled up the Strzelecki to inspect the site, and it's thought that Anglican missionaries may have travelled across to the Cooper, but ultimately the Lutherans settled at Killalpaninna, north of Marree on what was to become the Birdsville Track.

The first stock to be taken down the Strzelecki were a mob of horses, driven by an enterprising pioneer named John Costello in 1867. Costello was born at newly settled Yass in 1838, and grew up in the Goulburn district. However, as a young man in the 1860s he and other Southern Highlands graziers, such as the Durack family, were lured to Queensland's seemingly limitless opportunities.

Queensland had become an independent state in 1859, and had moved quickly to allow fourteen-year pastoral leases to be taken up across the sparsely populated interior, hoping to reap a revenue windfall in rents. Under Surveyor-General Augustus Gregory – the explorer had been snapped up by the administration – most of western and northern Queensland, an eighth of Australia's landmass, was opened to leasehold between 1860 and 1864.

Costello's sister married into the Durack dynasty in 1862, and in 1867 Costello and his brother-in-law Patrick Durack and their families moved to Queensland, initially taking up land at Mobell Creek (now Moble Creek), south-west of Quilpie. Costello named his station Burtna, the Aboriginal name for the waterhole where the homestead was built. Later that year, he had 200 horses ready for market and decided to take them to Kapunda, just north of Adelaide in South Australia.

Costello was highly regarded as a drover and for his ability to navigate his way through untracked outback country. He took charge of the droving himself as he attempted to become the first drover to take stock through land that remained wilderness. The mob was made up of unbroken colts and fillies, and reputedly the young horses were in such good condition that they played up all the way to South Australia.

The untrained horses rushed nearly every night, and rounding them up as they galloped through the bush was a test of courage and skill. If there were any incidents involving Aboriginal people, his descendant Michael Costello made no mention of them when, decades later in the 1930s, he recalled John Costello's droving trip. The Strzelecki must have had good water, as despite the risks and dangers involved, Costello managed to get the stock through to Kapunda without losing a single animal. There they reputedly achieved good prices at auction, by some accounts as much as £3000.

Within a couple of years Patrick Durack had shifted to Thylungra Station, north-west of modern-day Quilpie, and John Costello had established Kyabra, west of Quilpie. Costello was particularly active in exploring the country 'further out' and expanding his properties. During the 1870s he built up a holding covering 33 670 square kilometres between Kyabra and the Diamantina River.

It was in 1870, while exploring country around Cooper Creek, that Costello saw the first evidence of the most famous cattle-duffing episode in Australian history – the tracks of hundreds of cattle heading south-east. To Costello, the tracks looked highly suspicious as there were no stations for 700 kilometres in the direction the cattle were headed, and cattle duffers had tried to hide out on the Cooper at least once before.

In the mid-1860s a duffer named James Harnell, who went by the nickname Narran Jim, had taken stock he'd stolen from the district around the Culgoa and Narran rivers across Queensland to the Cooper. Along the way he stole a number of weaners from Bulloo Downs Station as well. An alert Bulloo Downs stockman contacted the police, and when Police Inspector Fitzgerald and eight Aboriginal troopers tracked Narran Jim and surrounded him while he was sleeping, the cattle duffer woke to find himself looking down the barrel of Fitzgerald's revolver and seven years in jail.

Not long after John Costello returned to Kyabra from his visit to

Cooper Creek, Thargomindah's Police Inspector Gilmour paid one of his regular visits, whereupon Costello informed him of this latest find. To this day in the remote parts of Queensland, police perform most of the government's administrative roles. For Gilmour in the 1870s, this included the job of stock inspector. Like Costello, he didn't know of anyone who had sent away a large mob of cattle, certainly not down the Strzelecki to Adelaide, and he too suspected cattle duffing.

It transpired that the cattle had been taken from Bowen Downs, a station established by a syndicate that included the famous explorer William Landsborough, who'd been involved in the search for Burke's expedition, and the brilliant drover Nat Buchanan (see Chapter 6). The 250-square-kilometre property had since been taken over by the Scottish Australian Investment Company, whose lax station managers at first dismissed the suggestion that hundreds of their cattle might have been stolen. However, when they mustered the station at the end of 1870, they found they were down at least a thousand head. They also found the tracks of a mob of cattle that size heading towards the Cooper.

In January 1871, South Australian police arrested a drover from Blanchewater Station in possession of cattle carrying one of the Bowen Downs brands. He maintained the cattle had been bought from a drover coming down the Strzelecki. At the time, Blanchewater had been enjoying a particularly good season and had been keen to restock. When over a thousand head arrived unexpectedly on their doorstep and were offered for sale at a bargain price, Blanchewater's manager was perfectly prepared to swallow whatever story he was told about where they'd come from, and bought the lot.

The case caused a sensation, especially when what looked like a watertight case was brought against the duffers' ringleader, Harry Redford. However, the trial conducted at Roma in February 1873 resulted in a controversial verdict of not guilty.

What helped Redford was the fact that he'd firmly established the viability of a new stock route to southern markets from the now increasingly settled western Queensland. The bad reputation of the region he'd passed through had been formed by the negative reports of Eyre and Sturt, and the deaths of Burke and Wills. Men like Augustus Gregory and John Costello had subsequently found otherwise, but it was Redford who shattered such illusions with his feat of droving more than a thousand cattle. Following a major flood down the Cooper and Strzelecki, rather than encountering arid wastelands, he'd been forced to make detours around waterlogged flood plains lush with fodder.

Redford may have thought he would avoid detection by taking cattle through such a remote region but it may have been more widely used than he realised. Two of the stockmen who had helped him drove the cattle down the Strzelecki had apparently taken the same route on their way from South Australia to Queensland. In the summer of 1870–71, station manager George McGillivray had also travelled the track with a young Aboriginal named Jerry. McGillivray had been trying to get from his station, near Normanton, down to the Paroo River, but had lost his way. He was forced to abandon one of his horses, lame and exhausted, along the Cooper. He and Jerry then nearly died of thirst as they tried to travel down the Strzelecki in the hottest part of the year.

Even as the ink dried on the 1873 reports of the Redford trial, stations were being established along the Cooper and Strzelecki. Two settlers, John Conrick and Robert Bostock, were already moving stock towards the Cooper while the trial was under way, and they reached the Cooper's junction with the Strzelecki in October 1873. Bostock took up Innamincka Station, actually in South Australia although he wasn't aware of it at the time. Conrick took up Nappa Merrie Station, not far from the famous Dig Tree on the Cooper, in Queensland. At the southern end of the Strzelecki, Tinga Tingana station was taken up in 1874.

When Robert Bostock discovered that he'd settled on the South
Australian side of the border, even though he'd been paying his lease
to Queensland for the previous six years, he was faced with tighter
regulations and in 1879 he quit the station. John Conrick stayed on
at Nappa Merrie for most of his life, and his experiences mirrored the
shifting fortunes of the Strzelecki Track.

It was immediately obvious that the closest source of supplies, as
well as the closest market for cattle and wool, was South Australia.
It was 600 kilometres to the nearest South Australian port, Port
Augusta, compared to 1200 kilometres to the nearest Queensland
port, Ipswich. In addition, an old Aboriginal Conrick had befriended
told him it was only 'five sleeps' to Mount Hopeless Station, some 300
kilometres away.

Needing supplies, Conrick set out with two drays on his first trip
down the Strzelecki on 26 December 1874, in the height of summer.
He employed the Aboriginal man as his guide, paying him in clothing
and all the food he could eat.

It was a journey of contrasts. The Strzelecki watercourse comprised a wide flood plain, which at that time of year was reduced
to brown and white dust. Spotting waterholes was simplicity itself
because they were the only touches of green in an otherwise bare
landscape. Conrick and his heavily armed companions shot ducks on
the first few waterholes, and enjoyed duck meat all the way down the
Strzelecki. However, Conrick was already starting to realise the truth
of Augustus Gregory's assessment of the waterholes. He estimated
that none of them was going to last three more weeks in the furious
heat of summer, which meant the stock route couldn't be relied upon
in dry times. In a flood, the water would spread out over many kilometres, making it a tricky business to move stock in good times as
well as bad, which had been Redford's experience.

At Goora Goora waterhole, Conrick encountered a large group of
Aboriginal people. The water at Goora Goora was only about half a

metre deep, and when Conrick tried to water his horses, the Aboriginal elders started to object. Through his guide and a display of his firearms, Conrick made it clear that he was going to water his horses regardless of what they said. It turned out that Conrick's reputation for being firm but fair had preceded him. The elders exhorted the young warriors to attack but they refused.

That night Conrick, his Aboriginal guide and the man driving the second dray rolled out their swags under the vehicles to reduce the chances of being clubbed to death in their sleep. Conrick slept soundly. His assistant didn't sleep at all. The next day they continued on their way unmolested. They passed Artacoona Well, where the Walke brothers' Wallelderdine Station had been abandoned during one of the area's recurring droughts. All that was left was a slab hut and the stockyards that had once held the white bull they'd bought from Harry Redford four years earlier, and which had became a famous piece of evidence in the case against him. Conrick and his men travelled a further 14 kilometres to Carraweena soak, again half a metre deep, where they camped.

They took the day off on New Year's Day, then continued on their way, seeing more signs of attempts to settle the area and huts erected by parties searching for Burke's expedition. Where the Strzelecki veered west towards Lake Blanche, they left it and struck south over sandy country covered in trees. The ground was so rough they could barely stay seated in the bouncing drays. They passed between Lake Blanche and Lake Callabonna, which brought them to stony country.

They reached a soak at Yarla Creek but it was swarming with wasps. Despite it having good water, the horses wouldn't go near it. They pushed on to Mulligan Spring, called Mullachan by the area's Aboriginal inhabitants, where they found an outstation of Blanchewater.

In the sixteen years since Blanchewater had been established you could still count the travellers down the Strzelecki on the fingers of one hand. Now John Conrick had done the trip with a couple of drays. The outstation stockmen were astonished when he told them he'd come from Queensland.

Conrick managed to find a bush store beyond Blanchewater that saved him a journey of 200 kilometres or more to Port Augusta. He also tried to hire a bullocky to cart supplies to Cooper Creek on a regular basis. A bullocky named Kearns was offered £30 a tonne but when he saw the weaponry Conrick was travelling with, he said thanks but no thanks.

Conrick's return journey was complicated by heavy rains not far from Mulligan Spring. The drays became so deeply bogged that there was nothing for it but to leave them and seek help back at the Blanchewater outstation. When the weather cleared, the drays were pulled clear with the help of some station horses. Conrick turned north to travel up the Strzelecki, knowing that the rains might have made the ground boggy, but his concerns about the waterholes drying out no longer applied.

Conrick had travelled 30 kilometres when he encountered one of his partners in Nappa Merrie, George Ware, who'd ridden down the track to see how he was getting on. Together they made the return journey to Nappa Merrie, establishing in the process that it was feasible for drays to make the journey along the Strzelecki Track. Many years later, Conrick reminisced that:

> Along this route hundreds of thousands of sheep and cattle have since been travelled, and scores of thousands of bales of wool have been sent via Farina and other northern trucking stations.

The route might have been feasible, but it was seldom easy. In 1876 John Conrick had to travel for supplies in October. It was late spring but the country was already in drought and temperatures were

ABOVE: *The Cowpastures,* circa 1874, by A. Arthur Willmore. This area was where the First Fleet cattle that escaped in 1788 were found, breeding rapidly, seven years later. *(National Library, an7372821)*

BELOW: *Overlanders,* S.T. Gill, 1864. Overlanders were the precursors to drovers, often taking livestock on speculative 'run-hunting' ventures. A boss drover would chip these two for being too close together, like 'two men on one horse'. *(National Library, an7149189)*

ABOVE: Cattle watering at a lake near Mount Kosciusko, 1946. Drovers who took cattle to the highest alpine regions ran the risk of encountering blizzards at any time of the year. *(Charles Kerry Studio, Powerhouse Museum)*

RIGHT: 1934 cover of *The Queenslander*, depicting the distinctive dress style noticeable among many drovers. *(John Oxley Library, State Library of Queensland, 191949)*

FAR RIGHT: Hereford cattle grazing near Kiandra were trapped by heavy snow falls late in the season, in May 1957. *(W. Pedersen, National Archives, A1200:L22767)*

The Queenslander
ILLUSTRATED WEEKLY
6

POSTAGE: Commonwealth, N.Z. New Guinea, Mandated Territories, and Fiji, 5d.; Britain and Ireland, 5d.; all sea route 5d.; other parts of the British Empire, 5d.; U.S.A. and Foreign Countries, 6d.

May 10, 1934.

LEFT: Whites River Hut and the slopes leading up to the Rolling Grounds, near Guthega, circa 1930s. Stockyards can still be seen. This hut was eventually shared with a ski club, which now maintains it. *(George Day Collection, National Library, vn4235951)*

TOP: Cattle being mustered in the Victorian Alps at the end of the 1984 summer grazing season. *(National Archives, A6135, K2/7/84/44)*

BOTTOM: Cattle being driven out of a pasture due to the Snowy Hydro-Electric Scheme, 1960. In 1957, New South Wales ended cattle grazing in its High Country areas after the scheme established, with scientific backing, that grazing was harmful to the catchment. However, many drovers ignored the ban until 1969. *(National Archives, A11016:16786)*

TOP LEFT: Huts such as Broken Dam, photographed here in August 1997, have been protecting High Country drovers and adventurers since William Brodribb found shelter in one as early as 1848. *(Jane Wheaton, National Library, vn3259785)*

TOP RIGHT: After fire swept the Kosciuszko and Namadgi national parks in January 2003, twenty-four High Country huts, such as Boobee Hut, were lost. Volunteers with the Kosciuszko Huts Association have been rebuilding them ever since. *(Andrew Wilson, National Library, vn3092201)*

PANORAMA: High Country drovers have argued that grazing and controlled burning in alpine areas reduces fuel loads. Without them, wildfires of unprecedented ferocity, such as this fire in the Victorian High Country on 11 January 2007, are now commonplace. This photograph was taken looking towards Dargo from Swifts Creek. *(Henry Firus, Flagstaffphotos)*

TOP: On poorly watered routes through central Australia, such as the Birdsville and Strzelecki tracks, camel trains were a common sight from the 1870s to the 1950s. They transported goods of every description, and on occasion were used on droving trips. This string is on the Birdsville Track, circa 1940s. *(John Flynn, National Library, an24230028)*

ABOVE LEFT: To improve the reliability of the Birdsville Track, artesian bores were sunk along its length between 1889 and 1916. Maintenance issues saw many fall into disrepair and spill boiling water across the ground, as here at Lake Harry Station in 1924. *(State Library of South Australia, B48852)*

ABOVE RIGHT: Murranji Waterhole, circa 1980. The waterhole and the Murranji Track are now almost completely overgrown. *(Darrell Lewis Collection)*

ABOVE: The Murranji Track after it was widened in 1943. This photograph was taken by Northern Territory Administrator Charles Abbott, while on a tour of the region. His caption read: 'This year there are wide boulevardes . . . along the Murrunji.' *(National Archives, M10:4/107)*

soaring. The Strzelecki was dry for 160 kilometres south from Cooper Creek. Men hired to bring his supplies through had abandoned them at the Mulligan Spring outstation. To get them, Conrick took a dray with two horses, an assistant named Ogilby and his horse, and 180 litres of water.

Conrick walked beside the dray horses while Ogilby rode. They started late in the day and covered the first 40 kilometres at night. They took a break at 2 a.m., got going again at 4 a.m. and covered another 40 kilometres, by which time the sun was burning in a cloudless sky. When it became unbearably hot, they watered the horses, hobbled them, and rested through the heat of the afternoon.

As the sun started to set and the air cooled marginally, they set out and covered 20 kilometres to Mudrabarcoola, the site of two native wells. They found water but the well had two dead and rotting dingoes in it. They had no choice but to press on another 30 kilometres and try to reach Yerungarrowie soak, where Conrick hoped they would have a better chance of getting water.

First, they had to get there. One of the horses in the dray had all but given up pulling, and the other was doing all the work. Ogilby's horse was trembling and stumbling as it struggled over the sandy ground. Ogilby, now on foot, wasn't doing much better. Night had fallen but it remained unbearably hot. They struggled on until at last they reached Yerungarrowie.

The sandy bottom was completely dry. With fading hopes, Conrick started digging. Half a metre down there was still no water. He kept at it until, at last, he was rewarded with a trickle of water seeping into the hole. Slowly but surely the soak yielded enough water for the horses and men, and their empty water casks. Conrick decided to rest at the soak for a couple of days. There was dry feed for the horses, which helped them recover.

There was water in the soaks from Yerungarrowie to Mulligan Spring, where the horses were given another spell before they started on the return journey. The dry stage presented a real problem, as the horses now had to face it while pulling a much heavier dray, laden with flour and sugar.

The weather was only getting hotter. At Monte Collina well, a group of forty Aboriginal people tried to prevent them getting water but Conrick insisted and they relented. At Yerungarrowie, the last place they could be sure of water, the horses were rested, the water casks were filled and the harrowing dry stage began.

Conrick started early in the morning, but as day broke the temperature rose and rose. It became extremely hot, conditions made more uncomfortable as it became increasingly humid. As they covered the 30-kilometre stretch to Mudrabarcoola, the sky clouded over and grew darker. The cloud did nothing to reduce the building heat.

Conrick might have been hoping that the water at Mudrabarcoola had improved in the couple of weeks since the dingoes had been removed from the soak. However, when he was a kilometre away this became academic. There was a rumble of thunder as a storm swept in and lightning struck all around them. A tree near the dray was hit and exploded into flaming splinters. Drops of rain threw up puffs of dust from the parched ground before the heavens opened and heavy rain poured down.

After the storm passed, Conrick went to the highest ground he could find and observed a sheet of water extending for kilometres in every direction. The next day, they emptied the water casks, thinking they wouldn't need them. As luck would have it, though, they hit bone-dry country again within 15 kilometres.

Chastened by their hastiness, when they came upon another area where a storm had passed, they refilled the casks. From that point on, though, the country was waterlogged, which meant that the horses struggled in boggy conditions and could only manage about 15 kilometres a day. After three days and 50 kilometres of slogging through mud, a station manager appeared with a pair of draught horses to help pull them through.

The rains of 1877 heralded a run of good seasons, and by 1878 many of the Cooper Creek stations were in a position to send cattle to market down the Strzelecki Track. John Conrick sent seventy-two bullocks away in the middle of the year, leading the droving himself. He went all the way to Adelaide, selling one bullock at Orroroo, twenty-seven at Burra for £208 and the remaining forty-four in Adelaide for £390.

Around the same time, the South Australian government moved to improve the reliability of waters on the Strzelecki Track by constructing three earth dams. However, the combination of low rainfall (around 150 millimetres per annum) and high evaporation rates (around 3000 millimetres per annum) meant they made little difference.

In 1882 the South Australian government implemented a water conservation policy and appointed a Conservator of Water, J. W. Jones, whose responsibility included the improvement of water supplies along all of South Australia's stock routes. However, the water situation in the north of the state was about to change dramatically.

In 1883 a test bore at Tarkaninna, north-east of what would become the town of Marree, struck South Australia's first artesian water. The presence of what became known as the Great Artesian Basin held the promise of a seemingly limitless supply of water and the end of inland Australia's water worries. The main drawback was that drilling was expensive. Faced with a limited budget and competing demands for bores in the north-east, in 1890 the South Australian government decided to concentrate its drilling efforts on the Birdsville Track, the most direct route south from Queensland's Channel Country (see Chapter 7). The Strzelecki Track had to struggle on with dams and wells dug by Jones and his men.

There was better news for the pastoralists who relied on the Strzelecki with the coming of the Great Northern Railway. In 1883 it terminated at what became the town of Farina, just two days' travel from the stations at the southern end of the track. The chain of waterholes down the Strzelecki became the supply line for many of the stations that were now operating in the boom-and-bust, drought-and-plenty country of north-east South Australia and south-west Queensland.

The difficult dry stages were made easier by the use of camels, with cameleers based first at Farina, then also at Marree when the line was extended further north. The cameleers were collectively referred to as Afghans, although they also came from India and areas that are now part of Pakistan. Their camel trains dominated inland transport along the Strzelecki and the equally dry sections of the Birdsville Track for the next half century.

The cameleers carried equipment and supplies north. On the return journey they carried bales of wool from stations such as Cordillo Downs, which initially operated as a sheep station until predation by dingoes and competition from rabbits forced the owners to turn to cattle. The last sheep were shorn there in 1942. Shearers were known to make the 500-kilometre journey from Farina to Cordillo by bicycle, a feat that can only really be appreciated by anyone who has travelled the long, hot, dry, rocky, sandy, bumpy route by any other means and still found most of it extremely uncomfortable.

As time went on, it became increasingly clear that the inland of Australia had an erratic and seemingly unpredictable cycle of seasons. Long periods of drought were sometimes, but not always, followed by a couple of seasons of good rains or floods that overflowed the rivers and brought up nutritious herbage or feed. Along the Strzelecki Track, stations were established to take advantage of good seasons, only to be defeated by a run of bad seasons. In particularly bad seasons, the track had to be closed as a stock route, as it could be dry and bereft of feed for almost its entire length.

The Strzelecki Track was always fraught with danger for unwary travellers but even experienced stockmen could be caught. In

February 1889, Henry 'Little Jack' Smith, the stockman in charge at Toolatchie outstation, a Strzelecki Creek waterhole on Innamincka Station, got lost on the property in 47°C heat. He may have been checking the condition of the waterholes or the state of feed in the area. In any case, he perished before he was found.

The uncertainties of the Strzelecki Track meant the problem for the station managers throughout the area was deciding when to move cattle out and how long to keep them on the property. In a good season, when feed was abundant, it was tempting to keep stock fattening until they were ready for market. However, if the feed on the Strzelecki was eaten out, they could be caught with too many stock as drought took hold and the stock route closed.

In 1894 a drought unlike anything that had come before gripped the outback. It lasted until 1902. The Strzelecki Track was reduced to bare dust and was closed for several years. Losses for stations whose stock were trapped were appalling. In an interview John Conrick gave the *Advertiser* in 1914, he detailed his experience:

> I was more fortunate than many others, for they had to abandon their holdings, and I was not quite reduced to that extremity. Still I had to strain every nerve to save the situation, and for a long time was feeding horses and cattle on mulga and minnaritchie [a species of bush similar to mulga]. The latter only grows in the watercourses and the stock are fond of the leaves. During those terrible eight years I lost 3000 cattle out of 4000 on the run, and about 7000 out of 12000 sheep. Those that survived, as you might expect, were not very robust specimens, but they soon picked up, and a couple of years after the drought broke one would never have credited, judging by the appearance of the country, that it had ever been in the deadly grip of those awful dry seasons.

Further north, Sidney Kidman tried to save 2000 bullocks by having them moved from Carcoory Station (now part of Roseberth Station) to Haddon Downs Station, at the top of the Strzelecki Track. All of them perished. Cadelga, in the same area, had been stocked with 24000 sheep, 10000 cattle and 300 horses. At the end of the drought there were 300 sheep, thirty cattle and a handful of horses. Cordillo Downs lost 59000 out of 66000 sheep. Arrabury lost almost all of its stock. Coongie Station, west of the Strzelecki on Cooper Creek, was left with 920 cattle from a herd of 19000. Up on the Georgina the situation was just as bad: Carandotta Station was running 100000 sheep and lost 90000; of 20000 cattle, 15000 didn't make it.

Shearers and drovers found themselves trapped at shrinking waterholes. One of them, Jack Button, recalled being camped on Kulyamurra Waterhole, on Cooper Creek near Innamincka. It was the last water left. He watched brumbies come in to drink then become trapped as they were too weak to climb the banks. He and the men with him killed bullocks and lived on their tongues, the only part of the animals that was still edible. When Kulyamurra started drying out, Button gambled his life and carried his swag down the Strzelecki, escaping the blighted country on foot.

In a classic case of too little, too late, the South Australian government, which had been extracting duties from stock entering South Australia for years, finally sank an artesian bore at Monte Collina, at the southern end of the Strzelecki Track, after the 1902 drought. However, as more bores opened on the Birdsville Track, the more direct route for stock coming down from western Queensland and the Northern Territory, it became the preferred route for stock. The Strzelecki was doomed to become the road less travelled.

Pastoralists had been lobbying for railway lines to Birdsville and Innamincka ever since it had reached Farina, but it never eventuated for either of the little towns. With the coming of Federation, the removal of border duties for travelling stock meant that many border towns that sat astride the great stock routes through western Queensland went into decline. Not that everyone was sorry to see the duties go. John Conrick, who was charged every time he took his stock from his Queensland property to his nearest market in South Australia, commented in the 1890s:

It is now 21 years since I first opened the Strzelecki Route to South Australia, and although the country was then inhabited by savages only, I travelled through unmolested: and now after two decades this beautiful territory has become so thoroughly civilised that I am asked to arm myself with a permit before I can cross the border or run the risk of having my horse and buggy confiscated.

The township of Innamincka, at the junction of the Strzelecki and Cooper Creeks, had been in existence since a police camp was established there in 1882 to discourage stock duffing. The pub was licensed in 1885. The town might have weathered the departure of stock inspectors after Federation but the difficulties of travelling stock down the Strzelecki were made harder by a succession of terrible droughts in the first half of the twentieth century. Those stations that had struggled through the 1902 drought were hammered again in 1914 and 1925. In the 1925 drought, Durrie Station, on the Diamantina, lost 30000 head. The bodies of dead cattle were found densely packed around drying waterholes. In the drought of 1946, Innamincka Station was down to 2000 head when its management decided to destock entirely. The nearest station to the town had effectively shut down, the latest in a series of such closures. By then, most stations had also ceased running sheep and had concentrated on cattle, which were less labour-intensive.

By the end of World War II, the town of Innamincka had a population of only five. In 1952 the publican was told he had to upgrade the hotel. Unwilling to do so, he closed it instead. With cattle duffing pretty much a thing of the past, the pub was the main reason for the existence of the police station. Shortly after the pub closed, the police station shut as well.

In 1953 the Flying Doctor Service, which had run a nursing home in Innamincka since 1920, reviewed its operations. The nursing home was the only thing left in town. It still served the needs of the Aboriginal community and the few remaining stations, but the decision was made that their services could be provided by aircraft operating from Broken Hill. When the nursing home closed, the town of Innamincka was deserted.

By then, the Strzelecki Track was only likely to be used by drovers in good seasons. Otherwise, the bores on the Birdsville Track, sunk between 1890 and 1916, made it a better proposition. Stock coming down Cooper Creek could continue past the Strzelecki Track, following the Cooper's more reliable waterholes until it crossed the Birdsville Track. It was a longer journey but it involved less risk.

Fortunately, Innamincka's demise was short-lived. In the late 1950s oil exploration started in the area and soon oil was found throughout the region surrounding the town. The arrival of a new industry in the area saw road improvements, in particular to ensure that South Australia reaped the economic benefits of the mining activity, rather than Queensland or New South Wales.

With the new roads and growing interest in Australia's inland regions, tourism in the area also grew. Perched on a dusty gibber-strewn hill above the highest flood level of Cooper Creek, which between floods was a chain of idyllic waterholes perfect for a refreshing swim, Innamincka was an ideal stopping point. Visitors could use it as a base for exploring the sites related to the demise of the hapless Burke expedition. In 1972 a new hotel and shop were built in the town. The nursing home was refurbished and became a national park headquarters.

In recent years some other roads in the area have been given tourism-oriented titles like the Adventure Way. Not so the route that was once regarded by Augustus Gregory as the least difficult way into inland Australia. In fact, over the years the route turned out to be perilous at best. Nevertheless, it became one of the great stock routes of central Australia. It wasn't the best known, and certainly wasn't the most travelled, yet it retained connections with the famous exploits of Eyre, Sturt, Gregory, Burke and Harry Redford.

Today the road to Innamincka from Lyndhurst, just south of the ghost town of Farina, follows a less flood-prone route along higher ground east and west of the original stock route along Strzelecki Creek. For the last 100 kilometres a much rougher track can still be followed by those with stout hearts and stouter four-wheel-drives. The builders of the tourist road couldn't resist giving the route the name that still resonates throughout the outback – the Strzelecki Track.

What matter if the creeks are up – the cash, alas, runs down!

A very sure and certain sign we're long enough in town.

— 'West By North Again', Harry 'Breaker' Morant (1864–1902)

5

THE GREAT NORTH ROAD

The Overland Telegraph was one of the most audacious projects undertaken by an Australian state. When it put in a bid to build a line from the settled districts north of Adelaide, through the barely explored centre of the country, all the way to the newly established Port Darwin, on the north coast of the continent, South Australia was keen to secure a lucrative future as a hub for Australia's fledgling telecommunications network.

Over the years leading up to 1872, when the Telegraph was completed, thousands of men were employed along supply lines that extended 3000 kilometres across the country. As all those men had to eat, following in their wake came pioneering drovers seeking routes for sheep, cattle and horses through country that had defeated explorers only a decade earlier. Their names are all but forgotten, but their legacy endures in the country they opened to pastoralism and some of the greatest cattle stations in the world.

One of the longest overlanding expeditions, both in distance and in time, began even before the Overland Telegraph was thought of. Having heard that the South Australian government was prepared to pay £2000 to whoever was the first to drive 1000 sheep or 100 cattle overland to Darwin, in 1863 brothers Ralph and John Milner set out with several thousand sheep, intending to follow the explorer Stuart's route.

What the brothers may have heard was a garbled version of the government's reward for the first explorer to cross the country, but soon after they started they were caught in what became known as the Great Drought of the 1860s. Unable to travel north, they remained in South Australia until 1868, when the drought started to ease. By then work on the Telegraph had begun, and the hungry construction camps promised to be a ready market for large numbers of stock.

The Milners assembled fourteen men, twenty-five dogs (ten sheep-dogs, fifteen staghounds and greyhounds) and 300 horses, and headed for the properties run by missionaries at Killalpaninna and Koppera-manna on the Birdsville Track, hoping to acquire more sheep. However, while they were at Killalpaninna events took a tragic turn when Ralph Milner's wife died. She was buried at the station.

Finally, in September 1870, the Milners set out on their trek across Australia. The drovers included Ralph and John and seven other white stockmen, three Aboriginal men and an Aboriginal woman, who ran away a day after leaving Peake Station on the Oodnadatta Track. Their equipment included two bullock drays, a horse wagon and two spring carts, twelve months' provisions, material for making fifty pack saddles in case they had to abandon the wagons and drays, and between 4000 and 7000 sheep (accounts vary). The pay for the men was 25 shillings a week and a promise of half the government reward shared between them.

Details of the first part of the Milners' journey, which in its entirety was to take more than two years, are few and far between. What is known is that the expedition started at Kopperamanna, headed south past Mundowdna, then turned up the north-west track, following the telegraph line. They spent Christmas Day 1870 at Bulldog Creek, north of Mount Margaret Station, between William Creek and Oodnadatta.

Little is known about their activities in 1871, and the next record doesn't appear until 21 January 1872, when the *Advertiser* reported: 'A telegram from the Government Resident at Port Darwin announces that Mr J. Milner was murdered by natives at Attack Creek.' John Milner had been shepherding the flock at the creek in the Northern Territory, where the explorer Stuart's party had also been involved in a confrontation with Aboriginal warriors.

The rest of the men succeeded in reaching the Northern Territory's Top End towards the end of 1871. The reward, if it had ever existed, never materialised. As something of a consolation, Ralph Milner managed to sell the sheep to the Overland Telegraph construction project. However, his difficulties weren't over as the expedition had arrived in the middle of the Top End's wet season. Much of the country was boggy, if not impassable.

The feat of the Milners left a lasting impression on Alfred Giles, a South Australian farmer's son who joined the Overland Telegraph construction project as an assistant to John Ross, who established the exact route the line would take. Giles had already crossed the continent twice as part of his work, and was stationed in the Top End at Union Camp, near the junction of the Elsey and Roper rivers, when Milner's mob of sheep drew near.

On 7 December 1871 Giles heard from a party that had come up from the southern construction teams that Ralph Milner was on the Strangways River, with a flock of sheep, a mob of horses and a wagon. Giles, who was to become one of the pioneering settlers in the Top End, wrote in his memoir *Exploring in the Seventies*:

I could scarcely credit a flock of sheep being on the Strangways. Fancy, real mutton not more than 60 miles [100 kilometres] away! These were, undoubtedly, the first sheep ever brought overland from South Australia, or anywhere else, to the Northern Territory, and Mr Milner deserved the highest credit for this great pioneering feat.

Ralph Milner wasn't far to the south but it was to be two months before his sheep made it up to Giles' camp. On 3 February 1872 Ralph arrived at the camp on his own, saying he was optimistic that if the weather held, he'd get the sheep through within a few days.

After Ralph returned to his camp, the Top End was hit by more severe wet weather, and tremendous thunderstorms swept the country. However, Ralph was true to his word. He managed to get the sheep to the Elsey River, where, with the help of some of the Telegraph line workers, they managed to get the sheep over the wide, fast-flowing river. Wrote Giles:

> Some of the men carried them over on their backs, as there was no boat where the sheep crossed, which was at a point about three miles [four kilometres] above the junction of the Elsey and Roper Rivers, whereas the boat or line crossing was 10 miles [16 kilometres] higher up.

The sheep were in fairly good condition, considering they had walked nearly 2000 kilometres. By that stage they were carrying eighteen months' worth of fleece, having not been shorn since before they'd left South Australia.

On 11 February Ralph Milner reappeared at Giles' camp with fourteen horses, which had also been sold to the Overland Telegraph construction project. The sheep arrived later in the day, where they received a warm reception from men keen to enjoy their first fresh mutton after months of eating bully beef they referred to as 'red blanket'. Alfred Giles cast a bushman's eye over the flock and wrote:

The sheep, mostly ewes, were small and poor, averaging not more than 30 pounds [12.5 kg] dressed weight. I did not attribute their low condition wholly to the distance they had travelled so much as to their being heavily woolled, carrying an 18-months' fleece. The wool was of good quality and staple; the outer, or surface, was frayed and somewhat perished, but considering the unavoidable knocking about the sheep had had, this was not to be wondered at.

While the exact number of sheep Ralph started with isn't clear, he mentioned to Giles that he'd suffered heavy losses during the journey. On one occasion, at the Davenport Ranges south of Tennant Creek, he'd lost 900 head in a single night after they'd eaten a poison plant (*Gastrolobium grandiflorum*). A count of the sheep that reached the Top End revealed that from a mob that may have numbered between 4000 and 7000 when they started, only 1003 had survived.

Plans were made to distribute the sheep between the various construction parties in the Top End. Alfred Giles volunteered to take 300 head to the camp he was nominally attached to, but which hadn't been heard from for over five months because of the wet season. It was thought to be at or near Daly Waters, 250 kilometres south, where thirty-five men were under the command of a man named Burton. Having been out of touch for so long, grave fears were held for their supplies.

For Giles' 300 sheep, it meant retracing part of the journey they had already endured. On 13 February Giles counted out his sheep from the flock and set about getting them shorn, but it was soon apparent that the Telegraph men were deficient when it came to shearers. Wrote Giles:

Shearing in the Northern Territory was a novelty indeed, and among all the Government outfit no such article as sheep-shears was catalogued or thought of. Fortunately, Mr Milner was able to supply a few pairs.

Another remarkable fact was that out of more than 50 men in camp only one knew how to shear, and he happened to be the cook. Under his tutelage, four or five men started shearing, or, perhaps, I should say 'tomahawking'. The main thing was to get the wool off. There was no sorting or preparing. It was just chucked over the fence to rot, and would have grieved the squatter's heart.

The men weren't in any danger of breaking any records when it came to shearing, as they didn't finish until 1 March, two weeks after they started. Admittedly, the intervening period had been punctuated by a series of immense storms that inundated the country, making travel to Daly Waters impossible and the shearing of sodden sheep extremely difficult. Giles noted the fate of another mob of Milner's sheep that had been dispatched to another camp – they'd managed to cover less than 20 kilometres in sixteen days and still had 40 kilometres to go.

The wet season began to show signs of breaking, and by mid-March conditions had improved enough to allow the sheep to be moved. On 11 March, Alfred Giles and a colleague, Chris Bagot, rode over to the Elsey River and used a boat to sound the depth to see if the sheep could get across. At a crossing that was more than 200 metres wide, they found that in many places they couldn't touch the bottom with a long pole. They decided there was nothing for it but to boat the sheep over. The problem with that was the boat could only carry ten or so sheep at a time, which would mean at least thirty trips.

Reports from elsewhere in the Top End suggested conditions were worse on other river systems. In places, the Roper River was 10 kilometres wide. The north–south-running Strangways was impassable. When Ralph Milner tried to cross it, three of his horses were swept away, along with their packs and swags. While he set about trying to cross higher up, his men were living on nothing but mutton and water at his camp on Red Lily Lagoon, on the Roper River.

Alfred Giles was still convinced he could get across the Elsey. He rode to another camp and got hold of two coils of wire intended for the telegraph line, then rode back to the river. Securing the wire to a tree on the riverbank, he manoeuvred the boat to a tree in the middle of the stream, secured the wire and then tensioned it so it hung about a metre above the fast-flowing river. He then continued to the far bank of the river and secured the end of the wire to another tree. 'By these means,' Giles wrote, 'the boat would be propelled with greater speed, and straighter than with oars.'

On 14 March he built a yard on the opposite side of the river, to hold the sheep after they were boated across. The next morning he and his men brought the 300 sheep to the crossing place. They arrived at 3 p.m. and immediately started the boating operation. Giles soon discovered that even getting ten sheep into the boat meant cramming them in tightly. Most ended up in a 'sitting posture – in each others arms, as it were', as if they were out on a nautical excursion. On the first trip, things went awry.

> We had no oars but one man stood in the end of the boat, and, catching hold of the strained wire, pulled the boat along. When half-way across with the first load, the man let go the wire, and in trying to regain it capsized himself, as well as the boat and all the sheep. It was not a strong current, and we swam in, righted the boat, chased the sheep, and recovered them all, and by dark we had got 124 across. We started to boat again at daybreak the next morning, and got the whole 300 over by 10 o'clock.

Once begun, the operation proceeded remarkably smoothly, and several of Giles' colleagues who turned up to help were surprised when they found that the job was done before they got there.

Elsewhere the wet season was continuing to cause havoc. The mob of sheep being driven to the other camp had taken a month to cover

60 kilometres, an average of only 2 kilometres a day. The camp was on an open plain, and when the waters rose much of the gear had been swept away. The men managed to retreat to a rocky knoll a kilometre away, carrying stores, tents and swags through the rising water. All the heavy equipment was left behind, submerged. The drovers had managed to keep the sheep and horses to high ground, from which they looked out over kilometres of water where previously there had been land.

Amid the general inundation, on 17 March Alfred Giles started out from the Elsey River with his 300 sheep, bound for Burton's Camp at Daly Waters. With him were Chris Bagot, Albert Hanns, John Lowther and a man Giles described as a shepherd, Dave Johnson.

The men walked the sheep in the cool of the morning, from dawn until 10.30 a.m., when they reached All Saints Well, one of the many small bush camps set up by the construction teams. It was a journey of about 10 kilometres, under normal conditions an easy day's walk for sheep.

On 18 March they started out before dawn; leaving three sheep for the men at All Saints. Giles rode on ahead for 14 kilometres, scouting the route to a locality known as the Watertanks. When he got there, he set about building a yard in which to pen the sheep. That night it began to rain and a strong cold wind blew. It was unexpected weather for the tropics, and the recently shorn sheep suffered without their fleeces.

It continued to rain the next day and the ground was still so boggy that the men were forced to drove the sheep along higher ground, where they could find it. The consequence was that they were only able to manage another 10-kilometre stage, travelling the sheep across country.

This being only the second time anyone had attempted to drove sheep through the Top End – the first had been part of explorer Augustus Gregory's 1856 expedition from the Top End to Queensland – and

possibly the only time it was ever attempted in the wet season, Giles
and his men were learning as they travelled. Giles noted that 'There
were numerous tracks of the savages having been there, but we saw
none.' Unfortunately, this meant he was unable to record the Aboriginal response to their first encounter with sheep. On the Gregory
expedition Aboriginal people had visited his camps while they held
sheep but their reactions had gone unrecorded. Elsewhere in Australia, the Aboriginal people attached a natural comparison to the
strange-looking creatures. In New South Wales, Aboriginal people
called them jumbuks, meaning 'little clouds'.

When the weather cleared, the days grew progressively warmer
and it was only possible to drove the sheep in the cool of the morning and late in the afternoon. The tropical sun was quickly drying the
country, and they were soon travelling 12 kilometres a day and able
to use the road more often. Unfortunately, as the waters receded,
mosquitoes proliferated. Wrote Giles:

> The next day [24 March] we made the same distance, and camped
> on the edge of the 'Bay-o'-Biscay' [Giles' expression for impassable
> wetlands] in the company of millions of mosquitoes. They worried the
> sheep, biting their bare bellies and their ears. The grass was so long
> that we did not require to make a yard for the sheep. If we camped
> them on the road, we put a few bushes across the road in front and
> behind them and the long grass forming the sides held them safely.

On 27 March Giles and Chris Bagot left the other men to drove the
sheep and set out to locate Burton's camp, estimated to be about 40
kilometres to the south. So many months had passed since Burton
and his men had been heard from that there was no great certainty
as to their exact location.

Giles and Bagot took a packhorse and two days' provisions, so
confident were the two young bushmen that they would locate the

camp without difficulty. After all, how hard could it be to find thirty-odd men?

It wasn't long before they found the tracks left by Burton's carts, but in places they were washed out for many kilometres. Only through expert tracking and dead reckoning were they able to relocate them on the other side of 'Bay-o'-Biscay' country. In places the ground had completely dried out. In others areas they were forced to slog through the mud on foot, while they led the horses. They covered more than 30 kilometres, by the end of which their mounts were exhausted. Typically, Giles made no mention of his own fatigue or that of his colleague.

The next day the two men pressed on, following dray tracks for 12 kilometres before hitting another section of terribly boggy ground. They battled on until they reached Stuart's Swamp, 4 kilometres from Daly Waters, where they found fresh boot tracks. It was then a simple matter of following the tracks up Daly Creek to find Burton's camp.

The men were extremely glad to see the first new faces to appear in their incredibly isolated world after five long lonely months. Wrote Giles:

> The news that I had 300 sheep within 30 miles [48 kilometres] was most gratifying to the poor fellows, and they actually took off their hats and cheered us. They had been subsisting for two months upon three pounds [1.4 kilograms] of flour to each man a week, and any fish or game they could catch. They had been without tea or coffee during that time, and were drinking a substitute made from split peas roasted and steeped in boiling water. They called it coffee – most abominable stuff we thought it.

Although the men had been cut off and were almost starving, work had continued on the telegraph line, and 25 kilometres of poles had been put in place through wild and boggy terrain.

Men were assigned to help bring the sheep through. They included friends of Giles' named Ringwood and Bob Abrahams, and two other men, W. Edwards and F. Foreman. It took them two days, riding fresh horses, to reach the sheep camp. It was going to take a lot longer to bring the sheep through the boggy ground to Daly Waters. Giles detailed the trials and tribulations:

The weather continued beautifully fine. There were large smokes to the south-east and south in the evening – the first we had seen that year – and it was a sure indication of the drying-up of the grass and swamps and the end of the tropical wet season. On Tuesday 2nd April, Johnson, the shepherd, and I started with the sheep, leaving Abrahams and Edwards to bring on the packhorses at their leisure. We found we could only get the sheep three and a half miles [4.5 kilometres] easterly, as we had to dodge bogs and swampy parts. We then camped. I tried to cross the Bay-o'-Biscay country higher up and nearer the Birdum [Creek], but found it still too swampy. The sheep travelled very well. Next morning Johnson and I started at daylight, and at three miles [four kilometres] reached a sheet of water about a mile [1.6 kilometres] wide and from one to two feet [30 to 60 centimetres] deep. It took us four and a half hours to cross the sheep over it. We then reached a small patch of dry forest country and camped, thoroughly tired out with wading through the water backwards and forwards often carrying sheep from hillock to hillock, pushing them along, and pulling them out of bogs and crabholes. After more than 12 years among sheep, I never before encountered such difficulties when travelling as were to be met with in this country and at this time of year, when the grass was from seven to 12 feet [2 to 3.5 metres] high, twisted and tangled together so that the sheep could not face it. This, together with the floods, swamps and bogs of the wet season, which they had to be boated or dragged and tailed through, left it not only a matter of surprise that they had any condition at all, but that they lived through it!

Despite the hardships, Giles thought the Top End had plenty of potential for sheep. All that was needed, he believed, was a better understanding of the climate and a regime of burning the grass and overstocking for the first couple of years, to improve its land quality and give herbage a chance to come through. He also noted that the sheep Milner had brought from South Australia were merinos and that their hardiness had been proved by the long distance they had travelled and all they had been through over the last two years. He neglected to recall that 75–85 per cent of the animals had perished in the process.

It took six days to get the sheep through to Daly Waters, where, on 8 April 1872, 'all hands enjoyed a plentiful supply of fresh mutton . . . Everybody was pleased and reheartened, feeling that the bogs, isolation, and uncertainty were at an end. All looked forward to the speedy, and uninterrupted completion of this great work.'

The camp also received news from the south that the Overland Telegraph was now in operation between Tennant Creek and Adelaide, spanning more than half the continent. Soon the line from the north would reach Daly Waters and the intervening gap would be bridged by a pony express during the few months it took for the remaining line to be completed.

Later in 1872 Alfred Giles travelled to the Roper Landing, as the Overland Telegraph work was almost done. Roper Bar was the landing place for supplies being carried to the construction teams in the interior. During his journey he came upon one of the features that would mark the western starting point of the stock route that was to become the Gulf Track (see Chapter 6):

> We halted for dinner at Mount McMinn, a beautiful and high table-topped
> mountain close to the Roper River and 12 miles [19 kilometres] from
> the Roper Landing. On leaving this we passed through a remarkable

rocky gorge with immense rocks and twisted stones of every conceivable shape. It has, for some reason, been named Hell's Gates.

The Roper Landing was a bustling depot 120 kilometres up-river from the sea. More than 300 men had assembled there, and the numbers were growing as construction teams finished their tasks and converged on the depot from their camps inland. In September 1872 it had briefly been the most populous locality in the entire north of Australia. Rows and rows of tents were surrounded by wagons, drays and buggies, mobs of horses and teams of bullocks. The steamer *Young Australian* had tied up on the bank of the Roper alongside the camp, ferrying men and equipment to the larger steamer *Omeo* waiting in deeper water at the river mouth.

Most of the men at Roper Landing had been leaving the Northern Territory, never to return. Some, however, were left behind as part of the permanent staff of the completed telegraph line. They included drovers who were responsible for supplying livestock to the telegraph stations dotted along the line, especially in the early days when their vegetable and fruit gardens and herds and flocks of cattle, sheep and goats were being established.

While he was at Roper Landing, Alfred Giles recorded the arrival of the first stock to be overlanded from Queensland:

On 18th September, 1872, Mr Dillon Cox arrived with about 400 head of cattle, which, under the charge of his drover, Mr Wentworth d'Arcy Uhr, he had brought across from Queensland. These were undoubtedly the first cattle ever introduced overland into the Northern Territory, and it reflected credit upon Mr Cox and Mr Uhr for their plucky enterprise and endurance shown by droving stock across hundreds of miles of perfectly unknown country, risking floods or dry stages, as well as contending with hostile and treacherous savages.

From the scant accounts of the journey, it appears Uhr was a particularly hard man. Following the approximate route taken by Ludwig Leichhardt in 1844–45, he shot any Aboriginal people who dared oppose him. When one of his men pulled a gun on him, Uhr attacked him with a stockwhip.

The problem for Uhr and Cox was that they'd arrived too late. A big mob of cattle was no longer needed, as the telegraph construction teams were preparing to leave. They were slaughtering many of their own bullocks, no longer needed for the work, and didn't need more.

The upshot was that the Roper Landing saw its first court case, to settle a dispute between cattle-owner Cox and drover Uhr. The case was heard in a mess tent, presided over by Captain Douglas, Special Magistrate. Cox wanted Uhr to take the cattle on to Darwin, where he had some hope of finding a market for his beef. However, Darwin was several hundred kilometres away and Uhr refused to do the extra work without receiving an additional payment.

There was certainly no thought of stocking a run in the area with the cattle. Eventually a deal was struck and Uhr took the cattle on to what became known as the Cox Peninsula, west of Darwin, where they were slaughtered as required, then boated across and sold to the good citizens of the fledgling town.

Alfred Giles retained his association with the Overland Telegraph. Shortly after its completion, he overlanded 7000 sheep up the Oodnadatta Track, then along the telegraph line and the Great North Road. In 1874 he was asked to take another 5000 sheep north. In the process of mustering the mob, he met Harris Browne, whose brother W. J. Browne had taken up leases on Springvale and Bonrook stations, near present-day Katherine.

Browne asked Giles to overland stock to the stations in what author Ernestine Hill called 'the greatest cavalcade of droving ever seen in

Australia'. Involving 300 horses, 2000 cattle and 12000 sheep, it was certainly one of the biggest stock movements to the Territory. However, it would soon be eclipsed as vast areas were opened for pastoralism and a huge stocking operation got under way, as detailed in Chapter 6.

Despite Giles' initial opinion, sheep never did well in the tropical Top End. It was just too hot and humid. Freighting wool to market was also expensive, and the quality and yields were never good. Many sheep simply starved on the poor-quality grasses after arriving in the Top End, and within a decade it was almost exclusively cattle and horse country.

Giles eventually bought Bonrook Station from the Brownes, and remained in the Territory for the next fifty years.

Once the telegraph line was completed, the construction track became the foundation of the stock route known as the Great North Road. Sheep and cattle stations were established further north along the chain of mound springs that had been discovered, from Herrgott Springs (now Marree) to Alice Springs.

Repeater stations established a permanent European presence at the Peake, Strangways Springs and Charlotte Waters. North of the Alice, the construction gangs found gold at Pine Creek, which sparked a brief rush to the area, although the remoteness, primitive conditions and tropical climate made it one of the most lethal gold-fields ever discovered in Australia. It briefly provided a market for livestock that encouraged further settlement of stations in the area.

The further extension of the Great North Railway also aided development in central Australia. The railway reached Marree in 1884, and while pastoral interests in south-west Queensland hoped the line would be extended to Birdsville, the practicalities of supplying water to steam engines meant that over the next five years it followed the mound springs west and then north, through Coward Springs and

William Creek and on to Warrina. It reached Oodnadatta in January 1891. The Depression of the 1890s ended further progress until 1926, when the line was extended by the Commonwealth government north from Oodnadatta to Alice Springs with the famous Ghan line. It wasn't until the twenty-first century that the line to Darwin was finally completed, following a route west of the original Ghan line.

Long before then, sheep and cattle stations had been established along much of the length of the Overland Telegraph. Stock from central Australia, particularly around Alice Springs and Tennant Creek, travelled south along the Great North Road and Oodnadatta Track.

Within a decade of its completion, the Overland Telegraph wrought extraordinary changes in northern Australia. While it became a communications lifeline, the telegraph stations also became the backbone of other services in the sparsely populated region. The operators had to be almost totally self-sufficient, and sick or starving drovers soon found that the supplies and medical attention the stations could provide sometimes made the difference between life and death.

As the subsequent chapters in this book reveal, the stocking of the north would have been possible without the Overland Telegraph but it would have been accompanied by far more tragedy and disaster if not for the thin wire of civilisation that threaded through the loneliest regions of the country along the Great North Road.

Oh, may the showers in torrents fall,

And all the tanks run over;

And may the grass grow green and tall

In pathways of the drover

— 'Andy's Gone with Cattle', Henry Lawson (1867–1922)

6

TWENTY THOUSAND TO THE TERRITORY

There are few more potent examples of the ability of communication to transform the world than the arrival of a simple strand of telegraph wire in the Northern Territory in 1871. While the Overland Telegraph gave Australia virtually instantaneous communication with the world, within the space of ten years it changed the Territory from the almost exclusive domain of its Indigenous inhabitants to being the focal point of one of the greatest migrations of livestock the world has ever seen.

The telegraph line and the chain of telegraph stations that supported it were the first major pieces of infrastructure in the Territory, and would be the only major infrastructure for decades to follow. The South Australian government took over the administration of the Territory in 1863. In 1877, in order to encourage further settlement, it allowed large areas to be leased on extremely favourable terms. Leaseholders didn't have to stock their runs for three years.

The immediate reaction from speculators in the eastern states was a rush for grass. Much of it was leased sight unseen, then sold and resold by owners who would never set eyes or spend a penny on the land that was reaping them rich rewards. But the opportunity was fleeting. The deadline for stocking the first leases to be taken up was 1880, and as time ran out the only people left in the game were pastoralists who actually intended to stock their runs, something that was far easier said than done.

Stock had been travelling up the telegraph line to supply the telegraph stations since their establishment in the early 1870s, but as the stations in Queensland spread west during the same decade, an advantage over stock from South Australia soon emerged. The Queensland stations were much closer: from Adelaide to Darwin it was 3000 kilometres; from the Queensland border to Darwin it was about 1500 kilometres.

The first to attempt the journey was D'Arcy Uhr in 1872, droving 400 cattle from Charters Towers bound for the construction depot for the telegraph line on the Roper River, as detailed in Chapter 5. His violent reaction to any encounter with Aboriginal people meant that subsequent overlanders found the Aboriginal people along Uhr's route extremely hostile.

One trip in the 1870s, led by a man named William Nation, ended in disaster. Facing flooded rivers, Aboriginal attacks and crippling fevers, the stockmen deserted, leaving Nation and one stockman, named Elvey, with what remained of a mob of 500 cattle. Stalked by Aboriginal warriors, Nation and Elvey abandoned the cattle and concentrated on saving their own lives. Their flight was halted at the Limmen River, which was in flood, and they were forced to head inland. When Nation fell ill, Elvey continued on alone, trying to reach the telegraph line and summon help. To no avail. It's thought that Nation, after whom Nation Creek is named, starved to death.

Clearly the Gulf Track, as it came to be known, wasn't for the faint-hearted, but as 1880 drew nearer the pressure was increasing to get livestock through. Go west, young man, was the cry. But who would lead the way?

The answer came in the form of the greatest drover Australia has ever seen. That's a big call, but Nat Buchanan's achievements stand head and shoulders above anyone else. Born in Ireland in 1826, he migrated to Australia with his parents and four brothers in 1837, and grew up on a property on the New England plateau of New South Wales. In his lifetime as a drover and station owner, he pioneered stock routes from one side of the country to the other – from Rockhampton and Bowen, on the coast of Queensland, to Broome and the Murchison Goldfields in Western Australia. He also established, on his own or in partnership, two of Australia's most famous stations – Bowen Downs and Wave Hill.

In 1878 Nat Buchanan was asked to tackle the Gulf Track, taking 1200 head of cattle from Aramac in central Queensland to the newly formed Glencoe Station in the Top End. He got them there with the loss of one man, killed in an Aboriginal attack, but with more cattle than when he started (several cows calved along the way, and the newborns made up for cattle that had been speared by Aboriginal people or taken by crocodiles during the journey). In the process he established the route of the Gulf Track, which soon saw mob after mob following the trail he'd blazed. That alone was enough to make Nat Buchanan famous, but it was nothing compared to what came next.

In 1881 he embarked on what was recognised at the time, and remains to this day, a record droving feat. It created such a sensation that newspapers around Australia – Melbourne's *Argus*, the *Sydney Morning Herald* and Brisbane's *Courier-Mail* – all mentioned it. The *Northern Territory Times and Gazette* reported:

Mr C. B. Fisher, of Melbourne, has joined Messrs Maurice Lyons and A. W. Sergison in their extensive pastoral and agricultural properties in the Northern Territory of South Australia, and arrangements have been made to start immediately several herds of choice cattle, numbering about 20 000 head, under the supervision of Mr Nathaniel Buchanan. The owners intend soon to have 50 000 head of cattle on the country. They are also starting about 500 head of well-bred mares and necessary stallions for the above-mentioned runs, as the beginning of a large stud to breed horses for the Indian market.

The destination was Glencoe once more, and a nearby station at the Daly River. Buchanan had droved stock longer distances and done so through difficult country, but no one had ever attempted to take this many cattle at once. The ideal number of cattle in a mob was around a thousand. The challenge Buchanan faced was to drove twenty times the norm. The problems were endless: How many people would he need? How many horses? How long would it take? How much food and equipment was needed, in particular for the thousand kilometres of unsettled country where there was no opportunity to resupply? How many drays would it take to carry it all? And how would he keep such a big mob together? Should he split it up? If so, what size should each mob be? And how would he keep track of them all?

As Nat Buchanan rolled up his sleeves in May 1881, one thing was immediately obvious: he was going to need more than a few good men. In this he was particularly fortunate. He not only knew most of the best drovers in the country, he was related by marriage to three of them. W. R. (Wattie) Gordon, W. G (Willie) Gordon and J. H. (Hugh) Gordon were like peas in a pod – slender and upright, with typical flowing drovers' beards and piercing eyes accustomed to scanning far horizons. All three were more like brothers to Nat than brothers-in-law, so much so that when Nat's wife Kate had borne him their only child, in 1864, he was named Gordon.

The question of where to get 20 000 head of cattle was resolved by Messrs Lyons and Fisher, who owned several stations in southern Queensland, near the town of St George. It was decided to muster up to

16000 head from Noondoo, Carrawillinghi and Willmot stations, and make up any shortfall by purchasing more livestock from surrounding stations. The preferred beasts were three years and older, strong enough to withstand the rigours of travelling up to 3000 kilometres to the gulf and beyond. Older cattle were also more manageable than young cattle, a significant consideration given the size of the operation.

Huge cutting-out camps were established on the stations. As the drafts for the road were being assembled and branded, the growing mobs were held on camp by stockmen who circled them day and night. For many, a hard day of mustering was followed by a night watch with up to four more hours in the saddle. Under the circumstances, it wasn't hard to rack up sixteen hours a day on horseback. When they weren't working, the men slept – any time, anywhere. It was a taste of things to come. In a biography of his father, Gordon Buchanan (aged seventeen at the time) recalled:

> The cutting out camps were centres of furious activity and apparent confusion. Sweating horses and men were inextricably linked with the ever circling herd, amid the dust. But [the apparent confusion] was not so. The confined body of cattle with two horsemen, cutters out, riding through them, was very difficult to keep together. It required from six to ten men continually riding around the circumscribed area of the cutting out camp to prevent spreading and occasional breakaways from the bellowing, insurgent and rebellious throng.
>
> The good camp horse knows his quarry as soon as the whip or spur is popped on him and is the embodiment of speed, dexterity, intelligence and beauty. Propping, jumping, wheeling on his hind legs, anticipating by a fraction of a second every refractory turn of a beast. All his rider has to do is sit on him – not an easy job for some, but an intensely exhilarating one. He is the complete artist and is reserved almost entirely for this work.

Drays and drovers were also assembling around the mobs. The trip across central Queensland was through stations and towns where supplies were readily available, so when the mobs finally started out on the road north towards the Gulf of Carpentaria, probably around the beginning of August 1881, the drays were only lightly loaded. Swags, spare saddles, cooking utensils, tents, mosquito nets, basic medicines and hundreds of other items were packed in a highly organised manner so that anything that was needed could be found quickly. Things that were needed regularly, like swags, were packed where they were most accessible.

It was decided to divide the 16000 head of what became known as 'the southern contingent' into seven mobs of roughly 2300 head each. This was still twice the size of a typical mob of cattle, but with older cattle and expert drovers, Buchanan hoped they'd be manageable. He put Willie Gordon, the oldest of the Gordon brothers, in overall charge of the seven mobs; he was also boss drover of one mob. The other boss drovers were H. G. (Harry) Farquharson, W. (Big Bill) Farquharson, Jack Furnifull, Charley Craig, a drover named Kennedy and another named Scott.

When the cattle started their journey, the stockmen from the stations who'd helped with the mustering stayed with each mob for a couple of days to help the drovers train them for the new routine of travelling. Fresh cattle were more likely to rush. After a few days, they became accustomed to walking and grazing between 13 and 16 kilometres a day. They settled down more readily at their night camp and became familiar with the stockmen circling them on night watch.

Some drovers believed that cattle arriving at a camp that had just been vacated by another mob settled more easily. Others believed it made no difference. There were still rushes: all it took was one beast to take fright at something – a nip from a centipede, a stockman striking a match – and the effect on the mob was like wind through a field of wheat. The mob reacted almost as one: up and away.

At night, cattle will rush if they suddenly realise a stockman is nearby. So the stockmen 'make a bit of noise' so the stock always know where they are. Some recite poetry, most sing. One stockman told this writer he loved hearing Aboriginal stockmen singing in their language. An Aboriginal stockman said he preferred Tex Perkins.

When all the cattle were finally started on the road, the line of mobs stretched for over 100 kilometres. Having seen them on their way, Nat and a lively young stockman called Tom Cahill headed to Wood-house Station near Townsville to buy horses. Some were the 500 destined for the Glencoe and Daly River stations, while others were needed for the sixty or so men droving the mobs. When they had 120 unbroken horses, Tom, his brother Matt and an unnamed Aboriginal stockman drove them west towards Richmond Downs Station on the Flinders River, near the present-day town of Richmond.

Tom was not much bigger than a jockey, but he had more than his share of skill, energy and courage. His strategy for managing the untrained horses was to keep them tired and hungry. In the morning, with Tom in the lead and Matt and the Aboriginal stockman pushing the mob along from the rear, they trotted the horses along the road. They were given a spell at midday. Then they pushed on to night camp, again at a brisk pace, covering up to 50 kilometres in a day. At night, the tired horses were less inclined to stray far from camp while they grazed.

As they travelled, the three young men took advantage of any yards they came across to pause for a day or two to break in some of the horses. Some drovers believe that breaking in on the road has the advantage of the horses ending up being quieter and easier to catch, plus they learn their lessons better when they go straight from being broken in to working with cattle. After a week where they spend half a day behind stock, they're as good as many experienced horses. The one disadvantage is if an unbroken horse bolts or jumps out of a yard with a rope on. More often than not, they'll gallop in panic until they drop dead from exhaustion. If they survive, they're usually ruined for any kind of work.

Aware of the dangers, by the time the young stockmen were close to Richmond Downs, 300 kilometres from Woodhouse Station, most of the young horses were ready for work. They were so accustomed to the daily routine that Tom was able to leave his brother and the Aboriginal stockman to help Nat bring fifty more horses from Mount Sturgeon Station. Tom rode 160 trackless kilometres to reach the station, where he and Nat were in complete agreement on the method for droving small mobs of horses short-handed. The two of them set out for Richmond Downs with the fifty head and beat Tom's brother there.

The furiously busy Nat Buchanan had already organised the purchase of another 4500 cattle from Richmond Downs, and by the time they arrived at the station most of the mob had been mustered. Unfortunately, the entire mob rushed one night and flattened a large part of the fencing where they'd been yarded. The mustering had to start over, and with the yards destroyed the mob had to be held on camp, watched night and day by circling stockmen.

There were several bad rushes, and extra horses were kept ready for any emergency. Often the whole camp would be roused from sleep to ride out and turn the mob or round up strays.

The delays and rushes cost one stockman, Paddy Fitzpatrick, his life. He had galloped his horse to the head of a rush of 1200 cattle and was trying to turn the leaders when his horse fell. The rushing cattle ran right over Fitzpatrick and he was trampled to death.

Soon, though, the newly drafted and branded cattle were on the move along O'Connell Creek, down the Flinders River and towards the Gulf Track. Accounts put them in two or four mobs, certainly with boss drovers Hugh Gordon and 'Galloping' Miller, and possibly drovers Wattie Gordon and Tom Cahill.

As 1881 drew to a close, and the wet season approached, the Richmond Downs and southern contingent mobs converged on

the Leichhardt River. The two mobs may have formed into a single ponderous column just before reaching Leichhardt Crossing,
80 kilometres south-east of the tiny settlement of Burketown. Whether
they travelled in single or separate formations, the 20 000 cattle were
united in their struggles with mud as the first rains of the wet season
started to fall.

Several mobs were bogged down when the Flinders and Cloncurry
rivers burst their banks and spread over the flood plains until they
were 5 kilometres wide. Some cattle were caught on high ground
between the river channels, while the wiser drovers kept their stock
to the higher ground away from the flood plains. It meant the feed
and water for the cattle wasn't as good, but they were able to push
further ahead until more rain bogged their drays as well. Supply
drays from Normanton, 150 kilometres east, couldn't get through
either.

Eventually, they straggled on to the Leichhardt Crossing, near
Floraville Station, where the cattle were spelled (rested) in a fixed
camp and the drovers waited for a break in the weather. With the
mobs now assembled in one place, Nat Buchanan took the opportunity to assemble the supplies and equipment needed for the big
push west. Beyond Burketown, there was no chance to resupply until they reached Elsey Station, near the telegraph station at
Katherine, 900 kilometres away. Nat needed to procure everything
needed for about sixty men, nine separate droving teams and a trip
that would take at least five months.

With the temptations of Burketown not far away, there was soon
trouble in the camp. The first to go was 'Galloping' Miller, who
according to Gordon Buchanan 'exceeded the limit'. Presumably, this
means he went on a prolonged drinking spree, for he was replaced
by another boss drover, named Mooney.

Next, many of the stockmen went on strike. They said they wanted
more money, but it was suspected that many had already gone on the

grog and didn't want to continue beyond Burketown. Not far from the town was a locality called Hell's Gates, now the Hell's Gates Roadhouse, so called by drovers because the crossing into the Northern Territory took them into country where the only law was 'survival of the fittest'. At the other end of the Gulf Track was a gorge that would also be referred to as Hell's Gates in later years, as it was near the start of the Gulf Track for drovers bringing stock in the other direction.

Burketown was typical of frontier towns throughout the outback. In his memoir *Early Days in North Queensland,* Edward Palmer wrote:

> Burketown was the haven of refuge for all the inlanders and outlaws from the settled districts when they made other places too warm to hold them any longer. All kinds of characters made their way out to the Gulf in those early days. Men went there who had been wanted by the police for years. Horse-stealing and forging cheques were very common pastimes among the fancy, and Burketown society, in its first efforts to establish itself, was of a kind peculiarly its own.

Gordon Buchanan didn't entirely blame the stockmen for striking. He noted that wages ranged between 50 shillings to £3 and found, meaning that all meals and other incidentals were provided, but 'even in those days it was none too high'.

The strike put immense pressure on the drovers and stockmen who stuck to the job. Gordon Buchanan noted:

> The three Gordons and Tom Cahill with the help of the other boss drovers, and a few smart and reliable men and boys [possibly a reference, common at the time, to Aboriginal stockmen of all ages] who stuck to them, had great difficulty in holding the cattle. However, some of the men returned, and others joining, a start was made during a lull in the wet weather!

A combination of factors had ended the strike. In time-honoured tra-dition, the stockmen had handed all their money over the bar, and were broke. As the cattle started to move, they didn't want to be left behind without a job or money. Most had a horse or two of their own – Gordon noted that the total number of horses, including those being droved to Glencoe, was around 700 – but it was a long, lonely ride from Burketown to anywhere that might pass for civilisation.

The strikers had nearly three weeks to make up their minds, as the mobs started moving out, one after the other, a day or two apart. At that rate, it took between nine and eighteen days to get the great mass of cattle, drays, horses and men started.

The mobs soon settled into their rhythm as they crossed the Plains of Promise, the easygoing grasslands between Floraville and Punjab stations, south of Burketown. Big Bill Farquharson was boss drover of the lead mob. Next came young Tom Cahill. His age at the time isn't certain, but to this day drovers are fond of pointing out that there aren't many jobs where a sixteen-year-old can be put in charge of over a thousand head of cattle; they also point out that there aren't many sixteen-year-olds these days who could do it. The order of boss drovers in the following mobs isn't clear but included drovers Kennedy, Harry Farquharson and Jack Furnifull.

Willy Gordon was in charge of the last mob, and had the unenvi-able task of picking up the stragglers and weakened cattle that had dropped out of the mobs ahead. It was another sign of the esteem Nat had for his brother-in-law that he entrusted him with a position that demanded a tirelessly conscientious drover.

Beyond Punjab Station, the rains returned. The going was heavy, with boggy ground slowing progress. Up to that point the drays had been able to use the relatively firm Normanton–Burketown road – which suggests it may actually have been in better condition than it is today – although one cook and driver who pulled a dray off the track promptly sank it to the axles.

By now it was March or April 1882, and the wet season was drawing to a close. As the going started to get easier, Nat rode ahead to the Nicholson River where Big Bill Farquharson's mob was nearing Turn Off Lagoon, the appropriately named point where the Gulf Track began, heading north-west away from the westerly trending river, near the present-day community of Doomadgee, to skirt the Gulf of Carpentaria.

At the lagoon there was a bush shanty run by a man named Mick Cassidy. It was the last outpost of European habitation in western Queensland. A few of the men quit when they got there, rather than face the great empty spaces of the Northern Territory, much of it inhabited by Aboriginal people resentful of the growing stream of Europeans invading their lands.

The rest pressed on, now passing through country that was rapidly drying out after the Big Wet. The mud was replaced by dust that rose from the plodding lines of cattle, as the men in each droving team settled into their positions around the herd. Taking the estimate of sixty men spread across nine mobs, there were roughly seven men responsible for each group of animals. Each team had a cook who had breakfast ready just before dawn. The horse-tailer was up well before dawn rounding up the horses to be used for the day's droving. After the stockmen had eaten, they mounted their horses and got the cattle up and moving. While the cook packed up the camp, the tailer rounded up the horses that were being spelled that day and rode at a leisurely pace towards the next night's camp, sometimes helping the cook get the dray through difficult sections of the track. A crucial role for the horse-tailer was to find good feed for the horses; this was particularly vital for the stockhorses if they were to maintain condition despite the heavy workload they endured on a long droving trip.

The dray usually passed the grazing cattle during the morning. It might provide lunch during the afternoon, but more often the stockmen carried their lunch with them and met the cook at the night camp, where dinner was ready and the swags waiting for those who didn't have to go on night watch.

On such a long trip, scurvy was a potential problem, caused by Vitamin C deficiency. In settled areas, the rations Nat organised for his drovers included meat and fresh vegetables, bought from Chinese grocers who seemed to be able to conjure produce from even the most unforgiving land. As the stock travelled further into the unin-habited outback, dried fruit provided the necessary nutrition.

While Nat was riding up to 100 kilometres a day, he was known to get through a day in the saddle on just a pocketful of raisins. Even Aboriginal stockmen were impressed by his ability to get by with just a couple of mouthfuls of water.

The remaining five men in each team were responsible for drov-ing the cattle. One rode in the lead, checking the leading cattle so the mob didn't get strung out over too great a distance and become unmanageable. The lead stockman was usually the boss drover, often taking a position that was least exposed to the choking dust the cattle kicked up. Two men rode on the wings of the mob to turn back any strays and keep the cattle moving. The last two men rode behind the mob to poke the slower cattle along.

A sense of the scrub country beyond the Nicholson River can be gained on a drive along the modern road called the Savannah Way. In places, the bush is so dense it's only possible to see a few metres. Being a monsoonal rainforest, inundated for half the year and bone-dry for the other half, the trees tend to be short-lived, fast-growing and slender. The landscape can be unchanging for hundreds of kilo-metres, the monotony broken only by the many rivers that drain towards the Gulf.

For the drovers, the scenery might have been boring but the chal-lenges of keeping their mob together and in sight in the dense scrub gave them plenty to keep them busy and attentive.

In early autumn, the insect life around the Gulf has to be seen to be believed. At night in particular, the ground, trees and bushes come alive as billions of tiny creatures emerge to forage under cover of darkness in the coolest part of the day. To protect his men, in particular from disease-carrying mosquitoes, Nat equipped them with nets made from calico and cheesecloth. An opening in the net was just large enough for a man to crawl inside, then close himself in.

The nets didn't help Drover Kennedy, who fell ill, probably with malaria, and spent much of the trip being carried in one of the drays. However, the nets may have saved another man, George Hedley. Wrote Gordon Buchanan:

> It was through one of these nets a blackfellow on the upper Nichol-son got the surprise of his life. Sneaking in the bright moonlight on to George Hedley's camp, the occupant was apparently asleep. But the over-cautious nigger [Buchanan's word] tried to lift the foot of the net to make sure of his blow, and got the contents of Hedley's revolver. Hedley had not been asleep and was watching all his movements.

Gordon didn't elaborate on the fate of the Aboriginal who'd been shot, and the derogatory reference seems to have been published without demur when it appeared in the *Stock and Station Journal* in 1922. The attack was the first of a series of encounters with Aboriginal people – some violent, others less so.

The lead mobs were 80 kilometres west of the Northern Territory–Queensland border when Tom Cahill's team was approached by half a dozen Aboriginal men. The area around the Calvert River was regarded as a place where the Indigenous population was particularly threatening. The passage between the sea and the inland escarpment narrowed to such an extent that spears could be thrown almost with impunity at the unsuspecting men and beasts below. Nat had been threatened by Aboriginal warriors at the Calvert on the trip he made in 1878 to pioneer the Gulf Track.

In contrast to their feared reputation, the men who faced Tom Cahill appeared to be friendly. Tom's men had just killed a beast, and in an attempt to foster good relations he gave the Aboriginal men all the meat and bones they could carry.

The Aboriginal men returned to their camp, which turned out to be in a gorge 2 kilometres from Tom's night camp. It was a little too close for comfort, especially when Tom saw that hundreds of people were gathered, presumably for an important ceremony. When the men returned with the beef, there was such a roar of approval it was heard all the way down on the river flat where the cattle were grazing. Startled, the animals promptly rushed.

After the cattle had settled down again, another group of men approached the camp, bringing their women with them. Nat had a policy of not allowing Aboriginal people to stay in his camps; on his previous trip through the region, a stockman had been killed while making damper, and countless conflicts between European and Aboriginal men (indeed between men regardless of race, colour or creed) came down to fights over women. As soon as he could, Tom sent the new group on their way.

There was another encounter the following day. A single Aboriginal man, in ceremonial paint and headdress, waded across the river and called on Tom's camp. He may have been trying to negotiate for more beef, but the negotiations were soon interrupted. Wrote Gordon:

No unfriendliness was shown him, nor did he appear at all alarmed until the Malay horse-hunter, who was wearing a white hat (and excepting that and his colour in no way differing from the other drovers) appeared in the distance. When the Malay, who was on horseback, was nearing the camp, the blackfellow jumped up, gave him one look of horror and alarm, and ran for his life, disappearing over the river bank as if seven devils were after him.

No explanation of this terror was ever forthcoming. He may have imagined something supernatural in the Malay's appearance. On the other hand, the memory of some depredation by the Malays, who used to visit the northern coasts of Australia, may have filled him with fear. However, there was no further intercourse, friendly or unfriendly, with those blacks after that.

That wasn't the case for the drovers following. Harry Farquharson had several horses speared and noticed that one had been butchered for meat. This made him suspect the people around the Calvert were particularly hungry, because they normally didn't eat horse meat. Passing the cliffs, his drovers were threatened by warriors. Harry attempted to fire a warning shot at them, but his revolver jammed. That night, as he was cleaning the gun, it discharged and hit him in the leg, the bullet lodging in the muscles behind one of his knees. He spent the ensuing months in the dray. The bullet stayed in his leg.

Another thing that made life interesting for the drovers was saltwater crocodiles (*Crocodylus porosus*). Whereas subsequent European hunting would drive the crocodile population to the point of extinction, Aboriginal hunting and egg collecting hadn't dented their numbers or size. Many were certainly large enough to tackle the cattle, and on several occasions stock drinking at the water's edge stampeded when crocodiles attacked.

Tom Cahill was sitting on his horse in half a metre of water when he noticed a 1.5-metre crocodile swimming towards him. He was about to shoot when it swam off towards a cow that was also taking a drink. Later, a dead crocodile measuring 3.5 metres was sighted.

One hazard that was almost unique to the Gulf Track was the danger of striking a river where the water was salty or brackish. As Jack Furnifull's mob approached the Robinson River, 150 kilometres west of the Northern Territory–Queensland border, the cattle rushed the water before the men could pull them up. Some cattle went mad, and careered off through the scrub. The stockmen managed to turn a few to where the water was fresh and some found their way to it on their own. An unspecified number were lost, and in droving terms it was considered 'a bad smash'.

At the Wearyan River, one of the stockmen, W. Sayle, fell ill and died. The nature of his illness was never diagnosed. His body was buried on the track, another addition to the unknown number of lonely graves scattered throughout the outback, many of which have long since disappeared. Where a simple wooden cross was used, termites devoured any evidence. In places, a pile or ring of stones remains. In a few instances, iron surrounds and headstones can be seen, erected by grieving relatives long after their son, brother, husband or father had perished, far from hearth and home.

> And oft in the shades of the twilight,
> When the soft winds are whispering low,
> And the darkening shadows are falling,
> Sometimes think of the stockman below.

It wasn't all danger and tension. The long line of cattle averaged from 10 to 15 kilometres a day, and in places the country opened out to grasslands studded with woolly butt and ironbarks. The cattle were now well trained to the road, and many had their preferred positions in the slowly grazing mobs. Day after day passed without incident, but Gordon Buchanan maintained that droving the mobs was anything but boring:

> Besides [the stockman's] interest in the cattle, many of which were individually known and would at once be missed if not in the mob, the flora and bird and animal life often claimed his attention.
>
> The venomous green tree ant, which builds its nest in the gathered leaves of the branch end, and the rifle fish, which shoots insects by

squirting a jet of water at them, together with the corkscrew or panda-
nus palm, which lines the permanent watercourses, the feather palm,
green plum tree, etc., all came under his observant eye.

And in the bright starry nights with occasional meteors, on the
morning watch when the cattle were usually quiet, the heavens with
their wonder and mystery would lead his thoughts to the Great Creator
of all. The Great Comet [visible from September 1882 until February
1883] of that year was also an absorbing interest in the early morning.

As the procession continued, despite the best efforts of the tailers,
the horses began losing condition. They were more picky than the
cattle, and the mobs following had to contend with a stock route that
had already been heavily grazed. The horses hauling the drays were
starting to struggle, although the loads were getting lighter. Some
horses all but gave up, and had to be led rather than ridden.

Fortunately, the organisation of the massive operation was so good
that the provisions were holding up well. Some of the men made
johnny cakes with the flour that was still in plentiful supply, supple-
menting the horses' diet with stockman's tucker.

Once the first mobs hit the Roper River, the going got easier. Despite
the long dry season, along the river flats there was still plenty of good
feed. The country was open and the travelling to Elsey Station was
getting better by the day. By then, however, the mobs were strung out
over more than 150 kilometres. The lead mobs, guided by Nat, were
gaining condition on good feed and travelling fast. At the back of the
20 000 head, Willie Gordon was nursing the strays and stragglers on
what was left, as well as droving his own mob.

Other mobs of cattle were also pushing past Nat's trailing mobs.
Three drovers with 5000 cattle were also on the road to Glencoe:
Jack Warby, Fred Smith and Barney Keiran. Soon they were com-
peting with Nat's leading mobs to see who could reach Glencoe first.

Once Elsey Station was reached, the drovers were back in

civilisation, such as it was. There was a distinct road to the telegraph
station at Katherine, from where the telegraph line could be followed north-west to Glencoe. The progress of the mobs could also be
reported in the press. On 16 December 1882, the *Northern Territory
Times and Gazette* noted a telegram it received from the manager of
Elsey Station on 11 December: 'Warby passed Elsey yesterday with
1616 head of cattle. Also a mob of Buchanan's cattle. Both mobs for
Glencoe.'

Buchanan's mob may have been the one with Tom Cahill in charge,
as he and Warby arrived at the Katherine River crossing at almost
the same time. Big Bill Farquharson had already crossed safely but
early wet-season storms had brought the river up.

Warby got to the river ahead of Tom Cahill, but only just. He was
keen to keep his lead over the youngster and, throwing caution to the
wind, drove his whole mob straight into the fast-flowing water. His
stockmen were on hand to guide the mob across. However, when the
lead cattle got into the middle of the river and started swimming, they
panicked and tried to turn back. The weight of the mob behind kept
pressing forward and now the river turned into a white foam of more
than sixteen hundred colliding, thrashing, milling beasts. The current
swept them downstream as chaos reigned. Seventy cattle drowned,
as did one of the stockmen's horses, forcing the stockman to swim for
his life. A few cattle made it to the far side, but most ended up back
on the southern bank, a kilometre downstream, where it took Warby
a day to round them up.

Nat's confidence in young Tom was justified. When Tom arrived at
the crossing, he began by swimming a few of the leading cattle across
to the far side of the river before sending the bulk of the mob into
the water. The main body of cattle could see their mates on the far
side, the ones who tended to lead the mob anyway, and they swam
towards them. The whole mob emerged from the river on the far side
without incident. Too easy.

The rivalry continued for all of the remaining 120 kilometres to the stockyards at Glencoe. There the station manager insisted on counting the cattle as they were yarded. Wrote Gordon:

> Cahill's cattle were the nearer, but Warby met him between the wings as [Tom] was opening the big double gates, and with blustering challenge claimed priority.
>
> 'My lot is going through first, Tom. Get out of the way.'
>
> But Tommy, five feet two [155 centimetres] in his socks, stood his ground. His burly rival threatened to knock him down.
>
> Tommy's blue eyes flashed as he picked up a stout but supple yarding stick.
>
> 'Come another step closer, Warby, you bloody big bully and I'll lay you out. If this won't stop you, I have something here that will!' putting his hand on his revolver. Warby's was on his saddle some hundred yards away. Bluff or not, that staggered Warby.
>
> 'Go on then, yard 'em up you cantankerous little fat bastard.' *(From* In The Tracks of Old Bluey, *reproduced by kind permission of Central Queensland University Press)*

Over the next few weeks, the remaining mobs of cattle converged on Glencoe. They were counted into the yards, then the men were paid off. The greatest cattle drive in Australian history was complete.

For an operation of its size and complexity, the exercise had proceeded remarkably smoothly. One man had lost his life during the mustering. Another had died of an unknown illness during the droving. One man had suffered an accidental gunshot wound. One Aboriginal had been shot. It had taken just over eighteen months to muster and drove 20000 head up to 3000 kilometres, nearly a third of that distance through wilderness. At the end of 1882, the man responsible, Nat Buchanan, took ship in Darwin to return to his wife in Sydney. They had been apart throughout the year and a

half it had taken to achieve what remains Australia's greatest droving feat.

As it transpired, the 50 000 head of cattle sent to Glencoe and Daly
River stations did badly. The first cattle to arrive did well, as they
devoured the best feed, but what was left was insufficient for any
cattle to thrive. Rather than increasing, the size of the herds almost
immediately began to fall. Soon after, cattle started being moved to
other Fisher and Lyons leases. In 1884, Willie Gordon and the managers of Glencoe and Daly River stations mustered both properties
for stock to send to Victoria River Downs. They could only find 6000
head.

Daly River was subsequently destocked. Glencoe was left with
1000 head but was destined to become nothing more than a holding
paddock for stock travelling from the successful Northern Territory
and Kimberley stations in what would soon become a river of cattle
droved from one side of Australia to the other.

By the fiery dust storm drifting,

And the mocking mirage shifting,

In heat and drought and hopeless pain we take the stock away.

— 'With The Cattle', Banjo Paterson (1864–1941)

7

THE BIRDSVILLE TRACK

No sooner had the great stations of the Gulf Country and Northern Territory been stocked than the pressure to find markets for the cattle they produced saw mobs of livestock returning along the Gulf Track and later across the Barkly Tableland, another stock route pioneered by Nat Buchanan. From there they could cross to the watershed of the Murray-Darling and follow the stock routes down to the distant markets of Brisbane, Sydney or Melbourne.

However, as settlement moved further west, the extraordinary Channel Country was discovered. It was a region so highly valued by the state of Queensland that it had successfully had its border moved to include it. Settlement followed soon after. Roseberth Station was established on the Diamantina in around 1874. Carcoory Station, now part of Roseberth, was settled in 1877. South of the Queensland border, Pandie Pandie (which initially straddled the border) and Clifton Hills were settled in 1876.

All of these stations also sought markets for their stock, but for them the logical destination was Adelaide, 900 to 1300 kilometres south as compared to the 1600 kilometres east to Brisbane. The route to Adelaide followed the Diamantina River south for much of the way, but it was through country that explorers such as Sturt regarded as desert. In reality, The Channel Country has an extraordinary ability to put forth abundant, nutritious feed shortly after rain or a flood. In a good season, it's regarded as some of the best cattle-fattening country in the world. The feed is so good, station owners boast that cattle will fatten just by looking at it. However, in a bad season, when the feed runs out, stock can perish in their thousands.

The potential of the country soon saw mobs of cattle arriving at Camooweal, on the Queensland–Northern Territory border, where they could decide whether to continue east across the central Queensland stock routes or turn south for the Channel Country.

The south-bound mobs first followed the Georgina River system down to Boulia, from there continued to Bedourie, then on to the Cuttaburra Crossing, where the road to Birdsville crossed Eyre Creek. At the Cuttaburra the mobs left the creek and headed cross-country to the Diamantina, which they struck at Birdsville, where the river's channels narrowed to only a couple of kilometres.

The Diamantina tended to flood every three or four years and consisted of large waterholes up to 20 kilometres long. Many of them retained water even during prolonged periods of drought. The Diamantina and Georgina/Eyre Creek river systems joined about 150 kilometres south of Birdsville and formed the enormous flood plain known as Goyder Lagoon, on Clifton Hills Station.

From there the drovers could continue to follow a chain of waterholes – Little Lagoon, the Yellow Hole and the Fish Hole – down Warburton Creek towards Lake Eyre. The Kallakoopah, another river that emptied Goyder Lagoon, wound through the Simpson Desert before it, too, reached Lake Eyre. From the Fish Hole it was another 175-kilometre cross-country leg through Cowarie and Mungerannie

stations to Cooper Creek, and on to the next permanent water at Dulkaninna Creek.

With the extension of the railway line from Adelaide to Marree
in 1884, it was then a relatively simple matter to continue down to
the small but growing township that was rapidly replacing Farina,
40 kilometres further south, as the transport hub for the Channel
Country.

The route was pretty straightforward but even in a good season it still had problems. Goyder Lagoon effectively acts like a
giant sponge, soaking up the floodwaters from the Diamantina and
Georgina river systems. Only big floods make it beyond the lagoon
to replenish the waterholes further south. It was the same story
once drovers reached the Cooper. The Coongie Lakes upstream
absorbed most of the Cooper's floodwaters, and Strzelecki Creek
diverted more. It needed larger and consequently rarer floods to
fill the Warburton and lower Cooper, let alone penetrate all way
to Lake Eyre.

Floods and local rain were notoriously unpredictable in the
region, but one or the other was required to ensure sufficient feed
for droving stock. After becoming the first European to cross the
centre of the Simpson Desert in 1939, explorer Cecil Madigan noted
that while the average rainfall for the region was five inches (127
millimetres), this average meant little. 'It is characterised by several drought years in succession when there will be no more than
2 inches in the year,' he wrote in *Crossing the Dead Heart*. 'Then
perhaps a fall of 12 inches will come. It is better described as 10 inch
or nothing country.'

Given the climate, droving down the Birdsville Track quickly
became seasonal. From mid-autumn to mid-spring, a period of six
months, the daytime temperatures usually only reach the twenties.
Overnight, the temperature can fall to freezing. If water and feed is
about, it won't dry out and blow away in the cool conditions.

According to Madigan:

The present system is for cattle to be bred in the Gulf Country and
Northern Territory, from whose stations they are brought down on the
hoof, to be fattened in the Channel Country. Several pastoral companies
own breeding and fattening properties in these areas, running them in
conjunction; others buy stores to fatten in the south. But droving down
the long Georgina stock route is a slow, wasteful, inefficient matter.
A mob of stores may take four or five months to travel from the Barkly
Tableland to the Diamantina. By that time not only has the flood sub-
sided, but the top-feed has dried off. On the other hand, if there is no
flood, pastoralists dare not bring down big mobs, which might well
perish.

Summer is an entirely different story. Ephemeral winter feed will
disappear with the first hot winds, while only hardier grasses and
plants endure. Pools of water drop by centimetres every day. Without
water, survival can become the sole priority for man and beast. Drovers caught in such conditions suffered such terrible calamities that
the Birdsville Track soon earned a formidable reputation for death
and disaster.

Even in good seasons, the track wasn't popular. Author George
Farwell wrote of it in the 1950s:

Not that the great, sprawling Diamantina was one of the world's most
attractive corners. Drovers were by no means enamoured of its long
crossing, even if wood be plentiful and waterholes well spaced. There
seemed always a great wind blowing, dust, sandflies and heat; and it
had many eerie places, an atmosphere not easily defined. It was the
land of coochies, the debil-debils. *(Extracts from George Farwell's* Land
of Mirage *reproduced by kind permission of HarperCollins publishers)*

The area had more than its fair share of ghosts. Today, lonely graves dot the landscape, and landmarks recall tales of perished travellers and the massacres of Aboriginal people. Over the summer of 1885–86, the Birdsville policeman, Sergeant McDonald, recorded six deaths. On 13 September 1885, he wrote:

> Was informed today that the remains of Roberts the Haddon mailman who was supposed to have perished between Cadelga and Haddon last December has been found by the present mailman about 15 miles [24 kilometres] from Haddon, South Australia, on the present track.

And on 22 December:

> Traveller found a dead body. Three or four days old. Ten miles over the border in South Australia. Three men perished 10 miles from Clifton Hills Station, ten or twelve days ago. No water.

The three men referred to may have been part of an original group of four who set out to ride from Clifton Hills to Birdsville, possibly for a race meeting. They became lost and three of them decided to turn back. The fourth rider, believing he was still on the right track, continued on to Birdsville and arrived safely. The other three men, beginning to perish from thirst, eventually cut the throats of their horses and drank the blood. However, the blood's high salt content did them no good. The scene of their demise is known as Dead Mans Sandhill.

In February 1886 the Birdsville policeman recorded yet another fatality. A teacher from Birdsville, John Joass, had left the old location of Roseberth Station, 30 kilometres north of Birdsville, to walk back to town. He never arrived. On 20 February the policeman recorded:

> Charles Prince, stockman on Roseberth station, reported to the Sergt. that he was searching for John Joass and found his remains that day

about 8 miles [12 kilometres] from Roseberth and 12 [18 kilometres]
from Birdsville. About 2pm Sgt. McDonald and two men started with
a coffin to where remains were found, and dug a grave and buried them.
The flesh was all eaten and the inside torn away by the native dogs.

The stories were the same at the Marree end of the Birdsville track.
In March 1887 the Marree police were told that a swag had been
found on Killalpaninna Station. It was thought to belong to a man
named Jack Reed. There was no sign of Reed until four years later,
when the police recorded:

Police patrol with horses to Killalpaninna when manager reported that
two blacks had found at Kanuwaukaninna Creek human bones, supposed to be of Jack Reed, who had left Blazes Well 3/1/87 and perished
for want of water. Clothes identified.

Winter or summer, stock on the Birdsville Track faced dry stages. The
170-kilometre stretch from the Fish Hole to Dulkaninna was particularly testing. One old drover told author George Farwell:

You'd be surprised how far a bullock can go without water. He doesn't
perish till he's a heap of bones. We usually did it in four days. Came
into water on the fifth. Mob'd be in a pretty bad state, y' know, but
still walking. Just mooning along. When they come to the Lake, you'd
see 'em walk right in and not seem even to know what water was.
They'd be scared of it. They'd dip their heads in, and then pull back.
Dead scared. Bullock's memory don't go back more'n three days, they
reckon. Then again, if it was winter time, a mob might go a week without water. Keep travelling on, y' know.

I remember one time – a forty-mile [64 kilometre] dry from
Andrewilla to the Lagoon. Hot? It was getting close up summer time.
Mob all but perished. Wouldn't budge at all toward the end. Well,

I sighted a mob of Clifton Hills cattle coming into water. I got my boys
to turn them back into my bullocks. That saved things all right. My lot
just followed the others in.

The difficulties of the lower section of the Birdsville Track prompted
landowners and large pastoral companies to lobby the South Australian government to extend the railway line all the way through
to Birdsville. Even in the 1880s, it was becoming apparent that the
Birdsville Track was destined to become a major artery in the inland,
a key stock route for cattle from western Queensland and the Northern Territory to markets beyond.

Some cattle spent their entire life on the road, from the moment
they were old enough to travel until they were ready for market.
A calf born on the banks of the Ord or Victoria River in the Kimber-
leys could spend its life being droved across the Northern Territory
along the Gulf Track or the Barkly Stock Route. It might be sold and
resold along the way before being droved again down the Birdsville
Track to fatten in the Channel Country on its way south. The journey
might take three to six years, crossing the country from west to east,
then north to south – a distance of 3000 kilometres or more.

A railhead at Birdsville meant the freshly fattened cattle could
be taken from the heart of the Channel Country direct to market.
The cost of freight would be high – at times rail was five times more
expensive than droving – but the cattle wouldn't lose condition in the
couple of days they took to reach market, as compared to a journey
of three weeks or more down the Birdsville Track to the railhead at
Marree. The rail link would also mean stock could get through during drought and the region's stations could destock if the conditions
got too bad.

Unfortunately, when the railway was extended, the route followed the natural springs that occurred around the rim of what
would become known as the Great Artesian Basin. From Marree it

passed west of Lake Eyre, bound eventually for Oodnadatta and Alice Springs. The Channel Country landowners continued to lobby and in the early 1890s a royal commission examined their case. It delivered its finding just as the economic crisis of the 1890s swept the country – it would be years before South Australia was in a position to embark on a major infrastructure project such as a railway.

As with the Strzelecki Track, the scarcity of water paved the way for camels to dominate freight transport on the Birdsville Track. A famous photograph encapsulates the heyday of the cameleers – a string of some seventy camels crossing a bare plain, the line of burdened ships-of-the-desert shrinking into the distance before being swallowed up by a mirage on the horizon. A mural based on the photograph adorns the dining room of the pub in Marree to this day. The camel trains added a mystique to what at the time was one of Australia's most remote stock routes.

Birdsville was destined to remain a frontier town, a lonely outpost where border taxes were collected and drovers could resupply on their long journey south. In the days when the population numbered about 100, it was by all accounts one of the most lively stopping points. Wrote George Farwell:

Birdsville, when it had three pubs [in the 1890s], was one of the most rip-roaring of these towns. It was a hot and dusty track bringing cattle down from Bedourie, the nearest pub more than a hundred miles [160 kilometres] away, with over three hundred more to the next at Hergott Springs [Marree, 500 kilometres south, although a pub operated at Mungerannie, 300 kilometres south, between 1887 and 1894, and resumed operation since the 1980s]. Flash stockmen in for a spree would gallop their horses from one hotel to the next on the outskirts, the winner to shout for the bar. Publicans seasoned their rum by putting plug tobacco in the cask, adding raw spirits to bring up its strength. And, whatever the police were doing, duffers were always a jump or two ahead, for store cattle move slowly and news travelled as speedily as a stockhorse could gallop.

'You weren't safe to go about without a gun,' said Billy James, who first drove the Hergott–Birdsville mail coach fifty years ago. 'You didn't want to quarrel with the duffers, either. If you came on one of their yards, or some cove skinning a bullock, you wanted to look the other way.'

The customers the pubs served might have been of dubious character, but the publicans could give them a run for their money, in every sense. Stockmen, many of them illiterate, would pass their pay cheques over the bar and tell the publican to stop serving them when the money ran out. Soon they were too drunk to know how much they'd drunk, let alone what it had cost them. The arrangement seldom gave value for money.

Another practice in the Channel Country townships of Urandangi, Dajarra, Boulia, Bedourie and Birdsville was the use of what was called a 'shin plaster'. These were IOUs signed by publicans and storekeepers in lieu of actual money, and were given in change when a cheque wasn't completely spent. They were about the size of a large band-aid or shin plaster. Some bush publicans baked their shin plasters so they would disintegrate soon after they were given out.

Not all stockmen were taken in by the practices of the pubs. One Aboriginal stockman reputedly asked his boss if he could be paid with two cheques: 'One big fella, one little fella.' He gave the smaller cheque to the publican, and found that it made little difference to how long the grog lasted.

One bullock drover had an unorthodox approach to getting value for money. At a pub in the Boulia region, he was told after a big night that his cheque had cut out. As he was leaving, he asked for a bottle of rum, the usual gift after a customer had spent a large sum. The publican refused. So the drover hitched his bullock team to the pub's verandah posts and threatened to tear the place down. The publican hurried out with three bottles of rum, a small price to pay to save his establishment.

While the South Australian government couldn't afford to build a railway line along the Birdsville Track, from the 1890s onwards it started to take advantage of the discovery of artesian water north of Marree.

In 1889 a successful bore had been sunk at Marree, which supplemented the water for the steam trains that were following the mound springs west of Lake Eyre up to Oodnadatta. The following year a bore was sunk at Lake Harry, 30 kilometres north of the town, where a date plantation was established.

The depression of the 1890s put bore drilling on hold until the middle of the decade, when two factors saw it recommence. First, from 1896 drought gripped the region and the Birdsville Track became impassable. Second, from 1895 Sidney Kidman began buying up station after station in the region as owners gave up trying to raise cattle and sheep in such marginal country or were sent broke in the attempt.

Kidman's holdings were strategically located along the Birdsville, Strzelecki and Oodnadatta tracks. His strategy was to establish a chain of supply where cattle could be fattened as they moved from the northern stations at a leisurely pace towards the southern markets. His extensive use of telegraphic communication and reports from station managers effectively allowed him to droughtproof his operation, shifting cattle from station to station as conditions deteriorated. His cattle empire spanned the nation, and while it wasn't completely successful in protecting Kidman from drought, it gave the Cattle King, as he became known, considerable leverage when it came to getting things done in the outback. It didn't hurt that Kidman was South Australian, born and bred.

Thus, as Kidman acquired stations along the Birdsville Track,

Kopperamanna Bore was put down in 1897, Dulkaninna Bore in 1898 and Mungerannie Bore in 1899. The lower end of the track was now well watered, and Mungerannie was within striking distance of Goyder Lagoon. However, there was still plenty of potential for things to go wrong.

Around 1899, in the midst of drought, drover Jack Clarke got caught. Clarke had picked up 500 bullocks from an Elder Smith property, Warenda, north-east of Boulia, with instructions to deliver them to Kidman in Birdsville, although Kidman's headquarters were actually in Kapunda, near Adelaide. Clarke droved the stock down the Georgina, past Kidman's Glengyle and Carcoory stations, to Birdsville.

Kidman's agent wasn't there. There was a letter telling Clarke to push on to Andrewilla waterhole, where a Kidman drover would meet him. Clarke carried on through country that had been withered by drought for at least three years. There was virtually nothing for the cattle to feed on but he managed to reach Andrewilla, a long and deep sheet of permanent water 75 kilometres south of Birdsville, on the South Australian side of the border. When he got there, there was no Kidman drover to meet him.

Instead, there was a South Australian customs officer demanding border duties of £1000, which, not surprisingly, drover Clarke didn't have. The customs man eventually accepted an order from Elder Smith, still the legal owner of the cattle.

Eventually a letter arrived from Kidman saying he wasn't going to take delivery of the cattle unless they were brought down to Marree. Clarke decided to press on. He had just struggled over 650-odd kilometres of dry country, and whatever lay in store for him over the remaining 500 kilometres to Marree couldn't be worse than what lay behind. If he could just get from Andrewilla to Mungerannie Bore, he'd be right. Or so he thought.

Clarke sent a stockman ahead to scout for water. Goyder Lagoon turned out to be dry as a chip. The Round Hole, which was considered

to be permanent water, was empty. Down at Potato Tin Sandhill there
was just enough water for the stock to get a drink. Clarke moved
them down, then set out for Mungerannie. He got there without mishap and gave the stock a break.

Clarke may have been travelling the stock during the droving
season, but considering the cattle were being taken from a Channel Country station it may have been closer to summer. In any case,
Clarke decided to get the cattle moving at midnight on the long dry
stage to Kopperamanna Bore, 80 kilometres south. At nine the following morning, Clarke's luck ran out. In Farwell's *Land of Mirage,*
Clarke described what happened:

> The cattle were walking well. Presently a huge cloud, reaching as far
> as the eye could see, appeared in front of us. The bullocks walked very
> quickly and were inclined to break into a run. We steadied and stopped
> them, waiting for our packhorses to catch up. We wanted the men with
> them to go on and make camp for breakfast. We would spell in the heat
> of the day, then reach water on the Cooper before daylight.
>
> I said to Charlie Birkett beside me: 'Reckon that's rain or dust?'
>
> 'I think it's rain,' he answered.
>
> 'If it is, we're blessed,' I said, 'but if it's dust we're cursed.'
>
> A cool breeze blew up, as if coming off rain. The bullocks had their
> heads up, sniffing. Five minutes later we were smothered in dust.
> Horses, cattle and all turned their backs to the dust, huddled together
> in a heap. You couldn't see your hand before you.
>
> When we looked at our watches we had to put calico round them,
> and strike a match to see what time it was. Twelve o'clock came. There
> was no sign of it breaking. We hobbled our horses where they stood,
> and dropped the packs at their feet. Some of the packs were never
> found. They were buried in the sand. We couldn't eat anything. We'd
> had no supper nor breakfast either. Just about sundown the dust slack-
> ened a little, so we had to try to get the cattle to move.

Seventy of them were smothered. The ones that lay down were smothered, too. Then we got them to face the dust. Some would horn others that were struggling and dying. Their eyes were like balls of fire in the dust. They walked well for a couple of miles or more, till the dust came up thick as ever and we were wound up in a knot again. We were all knocked up, standing against a bit of a bush somewhere.

Toward morning the bullocks got very restless. They tried to get away in the opposite direction. Some did get away, but I held what I could. The dust didn't break till the sun rose next morning. We were then seventeen miles [27 kilometres] from the water. We travelled along in terrible heat, dropping the bullocks in little lots. When we came to the water we had only seventy-five head. The ones that got away had hit the Cooper ten miles [16 kilometres] from where we were, so I went back and tracked them up. It was hard to see the tracks in the dust. On the claypans between sand hills I managed to locate a few. They were walking one behind the other, slowly, lost, half-blinded, heads hanging. I found another thirty head – and twenty-eight of them were dead in salt water.

When we left the Cooper we had only seventy-two head out of five hundred.

When Clarke finally made it to Marree, Kidman refused to accept what was left of the mob. Elder Smith lost £4000, plus there was £1000 in duties to be paid on the perished cattle. There was some doubt about who would pay this and for a time it looked like Clarke might cop the bill. As word of this leaked out, drovers and station managers along the track rallied to help him. In the end Elder Smith paid the duties without question.

Kidman was to lose more cattle as the drought continued. In 1902 he tried to walk 2000 head from Carcoory Station to Durrie, and all perished. He tried to walk 1000 head to Pandie Pandie with the same result. In all, he's thought to have lost 85 000 head of cattle across all his holdings, unable to destock properties so remote from markets and rail transport.

Down on the Birdsville Track, the bore sinking went ahead at a governmental pace. Mount Gason and Mirra Mitta bores were sunk in 1904, Mulka and Goyder Lagoon bores in 1906, Clayton Bore in 1908 and Cannuwalkalanna Bore in 1916. Where desert had previously dominated, a well-watered direct route now ran south from Goyder Lagoon to Marree. Cecil Madigan described some of the bores as he saw them in 1939:

> The bore stream at Goyder Lagoon runs into a creek which was swampy at the time, and there were the usual flocks of ducks on it, of which I got another five, and clouds of noisy cockatoos. There were box gums and water plants along the creek but the bore was several hundred yards to the side on the bare gibber plain. Over half a million gallons [227 300 litres] of boiling water pours out of the bore day in and day out, and runs down a gutter to the creek. The gutter is fenced for the first couple of hundred yards to keep the stock off it till it has had time to spread and cool. On the lower ground there was a grove of acacias which made a very pleasant camping place, with the hot stream flowing past the door.

At Mount Gason Bore:

> There was a one-room building down by the track with a roof on, that was used by the passing drovers. The walls were decorated with charcoal drawings, some not without merit, and legends expressing very strong views on the character of certain drovers, with particular reference to the rations they provided.

The bores cemented the Birdsville Track as the primary stock route from Queensland to South Australia. With government-funded bores either on or near them, Kidman's stations stretched from north-west Queensland to his holding station, Mundowdna, between Marree and Farina. At Mundowdna, cattle ready for market walked straight onto the train.

However, the improved water supplies didn't mean the end of stock losses. In the 1914 drought Kidman lost 1200 head when a drover barely made it from Andrewilla Waterhole across a dry Goyder Lagoon to Koonchera Waterhole. There was water at Koonchera but the cattle were too weak to go any further and were trapped as the water gradually evaporated. All of them perished.

After 1917 drovers were given the option of avoiding the Georgina and Birdsville tracks if the season was bad. In that year the Queensland government completed a rail link to Dajarra, 150 kilometres south of Mount Isa, from which cattle could be trucked. Another line was extended to Quilpie, still 650 kilometres from Birdsville but able to service the needs of stations along the middle section of Cooper Creek. These days Dajarra is a sleepy backwater on the road from Mount Isa to Birdsville, but in its day it was one of the biggest cattle trucking centres in the world. In 1937 alone, a total of 11 300 cattle and 16 300 sheep were sent from there by rail. However, in a good season, triple that number of cattle were still going south on the hoof.

From 1912 onwards, one of the most remarkable figures in the Australian outback could be found at one of the stations midway along the Birdsville Track. Born in 1879, George 'Poddy' Aiston was a Boer War veteran who joined the South Australian police force in 1901, serving in a number of remote locations around the state.

The remote postings also meant he was responsible for the Aboriginal people in his jurisdiction, as Protector of Aborigines. George took a keen interest in the cultures of the Aboriginal people in his care, and recorded details of the rituals and tribal structures to which he was given access. He was noted for not having to patrol with a gun,

such was the respect he had earned. He was soon contributing arti-
cles about Aboriginal culture to scientific journals in Australia and
overseas.

In 1912 Aiston was transferred to Mungerannie Station on the Birdsville Track, where he became Protector of Aborigines for the Dieri and
Wangkangurru. He spent the next twelve years as the local mounted
policeman, by the end of which time most of his section of the track
was peaceful and law-abiding. Aiston's work was supplemented by
Lutheran missionaries at Killalpaninna Station, 100 kilometres south.

In 1924 Aiston resigned from the force and with his wife, Mabel,
bought Mulka Station from the Scobie family. It was a 1200-square-
kilometre holding with a government well on it, which Aiston leased
for £50 a year while providing water for travelling stock at a penny
a head. He and Mabel ran goats and cattle, and opened a small store
to sell supplies to passing drovers. At around the same time, George
published a book written with Dr G. V. Horne, called *Savage Life in
Central Australia*, based on more than twenty years spent living with
Indigenous people in the arid regions of South Australia.

In 1929 Aiston took two Wangkangurru men to Melbourne to dem-
onstrate traditional skills, art and crafts at the Melbourne Museum.
In 1934 he took five more men to Melbourne for the city's cente-
nary. It was the first time that Aboriginal people from the Simpson
Desert had been seen in the city. By that time Aiston was an honor-
ary consulting anthropologist at the Australian Institute of Anatomy
in Canberra, and considered an authority on the Aboriginal people in
the South Australian region.

While his career as a field anthropologist was earning him international standing, the fickle fortunes of the outback seasons were
hammering Mulka Station. The drought of 1934 saw the Birdsville
Track closed and no stock travelling down. The station's cattle were
devastated and there was no passing trade for the Mulka store.
George and Mabel barely hung on.

One of the attractions of the store was George's collection of Aboriginal artefacts, most of them purchased from their Aboriginal owners if they offered them for sale. However, George's interests extended beyond Aboriginal culture and included a range of collectibles. His assortment of weapons included pepperbox pistols that had been used at the Eureka stockade, a Chinese sword reputed to have been used to behead twenty men in the Boxer Rebellion, a French cavalry bugle from the Battle of Waterloo and suits of Persian and Japanese armour.

It was the most unlikely collection a drover could expect to find in a location as remote as Mulka Store. George Aiston's extraordinarily enquiring mind was even more unlikely. Yet this fascinating individual spent most of his life in the lonely outpost, selling flour, tea and sugar to passing drovers, while corresponding on a range of subjects with scientific colleagues around the world.

Aiston's health started to fail in 1943 and he was eventually flown out by the Flying Doctor and taken to Broken Hill Hospital. He died of cancer not long afterwards.

Mabel Aiston, herself an extraordinary character who had happily chosen life beside her husband far from the madding crowd, continued on at Mulka. She ran the store until 1953 and can be seen, wearing a floral dress and cardigan, meeting outback mailman Tom Kruse in the John Heyer film *The Back of Beyond*. The film described Mulka as the loneliest store on earth. When Mabel Aiston left Mulka, not long after the film was made, she donated her husband's collection and correspondence to the South Australian Museum, the National Museum in Canberra and the Mitchell Library in Sydney.

Mulka was absorbed into Mungerannie Station and the store was abandoned. The ruins can still be seen, 30 kilometres south of the Mungerannie Hotel. The barren landscape, fallen walls and consuming silence emphasise the extraordinary qualities George and Mabel Aiston displayed to embrace such a challenging location, creating an intellectual as well as physical oasis where body and mind could be nurtured at the halfway point of the long and dusty Birdsville Track.

The attitudes of drovers to such a presence on the stock route are not recorded, but it may not have been as out of place as one might imagine. Many drovers carried reading material to occupy their spare time, and often their books were collections of poetry. As Hector Barker put it in *Droving Days,* drovers' backgrounds ranged from former convicts to Oxford graduates.

While the water problem on the Birdsville Track was mostly solved, the issue of feed remained. Drought could still close the stock route. Drovers intending to bring cattle down from the north had to make other arrangements, but for local station owners it often meant they could only watch as their stock starved, with no way to get them out. Not that they didn't try.

From time to time camels had been suggested as having a role to play in droving stock, but this had generally been dismissed as something of a joke. Nevertheless, during a drought in 1929 that closed the track, Celsey Morton of Roseberth Station was offered the loan of some camels to help get 500 head of fat cattle down the track before the dry feed ran out and they perished. He decided he had nothing to lose.

The camels were used as packhorses, carrying oats and hay to feed the handful of stockhorses used to drove the cattle. The experiment was successful, although it was something of a last resort, and the stock made it down to the railhead at Marree without serious incident. Kidman's Durrie and Glengyle stations reputedly copied Morton's initiative shortly after, and it was repeated by another drover in 1935.

In the best seasons, the Birdsville Track took on a totally different aspect. When his expedition across the Simpson Desert reached Birdsville in 1939, Cecil Madigan found the Birdsville Track was a virtual highway of cattle moving south. There had been an average of 250 millimetres of rain across the Channel Country, with enough winter herbage coming up to feed millions of cattle.

The Diamantina was 'running a channel flood' all the way down to Lake Eyre. Pelicans, herons and ibis were flocking to its waters to breed and to feast on an explosion of aquatic life. Older drovers said they'd never seen the country in such good condition.

Mob after mob of cattle came down the Georgina and on to the Birdsville Track but they barely made a dent in the available feed. The country is so flat that when the water spreads over the Diamantina's flood plains, hundreds of square kilometres are covered. The flora of the region is perfectly tuned to the region's cycles of boom and bust, and explodes into vigorous growth. The grasses grow faster than stock can eat them, and the stock fatten just as quickly.

Madigan noted that when he was at Birdsville, six mobs of cattle were within one or two days' travel from the town. Although his expedition had achieved its objective, Madigan and some of his colleagues continued down the Birdsville Track, making scientific observations along the way. Madigan also witnessed aspects of droving on the track in that era.

Men were in great demand at this time and the drovers, the professional full-time drovers who own a plant and hire assistants, were having difficulty in holding their men.

It is quite a usual thing for a drover to have to fight his men to induce them to stay on. The extraordinary thing about it is that if the man loses the fight he seems quite willing to stay. The idea seems to be that the boss is then shown to be a good man to work for.

When I asked one drover about his difficulties he made a very wise remark that applies to leaders in all walks of life, and I have often quoted it since. He said a drover must know more than his men and do more than his men.

Madigan and his colleagues travelled at an easy pace down the western side of the Diamantina, past the idyllic, semi-permanent Dickeree waterhole, then the Eight Mile and on to the Karrathunka waterhole.

There we nearly overtook Tom Finlay, a drover with a mob of cattle who had given us fifty pounds [20 kilograms] of meat at Birdsville. We saw two of his men on their horses on the crest of a sandridge beyond our camp. The cattle were the other side and out of sight. Apparently they were not going to camp yet. They stood for a long time and watched us make camp, lonely black figures silhouetted against the grey and wintry sky. It was a cold, hard, comfortless time for them. I was reminded of the dingoes staring down on our desert camps. Then they disappeared. I thought if they camped soon they would come back to us, but we never saw them again.

Another party passed us on their way back to Queensland for more cattle. These men were in a hurry. Fifteen miles [24 kilometres] a day is about the rate for travelling with stock, but without them the drover travels fast, covering perhaps fifty miles [80 kilometres] a day. The drover has very high heels to his elastic-sided boots, to prevent his feet from slipping through the stirrups. Hard and permanent cones of grey clay had formed on these men's heels, making them even longer. I wondered how they managed to walk in them at all, not that the horseman does walk very much. Incidentally, the elastic sides are to help the foot to slip out of the boot in the case of being thrown and dragged by the stirrup.

Also on the track that year was a stockman named Tex Mintern. When he reached Adelaide he was interviewed for a feature in the *Argus*, which was published on 25 November 1939. His account covers the southward journey from start to finish.

Australia's 'big parade' of cattle-men takes place each year about February. In North Queensland may be seen an exodus of sun-bronzed men, some with swags, some with portmanteaux, but all with one purpose, going north to Camooweal to work for cattle drovers as horse-tailers, cooks and cattle-men.

They go west into the Northern Territory, north to the Gulf of Carpentaria, and south as far as Boulia, to bring herds of cattle to the railheads, principally to the two main North Queensland trucking centres, Kajabbi, north of Cloncurry, and Dajarra, to the south.

Theirs is an arduous task. My own experience on my trip last season is typical of most of these cross-country treks. I joined a droving plant in June as horsetailer, with forty-five head of Queensland's worst horses to look after. With the boss, the cook, and three cattle-men, we were to 'shift' 1,500 Hereford bullocks from Callulah Station, on the Leichhardt River, to Marree, the trucking centre in the north of South Australia.

For the first fortnight it did not cease raining. We were never dry. We had days of mud and slush. By the time we reached Marion Downs Station, on the Georgina River, our horses were knocked up after days of bog and wet weather. The cattle-men were riding the pack horses, which had had an easier time, and we were packing the broken-down saddle horses.

Shifting those 1,500 bullocks with only four men and weary horses was a big job. We averaged only nine miles [14 kilometres] a day. There were no roads to follow, and often we had to head across open country.

We reached Bedourie, and were among the sandhills of Central Australia. Some of these sandhills are tremendous, and very steep. They run only north and south, due to an almost constant south wind in the winter.

The spinifex, dead finish, and gidyea ridges of the north had been left behind. Wherever we turned now we saw saltbush, buckbush, needle-bush, turpentine, and now and then a stray stunted specimen of dead finish.

Every few miles we came across the bleached bones of cattle that had perished through drought. In one lot we counted as many as 13 skeletons, all within eight or nine yards [7.3 or 8.2 metres]; also the remains of horses. Every hundred miles [160 kilometres] or so we found the lonely grave of some son of the great outback, unnamed, marked only by a few posts and rails.

At night we cursed the dingoes, which surrounded our camp and gave us a mournful choir of wails. After 17 hours a day in the saddle seven days a week we could have done with the sleep that their wails interrupted.

By day we saw little but sand and crows. Our drinking water was so thick with sand and clay that we had to chew it. But we kept on across the desert wastes, and after 14 weeks we reached Marree, our destination. As soon as the last beast was on the trucks we headed our horses for the town and celebrated. And, after 1,000 miles [1600 kilometres] of mud, slush, and rain, wind, sand, crows, and desert wastes, I think we had cause for celebration.

The trucking season usually ends about August, as it is rarely possible to bring cattle long distances over hot, arid desert land as late as September. The feed, as a rule, has been scorched by the blazing sun, and most of the waterholes have dried up.

Every good season Adelaide buyers travel to North Queensland to buy cattle. Some of the big firms buy up to 10,000 head each, and sometimes many more, to be driven south to their depots. In Adelaide, as 'fats', the cattle bring from £10 to £20 a head.

But the real romance is for the men in charge of the herds. A few months' trailing hundreds of cattle across the dead heart of Australia is an experience that never loses its thrill. Ask any bullock drover, but before you do, remember that trekking hundreds of miles across a desert makes him a thirsty man. Thanks – I don't mind if I do.

To those unfamiliar with the Channel Country, the conclusion of Tex's interview may seem strange. The trip was exhausting and uncomfortable for weeks on end. Yet at the end of it, he regards it as being the experience of a lifetime. Of course, hardship is just part of the overall experience.

During a recent conversation I had with a station owner in Birdsville, we discussed the precarious financial balance involved in his operation. To the suggestion that he'd make more if he sold up and simply put his money in a bank, he pulled me up, 'You're missing the point. No one out here is doing it for the money. We do it because we love living here.'

Andrewilla waterhole was on Alton Downs, a station he part owned. With his permission I'd gone down there several times, sailing dinghies in the desert on its permanent waters. In his younger days the station owner had taken his family there to water-ski. It's a beautiful, improbable sheet of water surrounded by parched sand dunes. Cecil Madigan camped there in 1939 and was touched by the place as well. He wrote:

I watched a very wonderful dawn at this waterhole, one that has stood out clearly in my memory ever since, among the hundred dawns we saw. It was cloudless and calm. I lay in my bed on the bare ground above the steep bank, just beyond the thin line of trees that edged the waterhole. The moon was high, but its light was already paling and the shadows were gone. Orion still rode the skies, but the glorious morning star in the east was heralding the approach of the bold sun. The sky still held the dark blue of the night, but towards the east it changed to dove grey, then light grey and finally to a strip of tangerine that lay low on the horizon. They were not the brilliant colours of sunset clouds, but the most delicate hues of the sky itself. The black trees were silhouetted against these lovely tints. Gradually the stars faded and the mystic moonlight withdrew as night crept silently away, and objects took their true shape and distance in the hard light of day. A squawk was heard here and there in the trees, and soon clouds of cockatoos came to life and filled the morning with

their harsh screeching, tearing away the last soft trailing veils of night
as the sun came up.

In 1940 drought returned to the Channel Country. The average rainfall in the area was only 50 millimetres, a fifth of what it had been the
year before. There was no winter feed, and many of the waterholes
were drying out. With boom turned to bust, bringing cattle down the
Georgina and the Birdsville Track was a risky proposition once more.

It was another good year when George Farwell travelled through
in the late 1940s, and cattle were coming down in an endless stream
once again. Drover Ted Sheean told Farwell that he reckoned 30 000
had travelled the track south and eaten the country bare. Sheean was
facing the task of bringing cattle down from Dubbo Downs Station,
west of the Georgina, and had decided to try to bring them all the
way down to where the Georgina met the Mulligan River, right on the
edge of the Simpson Desert. In a country where rivers run to no obvious timetable, the Mulligan ran least of all. Sometimes the Georgina
rises so high that it crosses the enormous flood plains on Glengyle
Station and pours into the Mulligan on the other side. The two rivers eventually converge at Muncoonie Lake, flowing south as Eyre
Creek past the abandoned Annandale Homestead and on to Goyder
Lagoon, where it meets the Birdsville Track.

'We'll be right,' Sheean said. 'But we'll have to keep shifting.'

On his trip Farwell met another of the many great characters of
the Birdsville Track, Bill Gwydir. Farwell was out on a camel patrol
with Max Homes, the Marree policeman, when he met the drover
coming south with a mob of cattle:

Bill Gwydir rode a stocky grey with flowing white mane and tail. A spir-
ited well-tried gelding, it had fetlocks big as a young draught horse, and
he kept it usually for work about the camps.

Bill kept his distance, fearing the effect of our camels upon his grey, then swung out of the saddle with a lightness surprising in so large a man. His spurs clinked on the stony ground. A deep-chested, husky man in his early forties, flesh tanned like strong leather, he wore a tan leather coat with two belts that accentuated the breadth of his shoulders. Leather leggings and tight gabardines gave him an added stockiness. He wore a tall, broad-brimmed and weather-worn hat of incredible age. A pair of dust goggles were strapped about it, and the peak was worn away to a jagged cone, like a volcano. In this amazing hat was jauntily stuck the crimson-tipped feather of a black cockatoo.

Farwell was fascinated by Bill's manner of speech:

'By hell, Max,' he sang out in his husky, rather high, rhythmical voice, 'that turnout of yours'll scare my mob hell west and crooked. Once they smell camels they're gone . . . Yairs, there's a fair bit of feed yet, Max. Drying off, y'know. Hell, she'll be right on the Plain awhile. Been grass that high. And clover? There's whips of it. But didn't she blow last night? By the Lord God, she blew! I tell you, sure as God made little ponies, we're set for a dry summer. This track'll be hard as gin's heels!'

He did not talk, he sang. His husky, high voice was always rhythmical, pushing along with exuberance, the heavy stress upon the early syllables, falling away with a lilting cadence, to end with a last upward Irish twist. Now and again he dropped his voice, deep and deliberate, stressing some point, but always his vitality gained the upper hand. His big husky voice seemed to fill the wide plain, to bring colour to any company he kept. He laughed freely, spoke with pungency and wit, and even his obscenities were original and picturesque.

Bill Gwydir was more at home on a horse than on his own two feet. He'd been droving since the age of fifteen, when he'd started out as a horse-tailer, considered by many to be a particularly responsible position. A good horse-tailer ensures the working horses are always put on the best available feed, and can keep them in good condition as long as humanly possible.

At eighteen, Gwydir became a boss drover. He took a mob of store cattle from Marion Downs to New South Wales, where they gave him a bonus for delivering the stock in particularly good condition. He then worked as head stockman on Glengyle. He took a job in Sydney for a while, working in the Homebush cattle saleyards, but he didn't last long. 'City life,' he'd said, 'that's enough to kill a man. By hell, I went for my life back to the mulga. Out here a man's free as a frog from feathers.'

Farwell regarded Gwydir's accent as typical of the region:

> The leisurely, far-riding life of the cattle country, with its adventurous spirit and cyclic bursts of energy, gains its expression in something I like to term the 'Queensland voice'. It is a rugged, half-bantering, superbly confident voice, carrying an echo of ballad poetry and an Irish brogue.

It can still be heard in western Queensland today. Stockmen young and old, Aboriginal and European, will meet strangers with a confident, 'How's it goin'?' Driving in an unhurried manner borrows the droving term 'poking along'. Even babysitting is referred to as 'tailing the kids'.

One of Bill Gwydir's renowned exploits was bringing 600 head of cows and calves from the western side of the Simpson Desert to Mungerannie Station on the Birdsville Track, at the beginning of the drought of 1945. The feat hadn't been attempted since the turn of the century. The cattle belonged to another of the famous figures of the Birdsville Track, Jim Oldfield, whose family can still be found running stations in central Australia to this day. Jim was to meet Bill 80 kilometres east of Macumba Station with fresh horses, and they'd bring the stock through together.

However, most old hands were sceptical. 'You'll perish the cattle and you'll perish your men,' was the general verdict. They reckoned the lower Diamantina was all salt water, the result of the waterholes evaporating until only undrinkable brackish liquid remained.

While Jim scouted out waterholes along the Kallakoopah through to Lake Eyre, then tracked up the main, almost bone-dry channel of the Macumba, which in places spreads out to 40 or 50 kilometres wide, Bill was droving the cattle towards him, down the Macumba, but finding precious little feed to keep them going.

When Jim finally found him, Bill was out of supplies and his horses were thin and exhausted. From what Jim had seen of the country he'd scouted, turning back now seemed a good idea. The pundits might well be proved right if they chanced continuing their journey. But Bill had made it this far, and with Jim's fresh horses, he wasn't about to quit. The pair finally agreed to keep going.

A flood had come down the Macumba some months before, which meant there was still water about, although brackish. Summer was approaching, which didn't help matters. Nevertheless, all went well until they reached the Kallakoopah. There they managed to bog a dozen bullocks while trying to get them to drink. The men had to go into the water up to their waists to try to get them out.

When they ran short of supplies, Jim Oldfield rode ahead to Cowarie Station to get more. By then, Jim hadn't been heard from for weeks, and Bill Gwydir hadn't been heard from for even longer. Cattle might move slowly up and down the Birdsville Track but news travelled like lightning; at the time, most stations had pedal wireless sets. The general opinion had been formed that all the men and their stock were dead. It was a great relief to many, and a further enrichment of their legendary status, when Jim Oldfield rode out of the desert alive and well.

Eventually, the mob reached permanent water. Jim credited Bill with getting the cattle through without losing a single beast. George Farwell pointed out that without Jim Oldfield and fresh horses, it

would have been a much different story. However, the combination
of two of the great drovers of the region working together on such a
risky undertaking was probably the key to their success.

By the 1950s, many of the bores on the lower half of the Birdsville
Track were falling into disrepair. When first sunk, each bore was
maintained by a South Australian government employee: one for
each bore. The inefficiency of having someone spend most of their
time watching water flow out of the ground soon saw the caretakers' cottages, with their flowers and vegetable patches, replaced by a
more pragmatic arrangement.

The stations where the bores were located, and which benefited
greatly from their publicly funded existence, were given responsibility for their maintenance. They also had to ensure there was
a suitable water supply available for travelling stock. It seemed like a
good idea, except that the technical skills required to maintain bores
that were gushing water at near boiling point was beyond even the
most resourceful station managers.

In 1953 the South Australian government inspected the bores
along the stock route and found that many were in such disrepair
that they couldn't be used by travelling stock or anyone else for that
matter. In some places, it was only the topography around the bore
that allowed water to collect in places where cattle could drink. In
other places, shifting sand had buried the bores. Several were virtually out of control, their original casings having corroded, allowing
water to flow at an uncontrolled rate. Some were spewing several
million litres of water per day.

The report recommended that the stations be reminded of their
obligations, but the gap in technological know-how eventually saw
the South Australian Mines Department assume responsibility for
servicing the bores. The Superintendent of Boring, R. J. Wilson, got
the job.

To carry out the repairs, Wilson put on a head-to-toe rubber suit filled with cold water. He also wore goggles, gloves and rubber boots. He then stepped into the searing-hot artesian water and set about repairing the broken casings and pipes. He replaced broken parts as well. Despite his attempts at protective clothing, he was scalded several times. The discomfort as the cold water in his suit rose in temperature can only be guessed at.

After being roasted alive inside the suit, he often pulled it off to find the air temperature around the bores was in the 40s. He eventually repaired the bores at Goyder Lagoon, Mungerannie, Mulka and Dulkaninna. These days, the work around the bores is done using remote-controlled equipment.

The Birdsville Track remains one of the most famous roads in the outback, its fame assured in 1954 when John Heyer's film *Back of Beyond* achieved international success. The film, based in large part on George Farwell's best-seller *Land of Mirage,* put the rugged life of inland Australia onto the big screen for the first time. It made a star of one of the men who did the Birdsville mail run, Tom Kruse, but it also turned the Birdsville Track into a symbol of the hardships and adventures of living in central Australia. A generation of Australians, not to mention a large overseas audience, grew up believing that the Birdsville Track was where life was lived on a larger, more-dramatic scale than normal.

The track was as unforgiving as ever, but the drovers were joined by a new breed of outback traveller inspired to experience first hand the world they'd read about or seen on the screen. Few of the tourists who travelled the Birdsville Track realised that leaving their comfort zone meant they were entering a region where the margin between life and death can be extremely slim, and help can be a very long way away.

In 1963 the track was the scene of one of the worst tragedies the outback has ever seen. In the furious heat of December, English mechanic Ernest Page left Marree, where he'd been working, and headed north for 'a great holiday adventure'. With him were his wife and two young sons, aged twelve and ten. They managed to drive two-thirds of the length of the track without mishap. At Clifton Hills Station, they picked up their nineteen-year-old son, who'd been working as a ringer, and set out for Birdsville, 200 kilometres north, a couple of days before Christmas.

On 29 December their family sedan was found abandoned on the Birdsville Track, with a note: 'The Page family of Marree. Ran out of petrel [sic]. Are heading south. Have only sufficient water for two days. December 24th.'

The bodies of four members of the family were spotted by a searching plane beside the dry bed of the Coocheaperoonie waterhole on New Year's Day. A ground party located the remains of the eldest son on a dune one kilometre west.

Renowned outback author Ion Idriess was interviewed about the fatalities a couple of days later, and in explaining what might have happened he detailed the nature of droving on the Birdsville Track as he knew it. On 4 January 1964, he told the *Courier-Mail*:

> Unless the traveller panics, he cannot be lost on this track. Although it is often blotted out here and there by sandstorms, the experienced and cool-headed traveller knows it can be picked up again within half a mile or a mile [0.8 or 1.6 kilometres]. In the last 80 years hundreds of thousands of head of cattle have come down the Birdsville Track from the south-west stations in the Queensland Channel Country. These millions of hooves have left a track that is broad and can never be quite blotted out over more than short distances even by heavy sandstorms.

Even as the Pages were being mourned, the days of the Birdsville Track as a stock route were numbered. During the 1960s and 1970s, the roads between Birdsville and Marree and between Birdsville and Windorah were gradually upgraded to allow the use of road trains.

The number of cattle going to market on the hoof was rapidly overtaken by the number going by road and rail. In the case of the Birdsville Track, the emergence of Asian markets for beef meant that Brisbane became the focal point for shipping cattle overseas. Premium-quality Channel Country beef was destined almost entirely for overseas markets, so from that time onwards stock movements from the Channel Country tended to be to the east, rather than south down the Birdsville Track.

It was perhaps fitting that the last mob to travel down the Birdsville Track, in 1968, was droved by Bill Gwydir. By the 1980s road trains had completely overtaken rail as the preferred mode of transport. Marree closed in 1980. The rail line to Dajarra closed in 1988.

The changing priorities of the track saw the road that was being graded between Marree and Birdsville follow a different route north from Clifton Hills. The original road, along the stock route, followed the Diamantina River; the new route followed the wet-weather road that keeps to higher ground east of the Diamantina. The unsealed road still turns to slush after heavy rain but it usually doesn't go under water in a flood.

From just north of Clifton Hills homestead there are now two Birdsville Tracks – the original Inside Track and the new Outside Track. The Inside Track is often closed due to boggy conditions around Goyder Lagoon. However, visitors can usually travel some distance along it from the Birdsville end, and see some of the waterholes mentioned throughout this chapter. If you decide to make the journey, leave your travel details with Birdsville police and seek prior permission from station managers for any overnight camping or sightseeing away from the track. Contact numbers are available from Birdsville police or the Information Centre (www.diamantina.qld.gov. au/content/view/316/465).

A journey down the Inside Track after a major flood reveals the true nature of the region. When the waters recede, and rivers of grass rise in their wake covering thousands of square kilometres, it's easy to appreciate how this usually arid country was once a vital link in the great stock routes that spanned the entire country. Cattle and men could perish here, but in a good season the rivers of the Channel Country literally became rivers of cattle.

But to get to the head ere they scattered

out through the scrubs on the right.

So on with the dogs racing after,

we rode through the depths of the night

— 'Cattle Rush on a Night Camp', Charles MacAlister (1830–1908)

8

THE MURRANJI

It's long been said that if you build a better mousetrap, the world will beat a path to your door. Much the same could have been said of stock routes: find a good shortcut, and drovers would soon beat a path in your footsteps. It needn't have mattered that the shortcut meant running the gauntlet of difficult terrain and doubtful water-holes. In droving, time and distance meant money, so any shortcut, no matter how difficult, warranted consideration. Thus was created one of the most infamous stock routes in the country – the Murranji Track.

When Augustus Gregory explored the northern regions of Aus-tralia in the 1850s he had extolled the virtues of the Victoria River, a broad waterway that penetrated far to the south into the interior of the Top End. It had all the appearances of being some of the finest grazing land in Australia. Little wonder that it became the target of later explorers attempting to cross the country from south to north.

Unfortunately, as John McDouall Stuart found in 1861, the way

from central Australia through to the Victoria River was barred by
impenetrable scrub. Stuart was in the vicinity of Newcastle Waters in
mid-May of that year, trying to head direct for Victoria River country,
only 200 kilometres away. It was not to be:

> The scrub we were compelled to return from was the thickest I have ever
> had to contend with. The horses would not face it. They turned about in
> every direction, and we were in danger of losing them. In two or three
> yards [1.8 to 2.7 metres] they were quite out of sight. In the short dis-
> tance we penetrated it has torn our hands, faces, clothes, and, what is of
> more consequence, our saddle-bags, all to pieces. It consists of scrub of
> every kind, which is as thick as a hedge. Had we gone further into it we
> should have lost everything off the horses. No signs of water. From south
> to west, north and north-east nothing visible but Sturt Plains, with a few
> sand rises having scrub on them, which terminate the spurs of the stony
> rises. They are a complete barrier between me and the Victoria.

The belt of what he referred to as hedgewood comprised even
more forbiddingly named bulwaddy and lancewood. It remained an
impenetrable barrier for the next twenty-five years, forcing a 650-
kilometre detour to the north for those coming from the south or
east. When cattle stations in Western Australia's Kimberley and the
west of the Northern Territory were settled in the 1880s, the detour
became a significant imposition on overlanding trips that were measured in distances of 3000 kilometres or more. For stations such as
Wave Hill and Victoria River Downs seeking markets for their stock,
the hedgewood was an increasingly frustrating obstacle between
them and the population centres in the east and south.

The pressure to find a shortcut increased with Charles Hall and
Jack Slattery's discovery of gold in the Kimberley region in 1885.
What promised to be another Bendigo soon saw thousands trek
across the country or journey to the north-west by ship, hoping to

make their fortune. It promised to be a great opportunity for the cattle stations of the region, if only they could get hold of sufficient stock.

The first breakthrough in finding a shortcut through the hedgewood may have been achieved by two men who headed for the Kimberley as soon as the first reports of gold emerged. The *Northern Territory Times and Gazette* reported that former drover George Hedley (survivor of an Aboriginal attack, as detailed in Chapter 6) and a man named Morgan had arrived in the Victoria River district on 18 June 1885, after journeying direct from north of Newcastle Waters en route from Queensland. 'They had a rather rough time of it coming over,' the paper reported, 'owing to the scarcity of water on several long stages. At one time they had to do seventy miles [120 kilometres] without water.'

Little more is known of Hedley and Morgan's route and experiences in finding a way through the hedgewood. Some years later Gordon Buchanan wrote of their journey:

G. R. Hedley passed through from Newcastle Waters to the Victoria, safely negotiating a dry stage of eighty miles [130 kilometres]. Owing to the obstructive hedgewood, he was much delayed and only reached water in time to save himself and his party from perishing. He was the first to conquer this difficult region.

There are other claimants to being the first to cross the hedgewood, notably a drover named John Skuthorpe, who in 1905 claimed to have made the crossing in 1878. Charles Goodliffe also claimed to have been the first, in 1945. However, Hedley and Morgan's achievement was the earliest that was independently documented at the time, rather than claimed later.

It's likely that Hedley and Morgan inspired further exploration within a year. In mid-1886 Sam Croker, manager of Wave Hill Station, may have become the second man to find a way through the hedgewood when he was tracking stray bullocks. He travelled through to Newcastle Waters, possibly skirting the worst of it by looping around to the south and perhaps being helped in the reputedly waterless scrub by good winter rains across the region. From the sound of it, the cattle appeared to have been crossbred with homing pigeons and were trying to reach the place of their birth, as Croker continued tracking them halfway across the Barkly Tableland to Corella Creek, before returning with an unspecified number, possibly 150, to Powell Creek on the Great North Road.

As luck would have it, Sam was still at Powell Creek when his boss, Nat Buchanan, who had established Wave Hill and owned it in partnership with his city-based brother, William, turned up with a mob of 100 horses, bound for the station.

Among his many droving feats, in 1877 Nat had pioneered the stock route across the Barkly Tableland from Camooweal to Powell Creek, on the Overland Telegraph Line. The Barkly Stock Route could potentially cut off much of the northern detour, if only a way could be found to the west through the hedgewood.

With Nat was his son Gordon, who provided one of the earliest descriptions of the hedgewood's bulwaddy trees:

This appropriately named tree is apparently unknown in other parts of Australia. It grows in belts and irregular areas from a mile [1.6 kilometres] to several miles in extent. The branches start almost at the ground, each branch spreading at an angle of from forty-five degrees to almost horizontal, and interlocking with its neighbour. It reaches a height of from twenty to thirty feet [six to nine metres], and a single tree at a distance somewhat resembles a gigantic inverted skeleton umbrella without a handle.

It was now July 1886. Rain had been falling in the region, which meant surface water was available to make travel in normally

waterless areas possible. It was cold enough for the drovers to wake
in the morning with frost on their swags.

Sam had just crossed the hedgewood, and it's likely that both
he and Nat knew of Hedley and Morgan's earlier feat. It occurred
to both men that the hedgewood might not be so impenetrable
after all. Gordon explained: 'As cattle and horses were destined
for Wave Hill, two hundred miles [320 kilometres] or more by the
unknown direct route, but six hundred miles [960 kilometres] via
the Katherine, then the only known track, it was decided to explore
the shorter route.'

On 28 August the *Northern Territory Times and Gazette* belatedly
and not quite correctly reported the news:

> Messrs. N. Buchanan and S. Croker are engaged trying to find a road
> from Daly Waters [actually Newcastle Waters] across to the Victoria
> River, with a view to open up a route for fat stock to the Kimberley
> fields; if the attempt is successful, the road will be a great boon to stock-
> owners on the tableland, and save hundreds of miles of travelling.

It was a mark of Nat and Sam's ability that they were prepared to
attempt the pioneering effort with a mob of horses and cattle in tow.
It was also a mark of their confidence in information provided by the
local Aboriginal people, who told them there was a way through. Of
course, where stock was concerned, finding a route was one thing;
finding water along the route was another. Without water the stock
would surely perish, even in winter.

The Aboriginal people told them there was a good waterhole about
80 kilometres from Bucket Creek Waterhole, north-west of Newcastle Waters Telegraph Station. Beyond that, a similar distance away,
there was a second good waterhole. They agreed to show Nat and
Sam the way.

Leaving Powell Creek, the drovers travelled up the Great North Road to Newcastle Waters Telegraph Station. Just north of the station they came to a dry creek bed that turned north-west towards the hedgewood scrub. Nat found a tree stump and left an upturned bucket on it, to mark the point where the new stock route began.

According to Gordon: 'We camped for a few days at Frews Pond while Sam Croker made a preliminary investigation. Some friendly blacks led him to Murrinji [sic] Waterhole, about fifty miles [80 kilometres] out and now for the first time visited by white men.'

Reflecting on the events of 1886 in his 1933 memoir, Gordon listed the white men who were involved in the pioneering of what became known as the Murranji Track:

Of the six white men who opened up this track in 1886 I alone remain. Sam Croker was shot by a half-caste, Archie Ferguson was killed by a black in Queensland, Mick Barry died of fever in West Kimberley, and Willie Glass and Nat Buchanan passed quietly away in New South Wales.

While camped at Frews Pond, Gordon noted the steady stream of prospectors travelling north to Katherine to skirt the hedgewood scrub. Soon 6000 people would gather at the goldfield, but within two years the surface gold would play out and the rush would end as quickly as it had begun. At Frews Pond even the lure of gold couldn't tempt the miners to take the shortcut. As Gordon put it, when they were told what he and his father were attempting, they were 'one and all predicting disaster to us by the short route'.

One of the groups that passed was the Ragged Thirteen, a wild bunch of hard-living swaggies who soon gained a dubious reputation in the outback. Gordon wrote of them: 'At Daly Waters, about seventy miles [120 kilometres] north of Frews Pond, their free-and-easy ways developed into conduct that made the name notorious on the stations and towns of the north.'

When Sam returned from Murranji waterhole, the drovers prepared to poke the stock through the hedgewood. A dry stage of 80 kilometres was a long way for cattle and horses to go without water. If there were any problems, such as difficulties getting through the hedgewood, the stock would perish if they tried to turn back. Sam, Nat and the people with them might well share the same fate.

Droving stock through the narrow gaps in the hedgewood proved quite a challenge. In places the meandering passage was little more than a few metres wide, but it continued to provide a relatively unimpeded route through the claustrophobic scrub that pressed in on both sides.

For two days Sam and Nat drove their stock at a steady pace. Pushing them too hard would only increase their thirst. On the afternoon of the second day, the drovers started to peer through the trees, trying to make out anything that might indicate water ahead. At last, in the distance, they caught the telltale glitter of the sun shining on a small body of water. In this case, all that glittered was more precious than gold as the stock came in to drink.

The Aboriginal guides called the waterhole Murranji (generally pronounced Murrun-jie). There was 'plenty tucker' for the Aboriginal guides when Sam and Nat made camp, and the promise of more induced the guides to take the drovers through the hedgewood to the next waterhole.

Once again, the guides were reliable, and the drovers and their stock had left the worst of the hedgewood behind them by the time they reached Yellow Waterhole. There, two horses died from some form of poisoning that didn't affect the cattle. Several horses had also died at Frews Pond. The drovers were now just 50 kilometres from the Armstrong River, a tributary of the Victoria that would take them down to the stock route to Wave Hill Station and beyond. Not only had a watered route through the hedgewood been found, its viability for droving stock had been demonstrated at the same time.

The Murranji's success as a stock route was a different story. Only two waterholes along a stock route 200 kilometres long was precious few, as the water consumption of large mobs of cattle was considerably larger than that of passing groups of Aboriginal people. Drovers could arrive at either waterhole to find a mob had preceded them and left the site dry or churned to slush. They then faced a potentially desperate situation. Should they turn back, or press on and hope to reach the next waterhole and find sufficient water?

Several other factors meant that in its early years the Murranji was little used. The brevity of the Kimberley gold rush reduced demand for cattle, and stock movements fell accordingly. The establishment of port facilities in Wyndham provided an outlet for Kimberley cattle to be shipped to Perth markets. The imposition of duties on stock crossing state borders also reduced the viability of Kimberley cattle being moved into the Territory, while the prevalence of redwater fever led Queensland and Western Australia to close their borders to Territory cattle.

Given such circumstances, many Territory station owners found it a battle just to survive. By 1894 Wave Hill was struggling and Nat owed his brother a significant amount of money. William decided the station had to be auctioned. There was only one bidder – himself. William Buchanan got what was to become one of the greatest cattle stations in the country for a song. His brother, Australia's greatest drover, often recognisable for his use of an umbrella to protect his sun-sensitive skin, ended up growing lucerne on a 10-hectare holding near Tamworth. Never was there a more apt application of the saying 'put out to pasture'.

The years following Federation saw a dramatic change in the use of the Murranji. The establishment of the Commonwealth of Australia meant the abolition of trade restrictions between states. Suddenly, it cost nothing to move stock across the borders between the Kimberley, the Northern Territory and Queensland.

In addition, the severe drought of the late 1890s, combined with the losses to redwater fever and other diseases in Queensland, saw cattle numbers plummet in the eastern states. It's thought Queensland's herds may have fallen from 7 million to 2.5 million in the course of the decade. When the drought eased, in the early 1900s, Queensland properties were desperate to restock. Cattle prices rose rapidly. Moving stock from the Kimberley and Victoria River district became an increasingly attractive proposition.

In 1904 Sidney Kidman, who owned Carlton Hill and part-owned Victoria River Downs, and William Buchanan, owner of Wave Hill, Delamere and part of Victoria River Downs, decided to try moving stock down the Murranji and across the Barkly Tableland to Queensland. That year, 10 000 head travelled across the Murranji Track, most destined for stations in Queensland and New South Wales. One mob travelled on down the Georgina and Birdsville tracks to Marree. The glory days of Australian droving, when a river of cattle flowed from one side of Australia to the other, had begun.

However, the success of the early drovers didn't mean the Murranji was ever particularly liked as a stock route. As drover Dave Allworth said in an interview for this book:

No drover liked going through the Murranji. If they had touchy bullocks that were already rushing before they got up there, they were really worried. You could lose your reputation as a drover very quickly on the Murranji, if you had a bad smash. You might lose the lot, then get three-quarters of them back the next day but you'd never get 'em all back.

If you get a rush in the Murranji, you're going to lose cattle. Bulwaddy – you cannot ride through bulwaddy. You can ride through the lancewood, it's heavy scrub, but bulwaddy is the roughest, thickest timber. They rise up from the ground and branch out and they're solid.

I don't know of any old drovers who've never had a rush there. I went through the Murranji five or six times [in the early 1960s] and I never had a rush and that's just pure luck.

Some of the most vivid descriptions of rushes on the Murranji were written by Bob Lunney, years after he'd travelled down the track as a seventeen-year-old. On one occasion, while he was on night watch, he caused a rush.

Near the end of my watch, I pulled my tobacco tin out of my shirt pocket and rolled a smoke. I was riding past the lead bullocks. Half of them were still standing chewing their cuds. I had stopped singing to roll the smoke, and shut the lid of the tobacco tin with a metallic snap. A big steer jumped, driving his horn into another steer standing near him, and in seconds pandemonium reigned supreme.

With one accord, sixty of the standing bullocks took off. I wheeled my horse, dropping the cigarette and tobacco tin, and kicked Ginger into a gallop after them . . .

The country was fairly open and flat, and the light from the moon, which was well up in the sky, was good. The lead bullocks were rising and falling in an effortless, rhythmic, undulating motion. An air of fantasy developed as I tore along beside them. I felt I was on an immense merry-go-round with the animals moving up and down, but to the rumbling, thunderous roar of stampeding cattle . . .

The herd was stretching out as though it was an elastic lump of toffee, the fast-moving bullocks dragging a long, thin strand of cattle from the milling, confused mass that was the herd.

As I raced along about fifty yards [45 metres] behind the leaders, my mare veered sharply to the left, and bushes slashed at me as we rounded a large patch of scrub. She all but propped, then gathered herself and leapt over something I did not see, and was cantering as she hit the ground. I was nearly unseated. By the time I was draped along her neck again, she was back into a full gallop and cutting back in towards the fleeing leaders . . .

For no apparent reason, a bullock suddenly turned in front of the leading rider, whose horse smashed into the bullock, and both crashed to the ground, lost from my sight. I saw the second rider go up and over his horse's head in an arc as they smashed into the fallen horse or bullock, or both. Instinctively I slowed my horse, but there was no way I could get to them through the panic-stricken, surging cattle . . .

The only thing I could think to do was to get to the other side and turn the leaders towards my side of the herd, leading the ever thickening mob that would be following the leaders away from the accident. The leaders were four or five abreast, and I galloped along them until they were only two across. The mare fought the bit as I slowed her to the pace of the bullock beside me and then shouldered her into it, forcing it aside and into its running-mate. We shot through the gap we had made, as again I let her have her head.

The bullocks had slackened to a trot now, and as we came up to the leaders I viciously plied my whip, turning them. Within ten minutes I had them circling back towards the camp and milling around, their energy spent. *(From* 1500 Down The Murranji, *reproduced by kind permission Crawford House Publishing)*

The two riders who had fallen were badly injured. One had a broken arm; the other was taken from the scene unconscious with a suspected broken leg and several bad cuts. Such rushes also took a toll on the cattle. Calves were trampled under the mob, beasts were impaled on the limbs of trees.

On one occasion, drover Hector Barker was on night watch when lightning hit the ground near the mob, causing it to rush inwards. The pressure in the centre of the mob drove many of the bullocks upwards and one was seen tumbling back down over the heads of the animals at the highest point.

The lack of reliable water on the Murranji saw repeated requests for wells. In 1906 the wet season was late and the *Northern Territory Times and Gazette*'s Katherine River correspondent explained how stations like Wave Hill had a stockpile of 20 000 bullocks ready to go. They couldn't move them until it rained:

> Owing to the lack of water along stock routes, and the sooner the Government recognises the fact, and makes some serious attempt to open up the routes between Victoria River and Newcastle Waters, and between Powell's Creek and Camooweal, the better it will be for the NT. Dependable stock routes would be of vast assistance in the development and prosperity of the pastoral industry, and there would be no fear of cattle (as has happened in the past) dying on their runs from old age.

In 1908 one bore was sunk at Anthony's Lagoon on the Barkly Stock Route, through which most cattle could pass on their way from the Territory to Queensland. Further west, on the Murranji, there was still no action.

In 1911 the Commonwealth government took over responsibility for the Northern Territory from South Australia. A Commonwealth surveyor, Captain H. V. Barclay, travelled the region and recommended three wells be sunk at Bucket, Murranji and Yellow waterholes. Further surveys were conducted in the next few years but nothing was done.

It took the Commonwealth until 1917 to start sinking bores in the Northern Territory. However, despite years of requests for bores on the Murranji and Barkly, the government inexplicably decided to put them on the Great North Road, between the Roper River and Newcastle Waters.

The desperate situation on the Murranji was illustrated in 1919, when drovers with a mob of cattle set the record for what's thought to be the longest dry stage for cattle in Australia. According to Gordon Buchanan:

One of the greatest feats of skilful handling in the annals of cattle-droving was performed on the Murrinji Track in 1919 by the Farquharson brothers. By covering without loss the longest dry stage, one hundred and ten miles [176 kilometres], ever recorded their bullocks broke the Australian record. This achievement may have been approached by smaller and therefore more mobile mobs, or when aided by parakeelya or other moisture-holding plants, but these cattle [more than 1000 bullocks] had no such advantages and no adventitious aid except cool and cloudy weather.

The Farquharson brothers – Hugh, Harry and Archie – were cousins of Gordon's, from Inverway Station. His account, written in 1933, is closest to the event in question and may have been obtained first-hand. However, according to authors Ernestine Hill and George Farwell, it may have been a more significant feat than Gordon describes. They both maintain the trip took place in 1909 and was over 210 kilometres, effectively the entire length of the Murranji Track. The tale may have grown in the telling.

Nevertheless, in the *Pastoral Review* of 15 March 1952, Farwell quoted Archie Farquharson, whom he'd interviewed shortly before his death in 1950:

There was whips of feed. The big problem, of course, was water. Cattle going without water don't want too much feed. We had to take our plant of horses ahead of the mob to water them. We rode on to the Yellow Hole from the Armstrong, then went back for the cattle. Then we rode right on past the Murranji to the Bucket, watered them again and went back once more. The cattle were pretty quiet all the time, and they travelled well. Mind you, we had to watch them sharply. Double watch all the time. But we made that trip inside five days.

According to the various accounts the cattle were driven night and day. At night, a hurricane lamp was carried in the lead for the cattle to follow. One account has an Aboriginal stockman riding ahead with a board on his back to protect him from the heat of the lamp. Another account suggests the Farquharsons regarded their success as being due to night travel that reduced the moisture loss for the cattle and also gave them the opportunity to obtain water by licking dew from the feed they ate. According to Ernestine Hill, only five head were lost.

As with other stock routes in the remote parts of Australia, deaths were an all-too-common occurrence on the Murranji. In the 1880s, miners who travelled the track may have perished and been buried in anonymous graves. One story, recounted fifty years after the event, tells of a man and woman pushing a wheelbarrow from Queensland to the Kimberley goldfield. The man died near Yellow Waterhole, his wife buried him and continued pushing the barrow to Halls Creek, 700 kilometres west.

There have been reports of up to twenty graves around the Murranji Waterhole, but the wooden crosses, blazes on trees and other signs have long since disappeared. In the *Pastoralists' Review* of 15 August 1912, 'H7H', the pseudonym for drover Hely Hutchinson, wrote of a crossing he'd done in 1905: 'The dry stage between Newcastle River and Yellow Waterholes is dotted with little brown mounds, sad witness to the awful fate that overtook the poor fellows whose mortal clay occupies them.'

Deaths among drovers, as a direct result of droving, appear to be fewer. Ernestine Hill and George Farwell both described the deaths of three drovers after they were abandoned by a boss drover. Hill's version was that three men – two whites and an Aboriginal – were already suffering from fever (probably malaria) when the drover left them with food and a couple of drums of water while he pushed on with the cattle. The sick men were too weak to fend for themselves and the drovers with the next mob to come through found their remains. Ernestine wrote, 'One had travelled in circles till he fell. The others, a white and a black, sat back to back under the same tree in the listlessness of the dead.' (*Extract from Ernestine Hill's* The Territory, *reproduced by kind permission of HarperCollins Publishers*.)

The boss drover became known across northern Australia as Murdering Charley.

Exactly where and when these deaths occurred isn't clear, although it obviously predates Hill and Farwell's accounts published in the 1950s. One account suggests it was near a dune near Murranji Waterhole. A traveller in the 1960s claimed to have seen a tree at the waterhole carved with three men's initials and the date 1926, but the date and names may have been made by passing stockmen, rather than to mark a grave.

Other accounts suggest as many as six stockmen died of fever at Murranji. Again, their initials were also purported to have been carved into a tree. However, it seems unlikely that six deaths would go unreported in police records or journals of record such as the *Northern Territory Times*.

Those records list a man named Thomas Holden as being drowned in Murranji Waterhole in 1896 while hunting ducks. In 1899 Daniel Sheahan was reported to have died, causes not given. In 1905 a police report suggests two men died at Murranji – a man named Edward Connolly and an unnamed Aboriginal. How, or if, Connolly died isn't known, but the police reports suggests the Aboriginal died after a fall from a horse. In 1908 drover Sam Muggleton found the clothed skeleton of a European between Yellow Waterhole and Murranji, which may have been Connolly.

On 9 February 1906 the *Northern Territory Times and Gazette* carried what appeared to be an all-too-common report:

PERISHED FROM THIRST.

A TELEGRAM dated Powell's Creek, February 2, contains news of another of those painful tragedies with which the records of Australian bush life are so plentifully punctuated. The telegram in question states that Mr A. Muggleton reports having found a portion of the remains of a man named Lewellyn, about 25 miles [40 kilometres] from Armstrong's, Top Springs. All the surroundings went to show that the unfortunate fellow perished from want of water. Inquiries made affirm that the deceased man left Newcastle Waters Station in October of last year, wheeling a wheelbarrow, and with the avowed purpose of making his way overland, with this primitive outfit, to Western Australia. He knew at the time that he had in front of him at least one 150-mile [240 kilometre] dry stage, but was not to be daunted by this little obstacle – serious enough to give pause to a well-equipped party.

In 1908 stockman Jack Scott was reported as having disappeared on the track while suffering from fever. His remains were never found. A stockman named William Lenny was also reported as having died of 'malarial fever' at Murranji Waterhole.

A grave marked 'A. McDonald, died May, 1921' on a slab of bark was reputed to have been seen at Murranji waterhole in 1923. McDonald may have been Mulga Jim McDonald, who is thought to have died of malaria while taking a mob of bulls to Wave Hill.

The perilous state of the waters along the Murranji Track was finally addressed in 1921, when Syd 'Territory' Peacock was contracted to start work on the first Murranji bores. Peacock had previously put eight bores down on the Barkly Stock Route.

Lifting water was done by windmills, which immediately led to problems. During the Murranji droving season, primarily April to September, the area had long periods of windless days. It was known to be still for weeks on end. The consequence was that one mob would drink a tank dry, the windmill wouldn't fill it, and the following mobs would find there was no water.

Gordon Buchanan noted that the problems the Farquharson brothers experienced in 1919 persisted after the bores were sunk:

> Wave Hill cattle some years later were forced to travel ninety miles [145 kilometres] of this stage without water owing to the failure of the wind to operate several windmills which the government has placed on the bores that now divide the track into easy cattle stages.

Initially, some of the tanks that were installed were so small they barely contained sufficient water for one mob of 1200 to 1500 bullocks, let alone several mobs travelling through over the course of a few days. The situation was rectified in 1927 with the installation of 90 000-litre corrugated-iron tanks, which soon became covered in droving graffiti and drawings of varying quality.

Other problems continued to vex the stock route. Throughout the 1920s the maintenance of bores was largely neglected, while vandalism also occurred. The average distance between bores was 35 kilometres but there was a 70-kilometre stretch from No. 10 bore to No. 11 that relied on the Murranji Waterhole in between.

One of the biggest problems was the fact that the track through the hedgewood was very narrow. In places where a path had been hacked or burned through the scrub, mobs of cattle could end up being strung out over several kilometres. In such cases it was almost impossible to keep them together. If there was a rush, the cattle would be gone. And in the close scrub, rushes were common, especially among cattle accustomed to open country.

Just how narrow the track was in places is suggested by some of the requests made to governments to have it widened. In a letter to the Northern Australia Commission in 1928, a manager from English property holder Vestey, which had bought Wave Hill in 1914, pointed out that in Queensland stock routes had been cut through scrub 'one or two chains' wide. A chain being approximately 20 metres, the Murranji Track must in places have been much narrower.

In 1931, after Victoria River Downs lost 1000 bullocks in the scrub when the drovers couldn't head them, station manager Alf Martin suggested a track 400 metres wide would solve everyone's problems. A track 100 metres wide would be a good start. The government response, in 1932, was to have a 3-kilometre stretch of the worst scrub cleared by a contractor named Fred Colson. The track he cut and burned was only 21 metres wide.

The pattern of neglect continued until shortly after the beginning of World War II. The Murranji Track may have seemed as far from the conflict as it was possible to get, but when the Japanese bombed Darwin, Wyndham and Broome in early 1942, everything changed.

Before the bombing, just over 30 000 head of cattle were travelling the Murranji every year. When the bombing forced the closure of the meatworks at Wyndham and ended the shipping of cattle, the Murranji became the major focus of an exodus of cattle.

As the Commonwealth government gave serious consideration to abandoning northern Australia to the seemingly invincible Japanese, efforts were made to destock the Kimberley and the Northern Territory, thereby depriving the advancing enemy of valuable sustenance. In the eastern states, US armed forces started to arrive en masse and Australia became a strategic pivot in the Asia-Pacific theatre of war. The demand for beef soared, and plans were made to move cattle from the Kimberley and Territory to Queensland. Vestey got the contract to supply meat to the army and evacuate cattle.

As the 1942 droving season approached, Vestey's managing director, A. S. Bingle, wrote to the Government Secretary:

> I suggest that you should make a survey of the existing conditions of
> the various water improvements [on the Murranji] and see that they

ABOVE: Drovers on the Great North Road in 1968, rounding up a breakaway. *(Douglas Baglin, National Archives, B941: CATTLE BEEF/DROVING/MIXED/9)*

TOP: The graves of drovers James Thomson, Christopher Shoesmith and an Aboriginal stockman known as 'Chinaman', who were murdered by local Aboriginal people on the Canning Stock Route near Well 37 in April 1911. The killings haunted drovers on the stock route for years afterward. *(Battye Library, State Library of Western Australia, b1997428)*

BOTTOM: Today, more adventurers travel the Canning Stock Route each year than drovers have in its entire history. The numerous wrecked vehicles strewn along the route bear testimony to its continuing challenge to the endurance of man and machine. *(Jamie Paterson Photography)*

TOP: Kath and Edna Zigenbine surrounded by army soldiers when they passed through Elliott, Northern Territory, on a droving trip with their father in 1943. *(State Library of Victoria, H2002.199/1302)*

BOTTOM: An unnamed woman droving cattle on the Great North Road in 1923. *(State Library of South Australia, PRG 280/1/41/271)*

ABOVE: Drover Ronald Kerr with his seventeen-year-old wife Mavis and baby Johnny, circa 1955–6. *(Jeff Carter, National Library, an9070713)*

TOP: A typical night camp for sheep drovers in the Riverina District in 1947. *(National Archives, A1200:L8969)*

BOTTOM: In modern times, the basic plant has been updated but remains essentially the same – stripped to the essentials to ensure mobility. *(Ken Stepnell, National Archives, B4498:173C7)*

ABOVE: Drover Jack Hickery watches over sheep drinking
from a trough at One Tree in New South Wales, circa 1955.
(Jeff Carter, National Library, vn4557202)

TOP: Drover Charlie Rayment still pulling them up at age eighty-three, in a bronco branding competition at the Camooweal Drover's Camp, 2009. *(Evan McHugh)*

BOTTOM: Drovers with cattle on the bare plains of the Northern Territory. *(Douglas Baglin, National Archives, B941: CATTLE/BEEF/DROVING/MIXED/1)*

ABOVE: A mob being droved on the stock route outside Winton, 2009. *(Evan McHugh)*

are put in order for there must be no chance of a mishap, through lack
of attention, which will cause any undue losses among the travelling
cattle.

The government equipped two trucks with portable pumps for the
season and had them patrol up and down the Murranji Track and
Barkly Stock Route to try to keep up with demand. That season
47000 head of cattle – 30000 from Vestey's properties alone – all
but overwhelmed the resources of the Murranji. Stock movements of
such magnitude hadn't been seen since the original stocking of the
northern stations in the late 1870s, as detailed in Chapter 6.

In July the government's Northern Territory Administrator, Charles
Abbott, looked into the continuing complaints about the water supply, especially from Bingle, and reported that:

Many of these bores were put down at least 20 years ago and their flow
has diminished, apparently, in some instances, from corroded bore
casings. The majority of windmills pump into earth tanks and in most
cases the holding capacity of these earth tanks has been greatly diminished by a profuse growth of rushes and weeds in the tanks.

In 1943 the threat from the Japanese had eased but the cattle industry still remained a high priority for the war effort. In February 1943
a government conference recommended ensuring the supply of
material to improve stock routes. Fred Colson was again contracted
to widen the Murranji and provide 20-hectare reserves around
No. 11, 12 and 13 bores. This time he cleared a strip 110 metres wide
over a distance of 25 kilometres through the worst of the bulwaddy
and lancewood scrubs. By then Colson had access to a bulldozer, the
likes of which hadn't been seen since the arrival of the first heavy
road-building equipment in the Territory at the beginning of 1942,
when the Great North Road was improved.

World War II transformed the Northern Territory, if only by high-lighting the strategic importance of the region as a defensive buffer to aggression from the big, bad world to the north. The bores were improved and maintained. Maintenance trucks patrolled up and down the track throughout the droving season.

Despite the improvements, it was still a tricky place to take cattle. Dave Allworth took the fourth-last mob of cattle down the Murranji Track in the mid-1960s and recalled the various hazards along the way.

After leaving Top Springs, the first bore was Pussycat Bore. At Pussycat, cattle had to be dipped to get rid of the ticks that caused redwater fever. There were yards constructed for the purpose and a stock inspector to ensure that it was done.

Beyond Pussycat was a short steep climb onto a plateau and the start of the Murranji proper. Some drovers experienced difficulties getting cattle to climb the jump-up, but when asked if it was a major obstacle, Dave replied:

Not if you did it properly. It was a steep jump-up and stony on the side going up. Good on the top. You had to march the bullocks up there. You couldn't feed them up there. It would take about two hours to get your mob up. It was only about 300 metres high and about 500 metres up the jump-up.

You'd cut a lead out – that's the best thing. When you bring your mob up, start 'em up the jump-up; they start up and then they sort of stop because they don't like it. You get your men, all of them, and chop two or three hundred head off the lead and get in behind 'em and get into 'em with the whips if you gotto. Stand 'em up!

Force them to go up then the others would start drawing up behind 'em. You gotta do a lot of bloody stand 'em up, and do a lot of bloody floggin', and using your whip – not using your whip actually on 'em but makin' a lot of noise. If you keep that lead goin', drawing up the side, in a mob that's out on the road you'll always find the leaders. They're always the bunch in the lead and they're always there. And they're the ones, the real walkers, you get in behind 'em and drive 'em up onto the top, then if the other ones aren't drawing well enough you might go back and cut another lead off. Then they'll start following and the whole lot eventually draw up.

The technique was reminiscent of the methods used by High Country drovers taking stock up narrow climbs such as Hannells Spur, as detailed in Chapter 3. According to Dave, the big issue at the jump-up wasn't the climb, it was what was waiting at the top.

You had to have one man up there because if you had Wave Hill cattle they didn't know ironwood and it's poisonous for cattle. So he had to flog 'em off the ironwood. On the top there are all these ironwood suckers and if they get one mouthful, they're dead. They start scouring that night. The next morning they're scouring badly and by about 10 o'clock in the morning they're scouring so badly they drop out and by night they're gone.

On the Murranji proper there's not much ironwood. There's no ironwood in the bullwaddy and lancewood. When you get to those open forest areas you get the odd ironwood.

Up on the Murranji plateau, on the Top Springs side, the first water was at No. 13 bore, followed by Yellow Waterhole, which usually held water for six months during the cooler months, before it dried up.

Yellow Waterholes is real drummy ground. If you galloped over it you could hear it drummy, and it was holey, you had to watch out. The only good thing on the Murranji is there's no stones there – so you don't get sore-footed bullocks. The Murranji is on a plateau, you go up a jump-up to get onto it. There's stone down the bottom but no stone there.

Unfenced. Years gone by they bulldozed a track through. You had
about 100 metres of sort of track going through and then you had solid
lancewood or solid bullwaddy. You might go through four or five kilometres of solid lancewood or solid bullwaddy then you'd come out in a
little bit of open forest area, bloodwood forest where it's a little bit thin-
ner, and they're the places that you put your bullocks down at night.
You could ride around 'em okay, and if you had a rush, you might have
about 200 metres to put a bend in them before they hit the scrub. You
wouldn't have more than that. It's tight.

Travelling across the Murranji, boss drovers were always on edge,
trying to ensure they didn't lose any cattle. Dave reckoned it meant
losing a little bit more sleep. 'If you have a double watch,' he said,
'then the boss drover goes out there as the second man. If there's any
trouble the boss might go through the night and not get any sleep
whatsoever.'

During the day, the pressure didn't ease. With mobs travelling only
a few days apart, there was nowhere to pull up for a day or two.
Every mob had to keep to its schedule. Often a mob at the waterhole
waited directly behind another.

The narrow track also meant constant vigilance was required to
keep the mob confined to a small area:

You never let the bullocks string in the Murranji. You've got no control.
People think you've got twenty people around the cattle but you'd only
have three men on the cattle. You'd have 1200 to 1500 bullocks and
you've got three men, you've got a horse-tailer, you've got a cook – five
men. That's the whole camp. You'd have a man each on the wing and
a man on the tail.

Dave maintained that if the head of the mob got too far from the
tail, he'd send a man from the wing up to block them until the tail

caught up. Despite the challenges, he managed to get through five trips across the Murranji without a bad smash or rush. While the drover's reputation was the primary motive in delivering all their cattle in good condition, there was also a cash incentive.

Vesteys paid a bonus for 98 per cent delivery. I forget what it was but it wasn't terribly much. So any smart drover was picking up cattle and a few cleanskins particularly from the moment they started – and I'm talking about western desert, not inside. From the day you leave Wave Hill, you're lookin' for cleanskins. If you could get a couple and throw 'em; you had to throw 'em and earmark them, and bang their tails, because you can't have a cleanskin in your mob. They hadn't been inoculated and all cattle had to be inoculated before they went on the road. So when you get a cleanskin, you put an earmark and you bang its tail and that'll tell you it's a road bullock. Anyone going through the mob, like police or stock inspector or someone, it's hard to see the brands so they go on earmarks and bangtail. So you get two or three of those before you hit Top Springs.

Then in the Murranji, watering on the bores, there's always been a few drovers who've lost a few. Not necessarily from rushes; you see a lot on the Murranji if there's been a rush up ahead. Christ. They still come in and water on those bores because the bores have been maintained and there's water there. So you might get the odd one or two bullocks coming in at night. The bloke on night watch would come and say, 'There's some bush cattle comin' in.' I said, 'Let 'em come in, mate. We'll sort 'em out in the morning. Let 'em come and we'll see what they are. Don't let 'em out.' If they've got a Vestey brand they're quite acceptable. I've delivered over my number at Helen Springs [another of Vestey's stations, south-east of the Murranji]. Three or four over and they never queried it.

And the best thing about droving on the Murranji?

It's always a great moment to come out of the Murranji. The jump-up on this side is not a jump-up at all. It's just gradually sloping down over a half mile and you look down along through the bulwaddy and you can see that open plain about half a mile away. And the bullocks are walkin' in to water at No. 10 bore which is out on the plain. It's the one occasion you can let 'em string because they're only going to string out onto the plain. I'd tell the men on the wing, 'Just watch the lead and don't let 'em jog. Let 'em string onto the bore.' The bore's about half a mile away. And as you come down you think, 'Gee. It's a big relief to get out of the Murranji.' And you know from then on you've got the Barkly Tablelands and you can look your bullocks over every night and if you get a rush you've got as much country as you need to get 'em and put a bend in 'em.

The development of road transport in the mid-1960s rapidly put an end to the glory days of droving. In 1962, the number of cattle crossing the Murranji was 24 550; in 1967, the last year the Murranji was used, that number was down to 2653 head. In June 1967 drover Noel 'Pic' Willetts took the last mob over the track – 1390 head from Newry and Auvergne stations.

Old drovers lament the decay of one of the most famous and most testing stock routes in the country, for much of the Murranji Track is now overgrown, and the bores and tanks are falling into ruin. Access to the bore sites, which are now on private property, is possible after seeking permission from the relevant stations. They can be contacted through police stations, tourist information and roadhouses in Elliott and Top Springs.

The Buchanan Highway passes north of the original stock route. A more appropriate name for the highway would be the Hedley or Morgan Highway, or even the Croker Highway, after the pioneers who first penetrated the seemingly impassable hedgewood barrier. In the process they laid the foundations for the most daunting shortcut devised for droving.

Hardfaced greybeards, youngsters callow,

Some mounds cared for, some left fallow,

Some deep down, yet others shallow,

Some having but the sky.

— 'Where The Dead Men Lie', Barcroft Boake (1866–92)

9

CANNING'S FOLLY

In 1903 Western Australia completed one of the biggest and most audacious engineering projects Australia had ever seen. The fledgling state had succeeded in turning the entire Helena River inland, piping its waters over a distance of 450 kilometres from near the west coast through semi-desert to sustain the thirsty miners on the goldfields of Kalgoorlie and Coolgardie.

No further proof was needed that to bring abundance to the arid interior, all you needed was water. A healthy dose of self-confidence was also useful, and there was plenty on hand when the state's planners reflected on the virtually uninhabited deserts that dominated the Western Australian landscape.

The Tanami Desert, the Great Sandy Desert, the Little Sandy Desert, the Gibson Desert, the Great Victoria Desert – many had died attempting to explore these arid wastelands. They had crushed the hopes of those who'd survived. Nevertheless, the cocky Western Australians decided it was time the desert bloomed, and in 1906 the state embarked on a project to build a stock route direct from the settled south-west to the cattle country of the north-east. This was despite the unequivocal opinion of explorer David Carnegie on the country the stock route would travel. In 1896 he'd written: 'At least we have demonstrated the uselessness of any persons wasting their time and money in further investigations of that desolate region.'

Nevertheless, the route Carnegie had travelled was approximately the one preferred for what would become the Canning Stock Route. It was to travel from Wiluna, 850 kilometres north-east of Perth, through 1440 kilometres of undeveloped country to Halls Creek.

Such a stock route had been sought by Kimberley cattlemen since the early 1890s. For more than a decade they had been struggling with the difficulties of being so remote from southern markets in Western Australia, and from the rest of the country. The construction of port facilities in Wyndham had gone some way to alleviating their problems, but shipping cattle was as expensive as it had ever been. And as experience going back to the First Fleet had shown, many cattle lost condition during voyages of even moderate duration.

Adding to their woes, the East Kimberley and the Northern Territory were experiencing the devastating effects of redwater fever. First seen in the 1880s after cattle were imported to the Territory from Africa or Indonesia, the disease had spread across most of northern Australia by the 1890s. The fever was carried by cattle ticks, and it caused infected cattle to urinate blood. A mob of tick-affected cattle urinating in a waterhole could literally turn the water red, hence the name. Thousands of cattle were killed by redwater fever, and restrictions were placed on the movement of cattle from affected areas in an attempt to stop the disease spreading. The East Kimberley was one of the affected regions, and its stations weren't allowed to drove cattle through the unaffected West Kimberley.

Meanwhile, the rushes to the goldfields around what would soon become the towns of Kalgoorlie and Coolgardie had created a beckoning market of tens of thousands of hungry miners on the other side of the terrible deserts. Moving cattle through such a region presented no risk of infecting any other cattle. Without water, nothing could live there. There certainly weren't any cattle stations to worry about.

For almost twenty years other priorities took precedence over the development of the new stock route, though this didn't stop the cattlemen trying. In 1905 James Isdell, Member of the Legislative Assembly for the Pilbara, was still writing to the Minister for Lands outlining the advantages of the proposed stock route.

> In regard to tick-infested cattle bringing the pest over the desert into the south-west there is not the slightest danger. It is well known that ticks will not live in high tableland or in sandy country.

Isdell was correct in maintaining that the stock route wouldn't spread cattle ticks, but not for the reasons he understood. Cattle tick have a life span of eight days. After filling with blood, the ticks drop off the cattle and lay their eggs. If the newly hatched ticks don't get a meal of blood, they die. On the proposed stock route, the young ticks had to hook onto a new mob of cattle within a week if they were to survive. Even at the time the stock route was being proposed, that was unlikely, and it was to be borne out in reality as well.

Finally, flushed with the success of the Goldfields Water Scheme, the Western Australian government relented. On 27 April 1906, Alfred Canning, a surveyor with the Lands Department, was given the job of surveying and supervising the construction of the proposed stock route from Halls Creek to Wiluna.

Anyone who thinks surveying is a dull occupation could do well to consider the life of Alfred Canning. He had already proved himself a consummate bushman with the construction of Western Australia's rabbit-proof fence, an extraordinary barrier that extended from the state's southern coast near Esperance to its north coast near Port Hedland, a distance of 1800 kilometres. Now he was being asked to create a stock route through a wasteland of sand dunes and spinifex, where temperatures soared into the high 40s daily from early spring to late autumn.

Unlike other stock routes, which were opened up by drovers as the need arose and evolved over time to be well watered and travelled, what became known as the Canning Stock Route was purely the result of a decision by government. It wasn't unprecedented, but it was certainly an ambitious claim to say, 'If we build it, they will drove.'

Starting out from Wiluna in the cooler months of 1906, Canning and his survey party succeeded in finding many waterholes and soaks, often with the assistance of local Aboriginal people. However, as spring approached, temperatures became unbearably hot.

There were no problems while they could find water, but in mid-September Canning and his men were desperately thirsty when they reached Kuduarra Soak, only to find the water polluted by the rotting bodies of dead dingoes. Canning decided to press on 50 kilometres to Godfreys Tank, named after a member of David Carnegie's 1896 expedition, Godfrey Massie, and believed by David Carnegie to be a permanent water source. When Canning and his men got there, it was dry.

Canning decided to retreat to Kuduarra and try to clean it out. They were now in serious danger of perishing from thirst. As they staggered 50 kilometres back over the searing dunes, Canning's second-in-command Hubert Trotman and water borer Joe Tobin forged ahead, hoping to make a start on the waterhole before the others got there. When they reached Kuduarra, they were so thirsty they tried drinking the water as it was. It immediately made them violently sick.

'It's got quite a kick,' Tobin observed between convulsions.

The initial survey work was completed on 29 October 1906, when Canning and his men reached Flora Downs Station at the Halls Creek end of the stock route. He sent his report on 10 January 1907:

I feel certain when completed a well-watered stock route will be opened up, thus giving an outlet, much needed, to East Kimberley where they [the pastoralists] are rapidly becoming fully stocked not being able to get rid of anything but prime bullocks and even then at poor price.

On 27 February 1907, in advance of the main construction work, Alfred and his men set out to retrace their route, mapping it as they went and working on improving waters where they could.

On 5 April, at Waddawalla Soak (now known as Well 40), tragedy struck. Water borer Mick Tobin, brother of Joe, was attempting to communicate with an Aboriginal local when cameleer Tom Burke appeared, his string of enormous beasts bellowing as they scented water. As Mick turned to look at the beasts, the frightened local threw a spear at him, hitting him in the shoulder. The Aboriginal man fled as Mick started firing at him with his rifle.

'Let him go!' Canning shouted.

Mick either didn't hear or didn't obey, and when the man threw another spear, Mick fired again. Both men were hit, and both died of their wounds. Mick Tobin was buried near Waddawalla Soak. At the time his grave was one of the loneliest in Australia, but it wasn't long before he had company. Later that year, news came that a prospector named Stephen Grace had died after being speared in an Aboriginal attack in the Mackay Ranges, near the Canning Stock Route, 300 kilometres north of Wiluna. His last words were purported to be: 'Gold, gold, all for gold.'

The curious thing about Grace's death is that he was speared in August but died on 10 October. From his diary, it appears he didn't think the wound in his chest was too serious, and he continued prospecting with his colleagues. When the wound became infected, he grew steadily weaker and eventually died, probably from septicaemia. It's a measure of the remoteness of the region that the nearest medical help was probably more than 500 kilometres away.

Meanwhile, the Canning Stock Route construction team had no further trouble with Aboriginal people as their work went ahead. Their main problem was getting supplies. The logistics of transporting food to a construction team of twenty men, who at times were 700 kilometres from any kind of town, meant there were several occasions when they ran out of all but the most basic items. At one point they ran out of everything.

The first time supplies ran low the men went on strike, refusing to work without food. Canning was away trying to find out what had happened to the supply camels and there was nothing his second-in-charge, Trotman, could do. He simply continued working alone until, one by one, guilt or pride forced the others back to work. From then on, the men continued working whether they had anything to eat or not.

By the time the stock route was completed, in May 1910, the construction team had sunk twenty bores and opened up thirty-seven Aboriginal waterholes. The longest distance between wells was 26 kilometres. There was rejoicing in Wiluna when the construction team arrived, and the men were hailed as conquering heroes. Canning marked the culmination of four years of effort with an understated telegram sent to his superiors: WORK COMPLETED. CANNING.

Even before it was completed, the stock route was in use. The first mob of fifty bullocks was droved down from Flora Valley in 1909 by two members of the construction team, stockman Joseph Magee and an Aboriginal named Nipper, who was employed as a general-hand-cum-shepherd. The bullocks were all 'killers', destined to feed the construction team, and accordingly none made it all the way to Wiluna. Canning wrote to the Under-Secretary of Mines on 15 March 1910 that the cattle travelled well, despite the hot, dry conditions.

Also in 1909, a gold strike in the Tanami Desert saw prospectors travelling up the Canning Stock Route to the scene of the latest rush. They were able to take advantage of the waters along the route to sustain themselves and their horses.

With the stock route completed, a chain of wells and waterholes now stretched through the desert, with patches of good feed for stock. It looked like the audacious Western Australians had done it again.

However, it soon became clear that the government had made no provision for maintenance. As a consequence, the wells started to deteriorate from the moment they were finished. In addition, none of the wells had windmills, so water had to be raised by hand or beast, which made it slow to water cattle, limiting the number that could travel in a mob.

Drovers had to carry everything needed for a trip of up to eighteen weeks, as there was absolutely nowhere to resupply on the entire 1440 kilometres between Halls Creek and Wiluna.

The biggest problem of all was that there was no law along that distance except Aboriginal law. As far as the desert people were concerned, the drovers were trespassing. Indeed, Hubert Trotman noted the Aboriginal animosity when the stock route was being built. Despite his need for water, Trotman sympathised with the traditional owners of the land when he wrote:

> I can understand the blacks' fierce indignation for apparently they thought we deliberately trailed them with the object of depleting their waterholes which, of course, had to carry them over many rainless years.

Unfortunately, the flaws in the stock route were yet to be appreciated by the drovers who attempted to use it. The first to take stock down the whole length of the Canning Stock Route was George McIntyre, with forty-two horses and two foals belonging to a Pine Creek mine manager named Edwin Tamblyn. McIntyre was expected to take the coastal stock route but in October 1910 he was reported to be taking the Canning instead. He is thought to have travelled with a young Aboriginal named Nipper (not the same Nipper who had worked with the stock route construction team).

Only nine horses made it to their destination, Coorow, 275 kilometres north of Perth. The animals were sold for £90 – the cost of delivering them, £350.

The second drover to take stock down the Canning, William Mayberry, left a couple of months after McIntyre. He took seventy-seven horses and lost thirteen. In 1913 he wrote to the acting premier of Western Australia, detailing the condition of the stock route less than a year after it had been 'completed'.

> When we found a Well in a bad state and could not get water for seventy odd horses it was an easy matter to strike out for the next Well, but to think of trying to water a mob of mixed cattle and horses was impossible . . .
>
> When we got through we heard of [drover Tom] Cole starting with 350 head of cattle and 50 head of horses, I wired him that we thought it was impossible to bring a mob of cattle down as the wells were in a very bad state, the blacks had destroyed the good work that Mr Canning had done . . .
>
> The ropes were cut to pieces in many places, the buckets taken away, also windlass and troughing missing, and some of the Wells filled up with wood.

Forewarned, drover Cole took equipment with him to repair the wells as he went. However, he wasn't the next drover to take a mob down the Canning. In January 1911 James Thomson started down the route with another mob of cattle. His partner, Fred Terone, was forced to pull out before they got onto the Canning proper due to an attack of 'sandy blight'. This was the catch-all outback phrase for a range of eye infections usually caused by a lack of water to promote good sanitation and spread by a reliably generous supply of flies.

Without his partner, Thomson was short-handed. As Bill Mayberry predicted, when he got to the Canning he was soon struggling to water his stock. He decided to employ a local Aboriginal named Franky, who in some reports was described as 'half-civilised'. Now part of the droving plant, Franky and his wife (Lidia) were allowed to remain in the drovers' camp at night. What happened next made headlines around the country, and ensured the Canning's enduring fame.

In the first week of September 1911, readers of the *West Australian*, the *Adelaide Advertiser,* Melbourne's *Argus,* the *Hobart Mercury,* the *Sydney Morning Herald* and the *Northern Territory Times and Gazette* (to name a few) perused versions of the following report:

MURDERED BY BLACKS.

FATE OF TWO DROVERS.

POLICE IN SEARCH OF NATIVES IN CENTRAL AUSTRALIA.

PERTH. Wednesday.

Two cattle-drovers, Cole and Pennefather, arrived at Wiluna, in the North Murchison district, yesterday, from Hall's Creek, by way of the Canning stock route, and reported having discovered, on June 29, at No. 37 well, 450 miles [720 kilometres] north of Wiluna, and 450 miles from Hall's Creek, the bodies of James Thompson [sic], George Shoesmith, and a native employee, who left Hall's Creek, in the East Kimberley, last January, to overland a small mob of cattle.

The three bodies were found within a radius of 100 yards [90 metres] of the well, and were partly buried, the knees only showing above the ground.

Thompson's skull had been smashed in apparently by a heavy weapon; Shoesmith had a fracture of the left side of the skull, and

a spear-wound in the right side of the neck, and the body was also cut
in halves.

The native boy's body, supposed to be that of an aboriginal known as
'Chinaman', who left Hall's Creek with Thompson's party, was dismem-
bered, and buried about 10 yards [9 metres] from that of Shoesmith.

All three bodies were fully dressed, with the exception of boots, and
it is believed the victims were murdered while asleep.

Thompson's diary was found near the stock route on June 28, about
ten miles [16 kilometres] from the scene of the tragedies. The last entry
bears the date April 25. The diary of Shoesmith was picked up in pieces
near the scene of the murders.

The firearms, horses, and cattle were taken by the natives. The camels and horses were used by the natives until knocked up, and then
shot. The cattle were dispersed. One rifle, badly damaged, was picked
up near the scene of the murders in an abandoned native camp. A hundred miles [160 kilometres] north of this place Cole and Pennefather
saw natives wearing European clothing.

No. 37 well is within fifty miles [80 kilometres] of where Stephen
[sic] Tobin, of the Canning survey party, was murdered three [sic] years
ago. The natives in this part are apparently most treacherous, and a
menace to persons using the stock route. Thompson and Shoesmith
were ex-police constables, and Thompson was the son-in-law of August
Lucanus, hotel keeper at Wiluna, where his son and wife are living.
A strong police party is leaving Wiluna in search of the murderers, who
it is thought will be encountered within 20 miles [32 kilometres] of the
stock route, as the surrounding country is barren.

Australians outside Western Australia may not have known much
about the Canning Stock Route before the drovers' murders, but after
a report like that they weren't going to forget it in a hurry. Incidentally, Thomson's diary affirmed that many of the wells were in a state
of disrepair. In addition to damage caused by Aboriginal people, sand

had almost buried some of the cattle troughs. At some wells, Thomson was assisted by local Aboriginal people who knew how to operate the whip poles, ropes and buckets to bring up water.

Thomson's diary also noted the Canning Stock Route's ability to control cattle ticks. On 11 March, while still on Sturt Creek north of the route, he wrote: 'The ticks are very bad on the bullocks.' On the route, between Well 50 and Well 49, he wrote on 3 April, 'Not a tick on the bullocks that I can see.'

The Canning continued to make sensational news. In December reports were published that what became known as the 'punitive expedition' had 'dispersed' fourteen Aboriginal people found in the vicinity of the murders, 'all of whom were alleged to have been implicated in the tragedy'.

The punitive expedition, led by Police Sergeant Pilmer (some papers incorrectly refer to him as Palmer), reported the existence of severe drought conditions in the area. They believed it hadn't rained on the stock route for two or three years. With their camels rapidly losing condition, rather than turn back to Wiluna the expedition made a dash for Halls Creek, which, despite newspaper reports describing the location of Well 37 as halfway between the two towns, was significantly closer.

The full details of the expedition were revealed in February 1912. Again, newspapers around the country reported the extraordinary events from the outback, including extracts from Pilmer's diary. The *Sydney Morning Herald*'s headlines were typical:

A MASSACRE.
FATE OF TWO DROVERS. ATTACK ON PUNITIVE EXPEDITION.
NATIVES SHOT DOWN.

After providing some background to the expedition, the report went on:

The following extracts from Sergeant Palmer's [sic] diary of November
15 give details of a very bold attack made at midday by 25 blacks upon
his camp two stages north of the scene of the murder.

Sergeant Palmer attributes the massacre of Thompson [sic] and his
party to their carelessness in allowing a half-civilised black named
Franky and his gin to accompany the party and stay in the camp. From
Thompson's diary and from information collected en route Sergeant
Palmer considers that Franky was in league with the local blacks and
treacherously arranged for the surprise of the camp while the stockmen were asleep.

While the punitive party were whiling away the time reading,
25 natives made a determined attack on the camp. Fourteen natives,
forming an apparent advance party, came down Gravelly Hill, east of
the camp, at a run, each carrying two whackaburras [clubs]. Assistants
gave the alarm, and each member of the party stood to his rifle.

'I went just outside our camp to try and check the rush,' Sergeant
Palmer writes, 'and called upon and signed to them to stop and sit
down. They still came on. Divining their intentions to get at close
quarters, we opened fire simultaneously killing six in camp and one
20 yards [18 metres] distant. Three escaped wounded. About a dozen
on the Gravelly Hill decamped, and were followed some distance until
they were clear of our grazing camels. If this mob of natives had got
to close quarters with the party with their whackaburras the position
would have been serious, as the party would not have been able to
use their firearms, and the reserve natives would have come on with
their spears, with disastrous results. The attack was most daring, and
well planned, and would have done credit to more civilised people. The
eldest of these natives was not more than 30. They were a fine lot of
natives, remarkably conditioned. Two of the killed natives were wearing rope belts, and another a leather belt. Constable Leddin did good
work in protecting the left flank of the camp, and is deserving of special
praise. A large number of spears were afterwards gathered up off the

Gravelly Hill and destroyed. These natives were very bold and daring, and, in my opinion, were flushed with their victory over Thompson's party and its attendant spoil.

As always, the victors write the history, but it's worth noting that the supposedly emboldened Aboriginal people hadn't touched drover Tom Cole when he'd travelled down the Canning only a couple of months behind Thomson. The only accounts of what happened came from the punitive expedition itself, and it's not hard to find anomalies. First reports, in December 1911, spoke of fourteen Aboriginal people implicated in the murders being 'dispersed'. The more detailed reports of February 1912 described an attack by fourteen Aboriginal people that resulted in seven Aboriginal people being killed in self-defence, while three more were wounded and an additional dozen or so were chased away. Pilmer's official report referred to the presence of an Aboriginal woman, who had tried to grab his rifle.

The truth about what happened to the punitive expedition is open to speculation, and the question of what provoked the initial attack on drover Thomson and his men also remains unanswered.

Pilmer asserts that the motivation for the attack was the treachery of Franky. Of course, Franky's version of events, and that of the other Aboriginal stockmen on the drove, was not recorded. Deep in the desert country, the most likely provocation for the Aboriginal people would have been the sight of the third mob of stock in only a few months drinking their precious water supply. Another clue to what might have happened is the reference to Franky's wife, named by Thomson in his diary as Lidia. As previously noted, Aboriginal women were often the only source of companionship for drovers on remote stock routes, and whenever there was trouble in a stock camp, fights over women were never far away.

Despite his gruesome discovery on the Canning, drover Tom Cole thought it was a pretty good stock route. He'd got most of his cattle through to Wiluna and they'd fattened on the diverse feed found in sand-dune country. The stock had arrived in better condition than when they'd left Flora Valley Station.

Nevertheless, Cole's glowing opinion of the stock route overlooked its basic problems. Subsequent drovers continued to report the bad condition of the wells along the route. It was becoming established wisdom that mobs of 300 were the best one could hope to take down the Canning. Larger mobs were split up, if only to give the wells time to 'make' enough water and reduce the pressure of holding back thirsty cattle trying to get a drink.

The biggest problem remained the route's sheer isolation. Drovers could find themselves 700 kilometres from the nearest assistance, in an area where the Aboriginal population was demonstrably hostile. It couldn't have escaped the notice of drovers contemplating the journey that Thomson, Shoesmith and 'Chinaman' had been dead for two months before their bodies were discovered, and it had been another two months before news of their fate reached the world at large.

Over the years, nothing changed. As one drover told me, 'I've been down the Canning twice and I don't want to talk about it. I'm happy to talk about anything else, but not that.'

Another drover, who hadn't travelled the Canning but knew its reputation, explained: 'It was a pretty wild place. There were no police and those Aboriginal people out there had no respect for white law. You had to be prepared for anything, and I mean anything.'

The problems with the wells and fears of Aboriginal aggression combined to see the stock route seldom travelled after the initial burst of enthusiasm in 1911. Over the ensuing two decades, less than one mob per year travelled the lonely stretch of country.

In 1922 the dangers made news once again. At a campsite 50 kilometres south of Well 37, three oil prospectors were attacked after they'd gone to bed for the night. Two suffered serious head wounds.

A third, John McLernon, was fatally wounded and died at 6.30 a.m. His body is buried near Well 37.

Despite being unresponsive to calls to conduct regular maintenance on the Canning, the Western Australian government refused to give up on the track. In 1929 it contracted local identity William Snell to recondition the wells along its entire length. As it happened, one of the members of the reconstruction party was a survivor of the 1922 attack on the oil explorers.

Starting at Wiluna, Snell slowly progressed along the stock route, repairing wells as he went. At each well he planted vegetable seeds in the hope that the plants would flourish and provide fresh vegetables for passing drovers for years to come. His optimism gradually faded as the strain of repairing the wells or sinking new ones took its toll.

Snell managed to get more than halfway along the stock route before the work overwhelmed him. By October, he was at Well 35 and the approaching summer was already making the desert unbearable. One of the hardest aspects of travelling along that section of the Canning Stock Route at that time of the year is it doesn't get cool after the sun goes down. Explorers recorded temperatures over 100°F [37.7°C] after midnight. In the early hours of the morning, the sand can still be too hot to touch.

Snell buried his stores in anticipation of making a follow-up expedition to complete the work. However, amid controversy over the quality of the work he'd done, the government decided to replace him. Alfred Canning was asked to complete the job. At the time, he was seventy years old, but nevertheless he accepted the responsibility and started from scratch. Canning considered Snell's work substandard and ended up reconditioning every well along the length of the route. After eighteen months, the job was complete.

The reconditioning of the Canning Stock Route proved timely, as

Wiluna was the scene of a mining boom shortly afterwards. In the early 1930s gold, arsenic and other minerals were found in the area and the population rapidly rose. By 1932, when a railway from the south reached the town, the population had risen to 7000. Yet even that wasn't sufficient to send cattle streaming down the Canning from the Kimberley.

Only one station was regularly sending cattle down – Billiluna, at the head of the track, was the source of almost every mob. The station virtually had its own private, government-funded stock route, except that Billiluna's drovers often carried out maintenance on the wells themselves – it was that or see their cattle perish on the long dry stages.

Over the years, the tensions with the desert Aboriginal population continued. In 1936 a dingo trapper named Joe Wilkins was killed 25 kilometres east of Well 15.

A police investigation carried out after his body was found in mid-1937 revealed that Joe had been killed by three Aboriginal men named Chunga, Maloora and Yalyalli. The investigation revealed that Wilkins had been given one of Chunga's wives, but had then taken Chunga's other wife without his consent. Chunga had sought revenge, with the help of the other two men.

Maloora and Yalyalli were tried in September 1937 and sentenced to ten years in prison. Considerable debate ensued regarding the legality of compelling the wife of one of the men to give evidence against him. When Chunga was finally arrested in 1941, the Crown decided not to prosecute him. The other two men were released later that year.

While the dangers of the stock route were widely known, in 1940 they didn't stop Eileen Lanagan becoming the first woman to drove cattle down the Canning. Her husband, George, was taking 800 head from Billiluna to two stations near Wiluna and, despite warnings from the police and others, she was keen to experience droving first-hand. Eileen was related to Charles O'Connor, the talented engineer who had masterminded the Goldfields Water Scheme.

Eileen went on the eighteen-week trip as cook, with a young Aboriginal, Baroo, as her assistant. In addition to Baroo, the party included eleven Aboriginal stockmen, Eileen's husband and one other white man. Being the wife of the boss, Eileen was allowed two saddlebags for her personal items, instead of the usual one. In the extra bag she carried a pot of face cream, a diary and a revolver.

Fortunately, Eileen had no need of the gun. Her husband was well aware of the tensions between the Indigenous population and the drovers and was strict about not allowing them near his dinner camps. Yet he was also sensitive to their needs, and after killing a beast for his men he left the remains for the local Aboriginal people.

As with the other stock routes in northern Australia, in 1942 the Japanese bombing of Darwin and other coastal towns saw a rapid change in government attitudes to the maintenance of the wells on the Canning. The bombing of Wyndham and the closure of its meatworks suddenly saw years of neglect replaced with a sense of urgency as plans were made to destock northern Australia. In the case of the Canning, it was hoped that more than 7000 head of cattle could be evacuated in 1942. This was probably more cattle than had travelled the stock route in the entire thirty-two years since it had opened, though it was a paltry number compared to the 30 000 head travelling the Murranji every year and the 47 000 that did so in 1942. However, before anything like 7000 cattle could travel the Canning, once again the wells had to be reconditioned.

Despite the sense of urgency, work on the wells didn't start until July 1942, already near the end of what might be considered the droving 'season' on the Canning. Delays were caused by the perennial logistical problems of obtaining supplies and transporting them up the track. These problems were exacerbated by a rare occurrence on the Canning – floods.

Nevertheless, by the end of 1942 the southern team had completed its work on thirty wells, on time and on budget. The northern team had only completed ten of its allotted twenty wells. As a consequence, in 1942 only 400 bullocks were brought down the Canning by drovers Dowling and Terone, who passed one of the teams working on the wells on their way through.

The northern team continued to struggle with supply difficulties that revolved around having their depot located in Halls Creek. The further they got from the depot, the longer it took to ferry supplies to the distant wells. As a consequence, only five more wells were completed in 1943. Even using motor vehicles, and in one case a small aircraft, the northern team was no match for a man like Alfred Canning armed only with camels, determination and raw muscle.

In the end, the well reconditioning at the northern end of the Canning was never completed. The government documents relating to the last five wells are missing and all that is known is that the work was terminated in 1944, unfinished. By then the Canning was no longer the high-priority project it had been in 1942, when the Japanese were on Australia's doorstep.

While as few as a dozen droving mobs had travelled down the Canning in the thirty years up to World War II, in the years after the war as many as twenty trips were made. Again, most of them were from Billiluna Station.

Drovers from that era recall that the trip took around fourteen weeks, with the stock travelling down in winter. At times it was so cold that the drovers dismounted and walked beside their horses in order to keep warm. By that time, desert Aboriginal people were increasingly being employed as stockmen and their knowledge of the country made the going easier.

Jerry Pedro, a part-Aboriginal drover, recalled how on the darkest nights when they were moving stock, the Aboriginal stockmen could always find their way to the next well. As George Lanagan had done in the years prior to the war, after a beast was killed, its remains were always left for the people of the desert. Often the carcass would be gone within twenty-four hours.

According to Jerry Pedro, 'The next day you couldn't see where you'd killed the beast.'

Another drover, Ben Taylor, travelled the Canning Stock Route initially with George Lanagan from the late 1930s onwards. In an interview with Ronele and Eric Gard, he recalled his experiences. According to Taylor, the use of camels as pack animals wasn't only due to their endurance in the desert:

> One camel could carry as much as six or seven horses and they are a lot easier to handle. If we started off from Halls Creek we had to have at least 20 weeks rations, well if you had those split over . . . you would want 20 or 30 horses – you could put the lot on 6 or 7 camels. (*All Taylor quotes reproduced by kind permission of Ronele and Eric Gard.*)

The camels were also used to draw water from the wells. As a consequence, watering a mob was a time-consuming process that usually came near the end of the day, amid heat and dust made worse by milling, thirsty cattle. Said Ben:

> Once you start, it's all wells, like no windmills or nothing and every well was equipped with a whip pole, a windlass and a bucket. You had to be a navie who could ride a bit to be in the area. You pull [the water] up with a camel – through the whip pole. Like the camel, he had his harness on and he was hooked onto a long wire rope . . . The rope went through the pulley block on the ground at the back of the well and then through the whip pole pulley over the well shaft.

> We had a 25–30 gallon [110–135 litre] bucket and you'd pull the water
> up from the well . . . You had plenty of labour because in that coun-
> try where the bush blacks were, you had to have two camel boys and
> two tailers, because where the bush blacks are around one couldn't
> go on his own.

In 1959 George Lanagan was asked to take cattle down the Canning
from Billiluna Station for the last time. He arranged for drover Len
Brown to start off the cattle while he travelled to Wells 22 and 23 to
repair them. When Brown turned up, Lanagan took over and saw
the cattle the remainder of the way to Granite Peak Station, 200 kilometres north-east of Wiluna.

After 1959 cattle from the Kimberley stations either travelled east
along the Murranji Track or were trucked and shipped to market.
The reopening of the port facilities at Wyndham after the war, and
the emergence of Asia as a market for northern cattle, also accelerated the stock route's decline, a few years in advance of Australia's
other great stock routes.

The desert Aboriginal people could reasonably argue that they'd
beaten the white invaders. It's thought that the last of them – a family comprising a father, mother and seven children – left the desert as
recently as 1974. They were taken to a mission near Broome.

No cattle have made their way down the Canning in the last fifty
years, and they're not likely to do so ever again. 'It was never much
of a stock route,' one drover told me. 'You could only take about 300
head in a mob and with that many cattle and the distance involved,
it was hardly worth it.'

The optimism that surrounded the decision to construct the Canning Stock Route was never matched by the reality of its use. It was
the last great stock route to be opened in Australia, the longest and
most remote, and it remained a wild and dangerous place throughout its history.

However, in a curious twist, it's because of the Canning's bad reputation that the route has endured, though in a form never imagined by its creators. Today, four-wheel-drives regularly travel the Canning on what is considered one of the iconic adventures of the outback. Far more people traverse the road each year than they ever did in the entirety of its use as a stock route.

The first vehicles to drive the full length of the Canning did so in 1968, driven by surveyors Russell Wenholz and Dave Chudleigh from Canberra, and survey assistant Noel Kealley from Perth. At the time there was no defined track and the men travelled 2600 kilometres while trying to locate every well along the old route.

The Canning exerts a powerful attraction to travellers. It traverses stunning desert scenery that includes jump-ups, mountain ranges, natural springs and, of course, around 900 sand dunes. Much of the flora and fauna is unique. The route is dotted with historic graves and there are culturally significant Aboriginal art sites of high quality. Many of the wells and gravesites have been restored or maintained by volunteers who travel great distances from around the country to do so.

Yet the Canning still has traps for the unwary. The road is littered with broken vehicles, so far from roadside assistance that the costs and logistics of sending a recovery vehicle to get them are prohibitive. In April 2005 two men from New South Wales perished on the Talawana Track, 50 kilometres west of the Canning Stock Route, after their vehicle broke down. No one passed by before they died and it's thought two weeks passed before their bodies were discovered by a local stockman.

In May 2010 the Canning Stock Route celebrated the hundredth anniversary of its completion. Unlike most of the stock routes referred to in this book, it is still possible to travel its entire length. Permission is required from traditional owners to deviate from the route where it crosses Aboriginal land. Ronele and Eric Gard have compiled a traveller's guide to the Canning that has become a compendium of nearly every snippet of information regarding the stock route's history and those associated with it – from Alfred Canning to Eileen Lanagan.

It may have been folly to build a stock route through the middle of a desert, but today the Canning is one of the few ways to experience one of the largest wilderness areas in the country. It remains a monument to the courage and endurance of the drovers who faced its great emptiness, with stock, and got them through.

In the huts on new selections, in the camps of man's unrest,

On the frontiers of the Nation, live the Women of the West.

— 'The Women of the West', George Essex Evans (1863–1909)

10

SHE WAS A GOOD MAN

The annals of droving abound with the stories of famous men whose feats of endurance, courage and resourcefulness have become the stuff of legend. But to suggest that women weren't part of the droving life is to miss a significant part of the story. Sometimes their contribution is only hinted at. Sometimes it's deliberately skirted. Often it's difficult to recognise their role in droving history because the best women drovers were so highly regarded that, in a curious twist, they were stripped of their gender and came to be seen as men.

In *Flynn of the Inland,* Ion Idriess referred to legendary missionary John Flynn visiting an unnamed station, 'the home of the Five Sisters', when he was a patrol padre in the 1930s, travelling by camel around the outback. Two of the girls explained to him that the other three 'Jess, Bess and Tess are out on the run rounding up cleanskins with Dad'. Idriess added: 'The father had practically forgotten his only disappointment: just occasionally with wonderment he realised that his "boys" were girls.' According to Idriess:

They could ride any horse on the run, break in any 'outlaw' and enjoy the taming; could ride from dawn till dark on a muster for a month on end and find only joy in it. They had galloped before the thunder of a cattle stampede in the dead of night, had swum flooded rivers while clinging to their horses' tails.

They were dare-devils right enough. He [Flynn] had seen them in the stockyard among frightened plunging beasts and it fairly made his hair stand on end. He had sat on the rails with his heart in his mouth lest he should see those girls trampled to pancakes. They had laughed up at him and invited him to come down inside. Smilingly he declined.

(Extracts from Ion Idriess's Flynn of the Inland *reproduced by kind permission of ETT Imprint)*

Idriess concludes his catalogue of the girls' skills with the fairly tall story that three of them escorted the camel-riding priest on steers, which they intended to continue riding all the way to another station. The furthest this writer has seen a steer ridden could be measured in metres, not kilometres.

The reference to girls as boys is far from unique. Catherine 'Kate' Buchanan, wife of legendary drover Nat Buchanan, was described in similar terms while working on Mihi Creek Station, which was managed by her father. According to her son, Gordon: 'John Gordon, my grandfather, used to say long ago that "my boy Kitty is the most intelligent worker on Mihi Creek and my right-hand man".'

The gender confusion may have typified the prejudices of the time, but in its way it was the ultimate compliment a bloke could give. If a woman was doing the work of a man, and doing the job as well or better, she was considered to be a man, or as good as.

Kate Buchanan's skills as a rider came to the fore when the family travelled from Mihi Creek to a new station, Ban Ban, in Queensland. Shortly after setting off, Kate's father became critically ill. In *Packhorse and Waterhole*, Gordon Buchanan recounted what unfolded:

The nearest doctor was at Glen Innes, and the only possible messenger the sixteen-year-old Katherine [sic], who, indeed, was anxious to ride for succour. At the bridgeless Beardy River her horse would not face the boggy crossing. In desperation, she put him at the narrow channel higher up, cleared the water, but struck the sloping bank on the far side, her mount faltering but recovering. Then on a few miles to Stonehenge Station when another messenger was dispatched to the doctor at Glen Innes, who came at once to his new patient. If the dark had any terrors for this brave rider, the anxiety for her father and the need for speed and concentration on the road – or the unmade track – banished all other terrors on that hard and lone night ride.

Kate married Nat Buchanan in 1863, and shortly after went with him on a journey through unsettled country to the newly formed Bowen Downs Station, in central Queensland. For some years she was the only European woman in the district, living with only the most basic of amenities, although her enjoyment of an outdoor lifestyle was some compensation. However, when she fell pregnant with what would be her only child, her role as homemaker and mother increasingly tied her to the homestead.

Kate Buchanan raised Gordon while Nat spent periods of up to eighteen months on the road, often out of contact with the rest of the world and facing perilous situations. Kate endured long months without news, not knowing whether her husband was alive or dead, and dealing with her own hardships alone.

Henry Lawson identified the hardships of the women married to drovers in his famous short story, 'The Drover's Wife'. Alone in a remote bush shack, a woman battles snakes, bushfires, floods, pleuro-pneumonia, violent scrub cattle, marauding crows and eagles. She bears her children far from medical help and raises them alone. She defends them when villainous-looking swagmen come calling at her door. Sometimes she buries them alone.

For Kate Buchanan, her mercurial husband's visits were often all too brief. The reason she had only one child is not known, but perhaps it was because Nat was almost never home. Her lament may have been that suggested in the 1975 film *Sunday, Too Far Away*: Country women said of their relationships with their men that, when they came home for a weekend, on Friday they were too tired, Saturday too drunk, and Sunday too far away.

When it came to droving, however, some women chose to go with the stock. While I was researching my previous book, *Birdsville: My Year in the Back of Beyond*, I interviewed the then 79-year-old bookmaker Ron Murphy, who described his place of birth as: 'On the Boulia–Winton road, probably behind a mob of cattle. I don't remember, I was only one day old.' The clear suggestion was that Ron's mother gave birth to him while travelling with her drover husband.

White women may not have received much recognition as drovers or stockmen, but even less value was placed on the contribution of Aboriginal women. When George Farwell visited Clifton Hills Station in the late 1940s, he focused on renowned stockman and station manager Artie Rowlands. However, he does refer to Artie's Aboriginal wife:

Mrs Rowlands was a good mate for him, since it was her country, too. Born at Mungerannie, she was descended from the Dieri tribe through her mother, and was widely reputed to be as good at handling cattle as a man. For many years she rode out to the cattle camps with her husband, though latterly she was obliged to remain at home, because the Flying Doctor network insisted that someone be at hand to look after the radio.

Songwriter and author Ted Egan recognised the presence of Aboriginal women in his song 'The Drover's Boy'. The 'boy' turns out to be an Aboriginal woman who is killed when her stockhorse bolts and she suffers a fall. The gender mutation also conceals a relationship between the drover and the woman. Aboriginal women were often the only women in the remote areas drovers travelled. Some became sexual partners for brief liaisons; other relationships lasted longer and resulted in the women doing double duty as sexual partners and stockmen.

In either case, when drovers' yarns about their exploits turned to their sexual experiences, they invariably revolved around Aboriginal women, referred to as 'gins'. Few, if any, of the stories bear repeating.

As for their abilities with stock, in his book *Droving Days* author Herbert Barker detailed the skills of some of the Aboriginal women he encountered:

On some places there were good riders among the gins but they did not follow it up after they were fully grown, as a rule. The best work on horseback that I ever saw a gin do was cutting out cattle on a camp at Ethel Creek, a big cattle station at the head of the Fortescue River. There were about 500 cattle on the camp, and the head stockman and a gin, Bullockie by name, began cutting out. She could not have done better, showing plenty of headwork when bringing them to the outside and steering them to the nearest man on the face of the camp, opening their ranks just right for the face man to dive in and cut off the wanted one while she hunted the others back to the mob. It was most interesting to watch but rather spoilt by an odd man from the back of the camp chipping in to do a bit of cutting out himself. This is fatal, and I heard Bullockie on another occasion get cross with a boy for doing it. He was her son. *(Reproduced by kind permission of Hesperian Press)*

Despite the odds against them, a select few women managed to build reputations as drovers and stockmen. One of the earliest was Hannah Glennon. She was born at Toowoomba on 18 July 1872, the last of eight children of Irish emigrants John Glennon and Catherine Pickham, three of whose children died before reaching adulthood. John had worked as a bullock teamster before settling on a small-holding in the Westbrook district, south-west of Toowoomba.

A year after Hannah was born, John started to go blind, which threw much of the work of running the property onto Catherine and an older brother of Hannah's, Bill. In May 1874, John died. Soon after, Catherine married a man named Daniel Ryan. Bill eventually left home and went to work as a stockman on stations in western Queensland. He soon earned a reputation as an excellent rider and Hannah, fifteen years younger, had a ready-made role model whenever he returned to the farm. His stockman's outfit, rugged good looks, confidence and ability cut a glamorous figure for a young girl whose life comprised endless chores.

Twice a year, Bill returned home with a small mob of unbroken horses. Under the tutelage of her brother, Hannah became an expert rider and horse breaker. Learning at a young age, as many station managers will tell you, meant she was more willing to listen, and able to learn faster. Considering what life had in store for her, it was just as well.

In 1885, when Hannah was just thirteen, her stepfather died, and the weight of running the farm fell upon Hannah and her mother. Only a year later, however, Catherine also died. Hannah and Bill tried to keep the farm going but the work and returns just weren't there. The property was sold and Bill went back to work as a stockman out west. Hannah was too young to follow and was taken in by relatives of her stepfather. Her new family taught her the finer points of domestic life but her passion remained with horse work.

Her skills impressed William Beit, the son of a local grazier, who witnessed her horsemanship when she was still a teenager. In 1946, writing under the pen-name 'Pierie Remot' in the *North Queensland Register*, Beit recalled:

One day in the home yard, I saw her ride in breeches, boots and spurs. The horse was a low-set, short-backed, strong-boned animal, said to have been sent from the Lockyer District just to try Hannah out. He had already thrown the best riders on the Lockyer, and Black Peter Rouse from the Logan. She saddled him in the ring yard. Getting the reins righted, Hannah took a lug hold on him and landed on his back like a fly and rammed the spurs into him. The outlaw held his wind, giving seven or eight vicious bucks, and pulling to get his wind, he made two more desperate attempts to unseat his rider. It was a picture to see Hannah sitting calmly and unconcerned, like a 'Swell' in his Rolls Royce.

Horse-breaking and stock-riding are a dangerous business, and in 1888 Bill's luck ran out: he was killed in a riding accident on a western Queensland station. Hannah was devastated by the loss of her closest brother, but at the age of sixteen she thought she was ready to strike out on her own. She may not have had much choice, as she'd reached an age where she could reasonably be expected to go out to work.

Hannah was developing into a striking-looking young woman – tall and slender, with a mane of bright-red hair. She already had a reputation as an excellent horse-breaker, and a solid dose of self-confidence. Not long after her brother died, she gathered six saddle horses and three packhorses, and headed west in search of work.

At Wallumbilla Station in the Maranoa district, she was employed as a stockman. While there, she broke in a large number of horses. Next she became a horse-tailer for a drover. She may also have doubled as cook, putting to use the skills she'd learned with her kindly relatives.

Hannah may have known a bit about horses, but when it came to men she had a lot to learn. A year later, aged only seventeen, she was droving a mob of horses from Charleville when she met 26-year-old

Thomas Doyle, who was working as a boundary rider on Dillalah Station, 50 kilometres south of Charleville.

Doyle may have been sweetness and light at first, for in October 1889 the pair were married at a church in Charleville. After a week-long honeymoon the newlyweds returned to Dillalah, where Hannah's husband soon showed his true colours. He became abusive and threatening. On one occasion he tormented her by threatening to take poison. Shortly afterwards, he accused her of infidelity. By then Hannah may have been aware that she was pregnant, but nevertheless she'd had enough. She left her husband and went to stay with a sister at Cunnamulla.

Doyle attempted to reconcile with Hannah and she returned to him in February the following year. Their first child, Daisy, was born on 1 July 1890, but died only days later. Their marriage soon deteriorated. Six months later, pregnant with her second child, Hannah left Doyle again and headed for Adavale, where she booked into the Blackwater Hotel on 3 January 1891.

Doyle followed. His promises and threats made no impression on Hannah, who decided the break was permanent. Over the ensuing weeks he repeatedly visited the town, trying to win her back, but she refused. When begging failed, he threatened to harm her or himself.

On 26 January Doyle asked the proprietor of the Blackwater Hotel if he could borrow a gun to go turkey shooting. The following day, saddler Valentine Ganly heard a shot near the stables of the hotel and went to investigate. He found Doyle propped against a tree in the hotel grounds, bleeding from a gunshot wound to the abdomen. He had also managed to set his shirt on fire.

The dying man was carried into the dining room of the hotel. Despite his condition, when he saw Hannah, he called out to her: 'Don't go and leave me, Hannah. Come to me.'

'Tom, what made you shoot yourself?' she asked him.

'It was all through you, Hannah,' he answered. He died an agonising death at 3.40 the following morning.

Hannah left Adavale soon after, and despite her pregnancy headed 'further out'. At the age of eighteen she gave birth to her second child, Mary, on 10 July 1891. Hannah was now calling herself Annie, perhaps trying to escape her traumatic past, or simply because in a country where the letter 'h' is often superfluous, Hannah had become Anna and then Annie.

She then returned to the Blackall district, where in 1893 she apparently had another child, George, to an unknown father. Records also show that, as Annie Glennon, she married a man named Robert Watson on 22 November 1894. She was twenty-two, he was twenty-six. The scant records of the time reveal nothing more of this relationship.

Little is known of Hannah for the next three years. It is believed she was somewhere in central Queensland, droving, but there's no record of the location. Towards the end of the decade she was working in the Cloncurry area, where she eventually put her daughter in the care of a convent. The fate of her son is unknown.

In 1898 she was thought to be working on Mount Devlin Station, east of Cloncurry in the Hughenden area. In that year Michael Durack, son of Patrick Durack who had established Thylungra Station on Cooper Creek and several stations in Western Australia, was a passenger in a Cobb & Co. Coach travelling from Cloncurry to Hughenden. As the coach neared Hughenden it was flagged down by a woman riding a large black stallion. She and her horse were so striking that Durack recorded the details in his diary: 'One person encountered on my journey is worthy of special comment – a woman, tall, gaunt-looking and with bright red hair, who helped us rummage for her mail before riding away.'

When Durack made enquiries about her, the locals told him the woman's name was Red Jack. Her stallion was called Mephistopheles. Apparently the latest incarnation of Hannah/Annie Glennon/Doyle/Watson was thought to be the equal of her fellow stockmen, with a nickname and degree of fame that had male connotations. A legendary if enigmatic figure, she was a bit of a loner, which was perhaps not surprising given her experiences with men.

Hannah continued working as a stockman in central Queensland, the Gulf Country and the Atherton Tableland for the next four years. On 3 May 1902 she bore another child to an unknown father, a girl named Ada, at Fischerton, a tin-mining district south of Chillagoe, which was also a cattle region.

She was still in the area in 1904, probably mustering cattle on Chillagoe Station, when she suffered a fall from her horse. Alive but seriously injured, an attempt was made to transport her to Mareeba Hospital, some 100 kilometres away. Part of the journey may have been by rail but it was to no avail. Hannah died on 21 December 1904, aged only thirty-two. She was buried in Mareeba but her grave can no longer be located.

Yet Hannah's memory has endured, and she has become an obscure but legendary figure in the outback. She may also have made more of an impression on Michael Durack than he relates in his diary. In 1987, Mary Durack, author of her family history *Kings in Grass Castles*, published a poem, 'Red Jack', inspired by her father's story of his meeting with the remarkable woman with flaming red hair. Much of it appears to be fictitious – she is portrayed as virtuous, while Hannah's love life appears to have been robust. However, it does suggest that she enjoyed a reputation as a highly capable drover. The lines *Red Jack's as good as any man, / The settlers used to own* has a recognisable ring of truth.

Unfortunately, like so many woman (and men) before her, there is precious little detail of a life spent on horseback behind cattle far from journals of record. Nevertheless, the great chronicler of outback life, the late Marie Mahood, said this of Hannah:

She was only 32 but her name was legendary across North Queensland because she had dared the social conventions to do what she did best, to work in a man's world, where she was apparently accepted without question because of her extraordinary skill. *(Mahood extracts reproduced by kind permission of Central Queensland University Press)*

Much more is known about the woman who is credited with being the first female boss drover in the country. Edna Zigenbine was one of the generations of outback children born and raised behind mobs of livestock. She was born at Thargomindah, near the Queensland–New South Wales border, 1000 kilometres west of Brisbane, on 10 October 1926, the fifth of eight children of boss drover Harry Zigenbine and his wife, Ruby.

Moving from camp to camp, spelling on the edge of towns like Marree, Tennant Creek and Camooweal, Edna's mother struggled to raise her kids and give them the basics of schooling by correspondence. In later years, Edna looked back at what her mother went through and realised how hard it must have been for her. Every child was born in a different place. The youngest, Mavis, was born under a tree at the Butru railway siding, near Dajarra.

The older children were supposed to ride to school in Dajarra, but as Edna later told the president of the Drover's Camp Association, Liz Flood, 'Of course we didn't go. We used to go riding all day.' As a consequence, Edna never learned to read or write. Nor did most of her brothers and sisters.

Edna said she never knew how her mother managed to do the cooking and washing for eight kids out on the road. Even something as simple as a loaf of bread couldn't be bought – it had to be baked. Life on the road was hard, but it got harder when they came to town. That was where the men all got on the drink. This was especially true of Edna's father: a lot of his money went on alcohol instead of food for the family.

Renowned bushman and businessman R.M. Williams also witnessed Harry Zigenbine's drinking sprees, and the consequences for his family. In *I Once Met a Man,* he wrote of his first meeting with Harry, in Adelaide:

> Harry was a droving man, his wife and family were not kitted to visit
> towns, but there was a pub in the darker end of Adelaide that catered
> for such as Harry, a place to drink out a cheque, where elbows on the
> table was the custom. Word came to me that Harry Zigenbine would
> want to catch the Ghan train to Marree next day and could I see that
> he went? His family were parked on the edge of the town at Marree
> waiting for him – places like Marree don't support game, which is all
> Harry's family could expect to eat. Getting him from the pub to the train
> was a major problem, for in his present condition Harry was unwill-
> ing and Harry was heavy. *(R.M. Williams extracts reproduced by kind
> permission of the R.M. Williams estate)*

As soon as they were old enough, Edna and her siblings were in the saddle, working for their father round the clock, droving cattle and standing night watches. At a time when many outback men regarded their wives and children as a source of free labour, the average age that many youngsters left school and went to work was thirteen or fourteen. In the case of the Zigenbine kids, it was probably much earlier. Edna may have been exploited by her father, but she loved the life and in later years said she 'wouldn't change it for quids'.

Despite the attractions, in the mid-1940s Edna and her younger sister Mavis left droving and went to work as ward maids at the Tennant Creek Hospital. However, in 1950, her father found himself short-handed when R.M. Williams asked him to help take a mob of bullocks from Bedford Downs down the Murranji and on to Queensland after another drover pulled out. At the time Harry was at Hidden Valley Station, just north of the Murranji Track, and he called on his daughter to help him out.

Edna quit her job and at the age of twenty-three got back in the

saddle, along with her brothers Jack and Andy. Harry also provided the horses, and R.M. and stockman Jackie Cadell flew up
from Adelaide with a load of packsaddles. They rendezvoused at the
No. 12 Bore on the Murranji and brought the cattle through to Newcastle Waters.

Due to his business interests, R.M. had to leave them there. The
party continued on to the Ranken River, where the cattle had to go
through a dip to exterminate ticks before they crossed the border
into Queensland. The tick inspector used too much arsenic and the
cattle suffered severe burns. Harry sent R.M. a telegram along the
lines of: 'Cattle burnt in dip. Expect to lose the lot. Come at once.'
R.M. replied, 'Can't come. Sending nurse.' R.M. wasn't sure whether
Harry would enjoy the humour, but most of the cattle were saved.

Edna continued droving with her father. On a subsequent trip
he became so ill he had to pull out, leaving Edna and her younger
brother Andy with a mob of cattle still to be delivered. R.M. Williams
had first-hand knowledge of Harry Zigenbine's health problems.
He and Harry were at an open-air movie in Tennant Creek when
R.M. saw how things were. 'Came half time we went to the rough
hessian enclosed toilet. I noticed he was in trouble with blood red
urine – Harry had lived rough, drank heavy, travelled all the hard
roads. This was the end of the road.'

The 23-year-old Edna continued on with her brother (who was
the camp cook), three Aboriginal stockmen and one white stockman.
At Crow's Nest Bore some of the cattle came down with pleuro, but
Edna couldn't give them a break to recover because there wasn't
enough feed in the area. A stock inspector shot seventy head, but
declared the rest immune. At Elliott, on the Stuart Highway, one of
the Aboriginal stockmen pulled out. Edna's droving team was down
to five as they crossed the Barkly Tablelands.

At Lake Nash, near the Queensland border, the white stockman
pulled out as well. Fortunately it was a relatively easy ride down

the Georgina to Dajarra but it meant night watches of three hours instead of two for the reduced staff of four. And, of course, everyone drove the cattle right through the day. At Dajarra, 1600 head were loaded. There'd been no rushes. The cattle had been quiet the entire trip.

In droving, reputation is everything. Boss drovers who lose or mistreat cattle soon find no one will trust them with their stock. It was a testament to Edna's ability when, at the beginning of the next droving season, she was given another mob to drove, from Banka Banka Station 100 kilometres north of Tennant Creek. Says Marie Mahood:

> It was said of Edna that she was as good as any man with bullocks and steers and better with cows or a mixed mob. If a cow calved on the trip, Edna would pick up the newborn calf and ride with it to the cook's wagon. When they stopped for the night she would mother-up the cows and their calves and the next day the calves would get a ride on the wagon until they were strong enough to walk the daily distances with their mothers. With these mobs Edna often delivered more cattle than she had started out with. From the Kimberleys to Queensland Edna was first-choice drover for station owners who wanted to shift a mob which included cows.

R.M. Williams agreed, noting in *I Once Met a Man* that 'Edna took up where Harry left off to become the best woman drover in the west – she never knocked a calf in the head, seldom lost a cow, managed the roughest teams on the road.' In his autobiography, *Beneath Whose Hand*, R.M. added: 'The whole family including Edna, perhaps especially Edna, were accomplished drovers, and their feats were yarned about over a hundred campfires in every season.'

In later years many of Edna's friends and acquaintances pointed out that she couldn't abide cruelty to animals. They laughingly said she would always feed her horses before she fed them. Yet she also displayed qualities that had been learned from a lifetime around stock, and such qualities were valued by stock owners. Another woman, M. M. Bennett, explained why in a book about her father, *Christison of Lammermoor*:

> Quietly handled docile animals, habituated to the routine of being herded by day and watched by night, travel well and put on condition. It is the carefully bred, quietly handled bullock that fetches the highest price. Unfortunately, people are never merciful because it pays, but only if they are mercifully inclined, so men who ought to know better will gallop after cattle, knocking them about, terrifying them and making them wild – scrubbers only fit to be shot and left – and then boast of it to people as stupid as themselves.

It is worth noting that Edna was given her father's droving plant over any of her brothers. The fact that a physically slight, relatively young woman was shouldering the responsibilities and pressures of a boss drover attracted widespread attention and publicity. It didn't hurt that she was also quite photogenic. Wedding proposals started finding their way to her from all over the world.

Throughout the 1950s Edna continued droving with her father's plant. She was eventually joined by John Jessop, whom she married in the early 1950s. In 1954 she gave birth to her only son, also named John, and the small family continued on the road, as Edna's parents had done before her. In 1960 Edna and John separated. The writing was on the wall for droving and Edna headed for Mount Isa, where her lack of education didn't stop her getting a job with the council as a pound-keeper, responsible for tending to stray stock, particularly horses. Being settled in one place meant she had a chance to provide her young son with a better life than she had known.

Edna kept her own horse in the backyard of her house, and the verandahs of her house resembled those of a station homestead – piled

with saddles, bridles and swags. Her home became a handy stop
for passing stockmen, young ringers or old friends from her droving
days.

According to Liz Flood, who came to know her while running a
catering business next door and was with her the night she died:

> Edna was a very straight lady. She spoke her mind. She was completely
> illiterate but had a beautiful nature. She was a hard lady but she'd give
> you the shirt off her back. In all the years I've known Edna, I never saw
> that lady in a dress. I have seen photos of her at 19 years of age in a
> dress and she was a beautiful, beautiful young girl. But she was just
> one of the blokes. I don't mean that in the sense it is today. She mar-
> ried and she did have a son, she was a lady in her own right, but she
> was a drover.

Long after she stopped droving and even after she retired, Edna continued to attract considerable interest and publicity. However, Liz
pointed out that towards the end of Edna's life, when people were
writing stories saying she was a legend and a national icon, she
couldn't help feeling the words and notoriety weren't worth much as
she struggled from pension to pension.

Nevertheless, she never lost her generous spirit. Says Liz: 'You
could always go to Edna's place. If you didn't have a bed, the door
was always open, and many a night she'd have five or six blokes stay-
ing there. She had a heart as big as herself; she was only a little lady.'

Edna was also a keeper of the stories of the outback and droving.
Liz Flood recalls:

> I'll never forget the day I'd been asked to find out who this was in a
> book, there was a big picture and it was just a sepia photo, no names
> and so I asked Edna and she looked at it and started to cry. She said,
> 'That's my mother, my sister Kathy, my brother Jack and the Army

doctor at the Elliott Bore in 1942.' She was a great wealth of information. She knew 99.9 per cent of the drovers in this area or their
progeny.

Marie Mahood noted the understated praise that old drovers gave her:

> Edna's name is recognised by all and praise conceded by those who
> know themselves just how difficult the life of a boss drover could be.
> They are not given to extravagant praise, those old-timers. The top per-
> formers may rate only the comment, 'He was a good man on the job.'
> That's what they say about Edna. 'She was a good man on the job!'

Women are still droving. While researching this book, I came across
a mob of cattle being droved down 'the long paddock' (a droving
term for a stock route) just outside Winton. Two people were behind
the mob as it slowly fed along towards their dinner camp. One was a
man. The other was a woman.

While working on *Birdsville*, there were two young women working on Adria Downs Station – Jessica Gilby and Sigrid Manns. Sigrid
was supposed to work around the homestead but clearly wanted to
get out among the cattle. At the station one morning you could see
her disappointment when the day's jobs were being allocated and she
realised she was going to be left behind. Some time later she didn't
baulk at participating in a bronco-branding competition, despite having a broken arm.

On another occasion a mob of 300 Adria Herefords were being
walked to the Birdsville racecourse for a tourism promotion. The
Adria stockmen who were bringing them were having smoko when
I stopped for a yarn. While chatting, I noticed a cow start walking
away from the herd.

'That one's getting away,' I said, well aware that the station hands
didn't need me to tell them how to keep their herd together. As it

happened, to our mutual surprise I'd managed to notice something before they did. Jessica Gilby was the first to react. She leapt on her horse and trotted away, angling towards the cow to turn her back. The cow broke into a run but Jessica and her mount immediately accelerated to match it. In a moment she was galloping away, cutting off the beast and rounding it back to the herd. Within a minute Jessica was back, explaining that the cow was just trying to get back to her calf, somewhere back on the station. The young woman slid down from her mount and continued the interrupted conversation.

There are seven women members of the Drover's Camp Association. The organisation, of which Liz Flood is the first female president, is striving to document the lives of others that she's aware of. These days, female drovers are recognised as women, rather than men. While some are given credit for being as good as a man, a few are simply regarded as being as good as the best.

Emily Pankhurst aged 92 July 2014 is one.
The book written about her & her
Husband (deceased) is called
The Boss Drover.

Don't you hear the night-wind sighing
Through the cloud-bush, lute and lyre?
Can't you see the drovers lying
Head to saddle, foot to fire?

— Will Ogilvie (1869–1963)

I I

THE LONG PADDOCK

There's no romance in droving. People who think there's romance in droving are sheep drovers or they're from away down south. You get about five hours' sleep a night. The boss drover probably only gets about four hours a night for three months. The tucker's pretty basic. It's gotta be pretty basic tucker, otherwise you're not going to make any money. The men are used to that. You can sit back against the truck on dinner camps – when you're the bloke who's not on watch. There's always one bloke on watch – and after you've had dinner you can go to sleep just like that. You get used to gettin' by on four or five hours' sleep but your body's not used to it. Just like that. It's amazing.

The old Murranji drover was trying to put his life, with its moments of high drama and extreme danger, into perspective. A common theme emerges among drovers, or those who've known them. There was no romance; it was just dirty, dusty, exhausting work – hard on people, horses and equipment. It was a life characterised by the 'thousand-yard stare' and an ability to fall asleep anywhere, any time. But in the next breath many will confide that they'd still be doing it if they could.

The preceding chapters of this book have explored the lives and experiences of those who pioneered droving and stock routes. For them, the uncertainties of the country ahead were to some extent off-set by the pristine country they travelled. Often they had first pick of feed that had never been grazed by domesticated animals. Pioneering was full of challenges, but it could also result in the enduring fame of a Hawdon, Bonney, Redford or Buchanan.

Those who followed the established stock routes did so in almost complete anonymity. Any fame they enjoyed might only last their life-time, in the form of the quiet admiration of their peers. Nevertheless, some were destined to become famous as the last to travel a well-known stock route – George Lanagan on the Canning, Bill Gwydir on the Birdsville, Pic Willetts on the Murranji.

For them, as with countless others, droving was never about fame. In several interviews for this book, drovers remarked that most of the time droving 'the long paddock' was pretty mundane. Each day was the same as the last, with the cattle or sheep feeding peacefully along from one camp to the next. Yet they all had their stories.

There are many similarities in the backgrounds of drovers. Most left school and started working when they were very young.

Scrubba Watkins, now in his eighties after spending more than forty years in the saddle 'travelling all over Australia', got his educa-tion 'In a one-room school. I went in one door and out the other.' He was twelve when he did his first droving trip, taking bullocks with Gordy Oldfield down the Birdsville Track from Clifton Hills to Marree. 'It was a few weeks' trip, in 1939, and when we got to Marree that was the first we heard there was a war on.'

While accepting that the droving life wasn't easy, Scrubba still enjoyed it. 'They were the best years, happy days. You might get one bad mob but there were a hundred that were good. We loved the work; we were good at it. If you got a bad mob, you wouldn't go back. Same with the boss. If he was a bad boss, men wouldn't stay. Good blokes accepted responsibility.'

Dave Allworth started life in New South Wales but he was determined to work in the frontier world of the Northern Territory. In 1954, when he was sixteen, the Vestey firm of station owners sent him to Morestone Station in Queensland, to learn how to be a stockman. He said of the experience:

> You mightn't like it at the time, but if you get onto a property where there are hard men who know what they're about – good cattlemen, good horsemen – then they'll teach you. The manager threatened to give me a floggin' one day but that's the closest I ever got.
>
> They taught me how to shoe, pack horses, ride rough horses. They'd put me on a horse and say, 'He's a young horse, you can both learn together.'

As with many drovers, Dave did his time as a stockman on stations (in his case, in the Territory), before deciding to put a plant together. He ended up droving on the Murranji and Barkly stock routes in the final years that they were used.

Bob Savage was another drover who started out young. 'I was out droving from the age of twelve,' he said. 'I've taken cattle all over the country. Down the Georgina, through the Northern Territory and across in Western Australia. I've taken cattle down the Tanami Track to Alice Springs.'

Bob was one of the pioneers of the country on the north-west side of the Tanami, and the first to take up country there, at a station called Suplejack.

When we started out we were camped under a tree. I was building the place up and going away during the droving season to earn enough money to keep the place going. I was taking cattle down there until 1969. I took the last mob of cattle down. Well, I got someone to take cattle down the next year and they lost half of them.

Bob couldn't believe the Tanami when he first saw it. It was supposed to be desert, but there were Mitchell grass, Flinders grass and about twelve other different kinds of feed. There was tree cover and top feed as well.

Daryl Horkings was a drover who didn't mind the fences and enclosed spaces of the stock routes of southern New South Wales, where he was brought up. Throughout the 1970s and 1980s he was still one of many drovers feeding sheep and cattle along the stock routes around Deniliquin, putting condition on them before they went to market.

Daryl was born in Warragul, Victoria, in 1948. His family moved to Tocumwal in New South Wales soon after, and the droving bug bit while he was still at school: 'As kids we'd be allowed to watch the drovers go past,' he remembered. 'They were my heroes. That's what I was gonna do when I grew up.'

After leaving school he went straight to work as a stockman. Then he spent a few years breaking in horses before returning to the Riverina in 1973 to take up work as a drover for himself, based in Deniliquin. 'I did a lot of drovin' around that Riverina country – through the '70s and '80s. The long paddock, we were out feeding. We were never walking cattle or sheep from A to B. Wherever feed was we'd get 'em out there to get them a bellyful.'

For many drovers, the different stock routes they droved largely influenced their experiences. As Bob Savage recalled:

The best trip was that one down the Georgina. We took bullocks from Morestone to Avon across the Ranken Plain. It was downs country the whole way. There wasn't a tree anywhere. We had a competition once to try and find a leaf out there. There were windmills every 10 miles [16 kilometres]. You'd start out in the morning and you'd soon see the top of the next windmill, so you could already see where your night camp would be. And the cattle were a good mob. Bullocks. They'd stride out, 'cause you were only pushing them towards water. The only delays were when we'd stop to give 'em a good drink, because 1500 cattle take a lot of watering.

The worst trip was over to Halls Creek. On the track from Halls Creek to Broome a lot of drovers had bad smashes. They'd feel down because they'd hadn't done anything wrong and their cattle still rushed.

I was 20 miles [32 kilometres] this side of Broome at a place called Yawuru and the scorpions were crawling all over the cattle. They were this big. [He holds his hands about 30 centimetres apart.] I actually saw this scorpion on the face of one of the cattle that was lying down. It pulled back and the next thing you know it was up and away.

I had a smash there and the other drovers were going, 'You're not laughing now.'

And I said, 'I never laughed.'

I had plenty of rushes. I had one where the cattle rushed and wouldn't stop. We headed 'em and kept 'em on the stock route but they kept on rushing. They'd go along at a trot for a bit and then they'd gallop again. We just had to keep 'em going. It was pitch dark. By the end of it we were praying for the sunrise. Then they got out on the feed and pulled up.

Charlie Rayment is a typical drover, except for one thing. The best word to describe him is 'gentleman'. Now in his eighties, Charlie is quietly spoken and highly articulate – and sharp as a hawk. He still competes in bronco branding, the traditional western Queensland/ Northern Territory method for branding calves. Some older riders compete to show the world they can still ride a bit. Charlie is out there to win. He can rope calves and pull them up to the branding panel so fast he has to wait for his ground crew, including his mid-forties son Don, to keep up.

Charlie was raised in 'Waltzing Matilda' country around Winton, where he eventually acquired his own property and still resides today. Among many experiences in a very full life, the consummate horseman enlisted in World War II, only to find himself in the navy. He was serving aboard the heavy cruiser HMAS *Australia* when it was attacked and hit by kamikaze planes on six separate occasions.

He's another of the old-school drovers who doesn't mind taking the time to answer questions. Despite meeting him several times before, it was daunting to approach him for this book. Typically, he already knew what I·was up to and at the Camooweal Drovers Camp he came over for a bit of a yarn.

People from this country claim you. I met a lady I knew from Jundah. I've hardly been there at all in my life, I've mostly lived west of there (except for when I went away in World War II), but she claimed me. It's a bit like the Aboriginal people, who belong to the land. When you're raised here it's a bit the same. It feels that way.

It's the same as in those droving years. We knew a lot of drovers, ringers and station workers really well and yet we may hardly have met them – we knew their strengths and weaknesses and whether we could trust them in a tight spot.

I've been droving over different areas of Queensland, around Clermont and the Belyando River Country, Longreach and Winton, the Channel Country, Diamantina and Georgina River routes, and the country in between. A little in the Territory from Alroy Station and a little in the top of South Australia.

My first complete three weeks trip, as a fourteen-year-old, was with Brighton Downs fats to Winton. The boss was a half-caste gentleman, Johnny Williams. After World War II I worked for several boss drovers.

Then in 1950 I had my own pack-horse plant, mainly doing trips from the Georgina country to rail heads at Quilpie, Yaraka and Winton.

My longest trip was with 1500 Territory store bullocks down to the railhead at Trangie, NSW. It turned out to be a 26 weeks trip. I think it was 1952. I had four men and myself and 60 head of plant horses. It was an easy trip with plenty of feed and water.

We walked 'em down from Camooweal, down the gutter there [the Georgina River] and over to Dajarra. Then we went down, following the rivers and the soft country – crossed the Barcoo then on to the Paroo, followed it down, then crossed the watershed to the Warrego at Cunnamulla. Followed it down then crossed over some deserty country to the Darling, which was in flood and crossed the cattle over the old bridge at North Bourke.

We 'let go' a lot once we crossed the Queensland border, at the Barringun Gate. 'Letting go' means 'not watching'. They were broke-in bullocks by then, so we'd put them on camp at dark, settle them down and camp behind them. They would stay on camp most of the night, then towards morning they'd get up and stretch, then feed off the way we were going. You never 'let go' if they were thirsty or hungry. Next morning it was just a case of pushing them together, perhaps giving them a count, and you were already several miles along the way.

There's some bad country east of Bourke so we followed the Darling up on the east side to where the Bogan comes in, then followed it up through Nyngan and on to Trangie. I got to Trangie and them wheat stacks was gettin' higher and higher and closer together, and the fences were everywhere and I thought, 'That'll do me. Trangie was far enough.' The bullocks ended up at Hay on the Murrumbidgee, while the long trip back with the horse plant was ahead of us. No road-trains then.

That's the thing about the stock routes. They follow the softer country – the waters and the rivers – and avoid the stony ground. You wouldn't take cattle over the ranges to somewhere like Mackay if you

didn't have to. The roads these days stick to the ridges. Very few follow the stock routes, the softer country. So you get these people hauling
their caravans saying they've been over here and over there but they
haven't really seen the country. All they've seen is the bitumen. Their
rigs are too heavy to get in and see what the country is really like.

You get people like that who claim to be environmentalists. There
was this woman wrote an article and said she'd driven from Adelaide
to Darwin and hadn't seen a single kangaroo, so they must be endangered. She was probably in her motel room around sunset and didn't
know kangaroos have enough sense to find a little bit of shade during the heat of the day. She probably didn't have the sense to see their
droppings and tracks, but because she didn't see any she decided there
mustn't be any there. If anything there's more kangaroos today than
there've ever been because of all the waters that have been put down.
The only place there aren't many is that Channel Country, where the
cracky ground doesn't suit 'em.

For Daryl Horkings, droving 'inside' was a world away from the
long-distance droving in parts of Queensland, the Northern Territory
and Western Australia. However, it was typical of the experience of a
large number of drovers.

Deniliquin in the 1970s and 1980s was a huge sheep sale centre. Every fortnight 70 000 sheep would pass through the saleyards;
sometimes it was more than 90 000. The sheep came from as far
away as Queensland, but often the trucks dropped the stock with a
drover about a month's walk, around 160 kilometres, from the saleyards. Daryl recalled:

They'd put a lot of dollop on them in those four weeks on the road. It
would depend on what the [stock] routes were like. If you come to a
route and it was good, you'd just stay there. Sometimes you'd spend
a week on the one route. If you were there and they were improving on

the route, you'd have stayed there. You wouldn't be walkin' them miles if you didn't have to.

In those days you had to do 6 mile [10 kilometres] a day with sheep and 10 mile [16 kilometres] a day with cattle. If you were walkin' they didn't charge you agistment. Then when you get a good year and there's feed everywhere you could sit on a reserve. A reserve had something like 5000 acres [2000 hectares] on it and you could sit there as long as you wanted and just pay agistment. It was cheap in those days – half a cent a day for sheep and five cents a day for cattle. They'd only let you do that when there's 5000 acres of green feed there a foot high. You could stay there a bloody month and you wouldn't see what they'd eaten. It'd be growin' faster than they could eat it. I did that with sheep and cattle, some horses.

In those days there were eight or nine stock routes around Deniliquin and there were drovers on all of them. As many as twenty to twenty-five drovers would be travelling down the Hay Road, Moulamein Road, Finley Road, Conargo Road and others, all of them gazetted stock routes that had been used for droving long before cars made an appearance.

There were no bonuses here for bringing stock to the saleyards in good condition, but the drovers' reputations depended on it. It was what got them their next job. In good times or bad, they were focused on finding feed for the stock in their care.

When he could, Daryl tried not to lock his stock in yards at night. He believed they did better if they were allowed to roam free, just not too far. To keep them from wandering, he pegged dogs around them. If he was camped on a fenced stock route, he simply pegged four dogs at each end.

'They were just mongrels,' Daryl explained. 'They were just pegged there to make a noise to stop your sheep or cattle walkin' up the road. But the best dog of the lot was green feed. He was the best dog of the lot – green feed. He'd hold 'em.'

In addition, Daryl had six or seven working dogs. They were never used as peg dogs, but were kept in camp at night and well looked after. When he droved, Daryl often did so with only the dogs to help him. At the most, there was only him and another stockman:

> The dogs did most of the work, whether it was sheep or cattle. Each dog's worth three men. If you had to employ a couple of blokes, six or seven dogs'd do the same job and all you had to do was feed them. If you had a mob of sheep there was always enough killers in there for your tucker box and your dogs – old scraggers you'd get for killers. You'd pick old sheep up walking along the road – well they'd be dog tucker.

A truck and a caravan were the droving plant. Most of the time the caravan was only used to sleep. Daryl cooked inside if it was raining; otherwise he cooked at his campfire because he didn't have to clean up. 'You just peel your spuds and toss the peels in the fire,' he said.

In the 1970s and 1980s, virtually all the droving in New South Wales was based on feeding stock, rather than travelling them from point A to point B. However, from the mid-1980s onwards a series of severe droughts curtailed droving significantly.

Daryl also recalled that the traditional animosity towards drovers from local property owners hadn't diminished:

> Some of them cockies used to grow a lot of rice around that Deni area and they weren't supposed to do it but they'd drain their rice water out onto the stock route and these cockies'd be watchin' this feed growing and think, 'Oh, I'll put me cattle out there and eat that down.' And you'd come along with 5000 sheep and it'd be gone in a day. They used to hate us.
>
> I've had rows. One bloke used to leave his front gate open. Then your sheep or cattle end up going onto his place and he'd come down

screamin' and I'd just tell 'im, 'Shut your gate you so-and-so bastard.'
I'd be back at me camp a mile or so away and see 'em going in and
wouldn't bother goin' and gettin' 'em out. I might amble down in an
hour's time, or an hour and a half, and chase 'em out.

Like all good drovers, Daryl always finished a drove with the same
number of stock he started with. If he was ever short when he did a
count, he'd backtrack and usually find the missing stock in a cockie's
paddock.

I was never short when I handed them over. That's the art of droving.
I was travelling along the road one time and I see these sheep stringing
out into a cockie's paddock. There's two double gates and they're about
that far apart and my sheep are going through one at a time into this
paddock. So I put the dogs around 'em and went up and opened the
gate and brought mine back out. And as they're coming back there's
a few sheep of these cockie's came out with 'em. Well they went along
with the mob. And I had cross-bred ewe weaners at the time and they
were all cross-breds too, so they just matched in. So yeah, you took
your numbers back all right.

While Daryl mostly droved sheep, he preferred to drove cattle. Sheep
would hear a truck coming and walk straight in front of it. Cattle and
horses would look around and (usually) wait for the vehicle to pass.
If sheep didn't want to go somewhere, such as across a bridge, they
simply refused to move. He'd have to cut off ten or twenty and force
them over. With cattle, he could hold them up to the obstacle and,
while it might take a few minutes, they'd eventually start to move.
Daryl's verdict: 'Sheep are very bloody dumb.'

Stumpy Adams is one of those typical outback blokes who's a little
reticent on first meeting, but when he warms to you he'll yarn all day

and night. He's worked at everything from stockman to stock inspector, drover to camp cook. And no, he's not real tall.

Stumpy only did one droving trip, across the Ranken Plains, west
of Camooweal on the Queensland–Territory border. For him, a typical
day involved waking before dawn, rolling his swag, having a quick
breakfast, then getting going. The stockmen would poke the cattle
along until lunch, when they always had a camp. Someone watched
the cattle while everyone else had an hour's break.

'We just lay under a tree,' Stumpy recalled, 'put your riding boot
under your head and sleep like that for an hour. Then stand up and
say, "Righto, let's get goin'."'

After 'poking the cattle off camp', they let them feed all afternoon.
As other drovers have noted, well fed and watered cattle camped better at night if they weren't hungry or thirsty.

'Spider and me'd be bringin' the cattle up close and [boss drover]
Charlie'd be yellin' out, "Keep them cattle back." You know, keep 'em
feedin' up. You don't want to get 'em too early on camp. You want
'em comin' on camp just as the sun's goin' down.'

At night, Stumpy did the midnight to two o'clock watch. As he rode
around the mob, the habits of the mob soon became clear. Some were
camped near the fire, some preferred to sleep a bit further away. The
odd one would be trying to walk off. As he'd been taught to do, he
sang to the cattle or recited poetry, anything to make a continuous
noise so they knew he was there and wouldn't be startled.

'I tried to sing everything,' he said. 'If Van Gogh could've heard me
he'd've cut off his other ear.'

Stumpy reckoned droving was one of the best experiences he'd
ever had.

There's nothin' better than sittin' on a horse pokin' around looking
at the birds and the country. After that I always used to say to young
fellers, if you want to learn about cattle you want to go droving. Best

way you can ever learn is looking after cattle. Watching cattle, learnin' about cattle, how they act. Everything's different. The horses are different. It teaches you to be neat and tidy. Livin' in the bush is just like, you've gotta know where everything is in the dark. I was never in a packhorse camp thing but those fellas could pack up in the dark and have the horses ready on camp and the light'd be comin' through the trees and they'd be away.

Bob Savage took a more practical view of droving:

I wouldn't say I enjoyed the life; it was just what we grew up with. When the cattle were rushing it wasn't exciting or frightening. You were too busy concentrating on what you were doing, making sure you stayed in contact with them in the darkness. We just did what we had to do.

What makes a good drover is someone who knows how to handle cattle, what to do in a certain situation. The ones who don't last or can't handle the tough life tend to be a bit useless anyway. It's usually pretty simple. If you get your cattle to the night camp well watered and with plenty of feed, all they'll do is lie down and go to sleep. But if they're hungry or thirsty you'll get problems. If they're thirsty and they get the scent of water, they'll be away. So you have to be patient and not push the cattle too hard.

I was always lucky because I always had good men with me. When you've got people who know what they're doing, it makes for much less problems.

Daryl Horkings reckoned droving was a mixed bag:

Drovin' down that Riverina it was either the worst job you could have or the best job and there was no in-between. The worst of it – cold winter, freezing cold weather, bloody big frosts, drought time, no feed and not much water. And you'd be pushin' and pushin' and pushin' to do

your six mile. About four o'clock you're bloody worn out. It's gonna be
dark in an hour's time, the yards you're pokin' at are still a mile away
up the road and the frost is startin' to come in. You're buggered and
your dogs are buggered from pushin' these wet sheep along the road.
And you've gotta get there before it gets dark because a lot of times in
that country when it's gonna be frost there's also fog, thick fog. You had
to be locked up before dark, otherwise you'd lose 'em in the bloody fog.

So you'd get up to the yard, tie your dogs up and trot back to your
bloody truck, three or four mile back up the road. By the time you drive
back up to the camp it's absolutely bloody freezin'. You've gotta get
a fire going, feed your horses, rug your horses, do the same for your
dogs. By the time you did all that it'd be half past seven. You'd cook
yourself a feed and then go to bed, then do it all again tomorrow.

And the good times?

There was one year, '81, I had a mob of sheep, an old rodeo mate,
Bonny Young, had cattle, and we just boxed 'em together. We come along
together. We spent a fortnight on the one reserve. Just sit round the fire
drinkin' tea. There was nothin' else to do. The owner'd come out and
say, 'Gee, you're doin' a good job,' and we'd done nothin' but sit by the
fire. The other extreme you'd battle and work trying to get 'em a feed
and the owner'd come out and say, 'Gee, they're not doing too good, are
they?' because they've lost weight since he saw 'em two days ago.

Daryl reflected the attitudes of many drovers when he summed up
his thoughts:

I look back at those years I spent droving as the best of my life. Freedom. Total freedom. I suppose you're out on the road travelling like a
bloody gypsy – no worries and no cares. Even when I describe those
hard days they were still [about] freedom. That's what I like about 'em.

Admittedly, as the old Murranji drover suggested, Daryl *was* mostly droving sheep and he was from down south. Nevertheless, as Banjo Paterson put it, 'a drover's life has pleasures that the townsfolk never know'. If nothing else, it offered a choice for those who chafed at a desk job. They could throw it in, head outback and go droving.

Today, that option is no longer available, and it's hard not to think we're a little poorer for it. Where teenagers were once trusted with a thousand head of cattle, we no longer trust them with a single can of spray paint. Where once the passage of time was measured by the walking pace of livestock feeding slowly down the road, it's now parcelled tightly into a daily nine to five.

In recent decades there have been attempts to recapture the experience of droving with organised trips for anyone who can ride a bit and has the price of admission. More often than not such trips are touted as the last of their kind, but they've had more encores than Nellie Melba. And they're characterised by levels of comfort that real drovers never knew.

The old drovers are probably right when they say there's nothing romantic about droving, yet there's something about it that's appealing. From the High Country to the Murranji, the image of the drover stands apart. Freedom, adventure, resilience and resourcefulness – the qualities of the drovers remain those to which many of us aspire. Given the chance, we'd still trade places with a drover if we could.

I was a western bushman born and bred,

And so I loved the cattle, as men do

Whose life is to the dusty sandhills wed,

Whose world is bounded by a fence of blue

— 'The Overlander', Will Ogilvie (1869–1963)

EPILOGUE

In January 2009, years of drought in western Queensland came to an end in spectacular fashion with a rain event that sent an enormous wave of floodwater rolling down the channels of the Georgina and Diamantina rivers. It was the Georgina's third-biggest flood in recorded history, spreading up to 60 kilometres wide and inundating vast areas that soon sprang into verdant life as the waters receded. Where weeks before there had been a dust bowl, now there was feed for a million cattle.

For many of the stations in the area, the rains had come too late. Many had been forced to destock, in particular around the Boulia area. Now, with prodigious amounts of feed springing up, they didn't have the cattle available to take advantage of the boom times.

The problem for many landholders was that it was prohibitively expensive to buy store cattle and truck them in to fatten on the abundant verdure. The cost of fuel was too high. And the days of droving cattle in to fatten in the Channel Country had long since passed.

Or had they? One of the great cattle stations of the Australian outback crunched the numbers and decided that droving might still pay.

Lake Nash Station sits astride the Queensland–Northern Territory border and is watered by the mighty Georgina, when it flows. The station was established by the great pastoralist of the nineteenth century, John Costello, one of the first to head down the Strzelecki with stock and the man who discovered Harry Redford's famous theft of a thousand head of Bowen Downs cattle.

In good years, Lake Nash turned off prodigious numbers of cattle. Highly experienced and respected stock-and-station agent John Gilfoyle once went to inspect a mob of Lake Nash heifers, and wrote in his semi-autobiographical *Bloody Agents!*:

> What an eye opener? We drove out to the bore where a big mob of cherry red Santa Gertrudis heifers was being held up by the station camp. There seemed to be a lot of them.
>
> I asked the manager, 'How many are there?'
>
> 'About three.'
>
> I took that to mean three thousand. I had never seen 3000 cattle in one mob before, or since, let alone 3000 one age, one brand, one breed. (*Reproduced by kind permission of John Gilfoyle*)

When Lake Nash Station wanted to restock, it was never going to be a small operation. Early in 2009, the owners decided they wanted 6000 breeder heifers. That's a lot of cattle in any day and age, and getting them to Lake Nash from central Queensland, 1300 kilometres away, presented quite a challenge. Trucking them was out of the question. It was decided to drove them.

The station owners turned to one of the few drovers left in the business in Queensland, Bill Prow. Bill was still taking a couple of mobs a year from stations out west and knew the stock routes well.

By June he was on the road with the lead mob of 2000 heifers, travelling from Tambo through Winton, across to Boulia, then up the Georgina. Behind him were two more mobs of between 1500 and 2000 head, one with a young drover named Nathan Cooper, the other with drover Peter Little.

The trip took three months, travelling at an easy pace so the cattle would put on condition. Along the way the cattle became accustomed to feeding along and having people around them all day, which would make them quiet and easily handled by the time they reached the station. The other benefit of droving was that the cost compared favourably with trucking the cattle. And it was good fresh feed all the way.

'This is the first time we've headed north for a change,' Bill told ABC rural reporter Amy Phillips while on the road in June. 'Last year we had two mobs, one from Kynuna Station and one from Bull Creek, and we all went south. This year we're heading north so it is very uncommon. It makes organising where we set up camp a bit interesting, because I know the stock route very well, but you have to think for a change.' (*Reproduced by permission of the Australian Broadcasting Corporation and ABC Online.©2009 ABC. All rights reserved.*)

In September 2009, when I was travelling over part of the route Bill had taken a few months earlier, I came across a mob of Brahman cattle feeding along just outside Winton. They were being droved on horseback by two stockmen – one a man, the other a woman. Later that month, in central New South Wales, I came across a mob of sheep feeding along the road between Trangie and Warren. Recalling the observations of Darryl Horkings regarding the intelligence of sheep, quoted in Chapter 11, it made good sense to slow right down. While doing so, it was hard not to reflect that reports of droving's demise may yet prove to be premature.

Not far from Lake Nash, and only a few months after the station took delivery of its 6000 heifers, the small outback town of Camooweal held its annual Drovers Camp Festival. One hundred or more drovers from all over Australia journeyed to the town that was once the crossroads of some of Australia's greatest stock routes, the starting or finishing point for droving trips of thousands of kilometres and of three to six months or more in duration.

More than 150 drovers are members of the drovers' association that runs the festival and was formed in 1997 to preserve the memories of an era when thousands of livestock travelled the length and breadth of the land. A museum at the Drovers Camp contains files on many of the men and women who spent their lives behind mobs of cattle, sheep and horses. A gallery of paintings ensures that the faces of many will endure for years to come.

Even as the number of drovers diminishes each year, interest in droving continues to grow. Although many drovers are now in their seventies or eighties, membership of the Drovers Camp is increasing as more people from across Australia become aware of its existence. Many of the hundreds of visitors to the festival are there not just because they're passing through. They've arranged their holidays to coincide with it.

One of the main purposes of the festival is for old drovers to get together and reminisce about old times. Some are more than willing to talk to strangers about their experiences; others are reticent or feel they have nothing new to add to what has already been said or written on the subject. Sometimes, in the course of researching this book, the best approach was to stop asking questions, shut up and listen. Given time, the stories came.

In 2004 Liz Flood and her husband Col moved to Camooweal from Mount Isa to become volunteer caretakers of the Drovers Camp facilities and museum. Col was seventy-three and had just retired. Although she wasn't a drover herself, Liz was elected president of the Drovers Camp and she's held that role ever since. She runs the camp and festival on a voluntary basis, and spends much of her time between festivals compiling the stories of the drovers who belong to the organisation. When asked why our droving heritage is worth preserving, she replied:

> You look at the harsh conditions of the country. I drive home from Mount Isa in the summer and it's 46 degrees in the shade, and those fellas on horseback, in extreme weather conditions, I take my hat off to them. You get out on the Barkly Tableland and there's no trees in sight, it's just open plains. And in the winter you get the cold winds from the south-east that go straight through you. Being on the road and living the way they did, it wasn't easy.
>
> They're genuine, sincere old fellas. There's some that can be larrikins but they're just a different breed of people. They don't like accolades. They're a humble mob. The majority who were up here came from along the east coast, down inside, but at fourteen years of age. Some were only sixteen and in charge of a mob of 1600 head, 2000 head of cattle. You wouldn't do that now. They're just a different breed.

Now that the researching and writing of this book is complete, I still find it hard to reconcile the way drovers see themselves with the aura of fame others have given them. While they shrug and say, 'We were only doing a job,' our greatest poets have extolled their virtues. They're the subjects of paintings and films. The drovers' achievements have been etched into the landscape from one side of the country to the other, and are inextricably linked to Australia's sense of identity.

The drovers may see themselves as ordinary people, but their story shows they were capable of doing extraordinary things.

REFERENCES

Prologue
Historical Research Ltd, *Heritage of the Birdsville and Strzelecki Tracks*, South Australian Department for Environment and Heritage, Adelaide, 2002.

Chapter 1 – Follow the Cattle
Cunningham, Chris, *The Blue Mountains Rediscovered*, Kangaroo Press, Kenthurst, 1996.
Loney, Jack, and Stone, Peter, *Australian Shipwrecks: The Australia Run*, Reed, Sydney, 1972.
McHugh, Evan, *Outback Pioneers*, Penguin Books, Melbourne, 2008.
Watson, F. (ed), *Historical Records of Australia*, Library Committee of the Commonwealth Parliament, Sydney, 1915.

Chapter 2 – The Overlanders
Kain, Kevin, *The First Overlanders*, Gould Books, Ridgehaven, 1991.

McHugh, Evan, *Outback Heroes*, Penguin Books, Melbourne, 2005.

Mollison, Alexander Fullerton, *An Overlanding Diary*, Mast Gully Press, Melbourne, 1980.

Chapter 3 – The High Country

Alpine Grazing Taskforce, *Report of the Investigation into the Future of Grazing in the Alpine National Park*, Victorian Government, 2005.

Barker, Hector, *Droving Days*, Hesperian Press, Carlisle, 1994.

Brodribb, William, *Recollections of an Australian Squatter*, John Woods & Co., Sydney, 1883.

Carmody, Jean, *Early Days of the Upper Murray*, Shoestring Press, Wangaratta, 1981.

Hueneke, Klaus, *People of the Australian High Country*, Tabletop Press, Palmerston, 1997.

Kosciuszko Huts Association, www.kosciuszkohuts.org.au/history.html.

Larkins, John, *Story of the Snowy Mountains, Its History and People*, Reed, Sydney, 1980.

Lhotsky, John, *A Journey from Sydney to the Australian Alps*, J. Innes, Sydney, 1935.

Merritt, John, *Losing Ground: Grazing in the Snowy Mountains, 1944–1969*, Turalla Press, Canberra, 2007.

Mountain Cattlemen's Association of Victoria, Submission to the 2009 Victorian Bushfires Royal Commission, MCAV, Rosedale, 2009.

O'Connor, Maura, 'Mapping Australia's Transhumance: Snow lease and stock route maps of NSW', *The Globe*, Issue 56, 2005, pp. 13–24.

Peck, Harry, *Memoirs of a Stockman*, Stockland Press, Melbourne, 1942.

Chapter 4 – The Road Less Travelled

'On the Queensland Border: Life in the Interior', *Advertiser*, Adelaide, Saturday 25 April 1914, p. 7.

Costello, Michael, *The Life of John Costello*, Dymocks Book Arcade, Sydney, 1930.

Eyre, Edward, *Journals of Expeditions of Discovery into Central Australia*, T. and W. Boone, London, 1845.

Farwell, George, *Land of Mirage*, Cassell, Sydney, 1950.

Historical Research Pty Ltd, *Heritage of the Birdsville and Strzelecki Tracks*, South Australian Department for Environment and Heritage, Adelaide, 2002.

Litchfield, Lois, *Marree and the Tracks Beyond*, L. Litchfield, Marree, 1983.

Madigan, Cecil, *Crossing the Dead Heart*, Georgian House, Melbourne, 1946.

McHugh, Evan, *Outback Heroes*, Penguin Books, Melbourne, 2005.

———, *Red Centre, Dark Heart*, Penguin Books, Melbourne, 2009.

Tolcher, Helen, *Conrick of Nappa Merrie*, Helen Tolcher, Linden Park, 1997.

Chapter 5 – The Great North Road

Giles, Alfred, *Exploring in the Seventies*, W.K. Thomas, Adelaide, 1926.

Hill, Ernestine, *The Territory*, Angus & Robertson, Sydney, 1951.

Historical Research Pty Ltd, *Heritage of the Birdsville and Strzelecki Tracks*, South Australian Department for Environment and Heritage, Adelaide, 2002.

Litchfield, Lois, *Marree and the Tracks Beyond*, L. Litchfield, Marree, 1983.

McHugh, Evan, *Outback Heroes*, Penguin Books, Melbourne, 2005.

Chapter 6 – Twenty Thousand to the Territory

Buchanan, Bobbie, *In the Tracks of Old Bluey*, Central Queensland University Press, Rockhampton, 1997.

Buchanan, Gordon, *Packhorse and Waterhole*, Angus & Robertson, Sydney, 1933.

———, 'Pioneers of the Far North', *Stock and Station Journal*, various issues January–February 1922.

'Pastoral Occupation of Northern Territory', *Northern Territory Times and Gazette*, Saturday 4 June 1881, p. 3.

Chapter 7 – The Birdsville Track

Advertiser, Adelaide, 13 and 14 August 1957.

Courier-Mail, Brisbane, 1–4 January 1964.

Farwell, George, *Land of Mirage*, Cassell, Sydney, 1950.

Historical Research Pty Ltd, H*eritage of the Birdsville and Strzelecki Tracks*, South Australian Department for Environment and Heritage, Adelaide, 2002.

Litchfield, Lois, *Marree and the Tracks Beyond*, L. Litchfield, Marree, 1983.

Madigan, Cecil, *Crossing the Dead Heart*, Georgian House, Melbourne, 1946.

Mintern, Tex, 'A Cattle-man Gives a First-hand Account of One of Australia's Most Arduous Jobs', *The Argus Weekend*, 15 November 1939, p. 1.

Chapter 8 – The Murranji

Buchanan, Bobbie, *In the Tracks of Old Bluey*, Central Queensland University Press, Rockhampton, 1997.

Buchanan, Gordon, *Packhorse and Waterhole*, Angus and Robertson, Sydney, 1933.

———, 'Pioneers of the Far North', *Stock and Station Journal*, various issues January–February 1922.

Hill, Ernestine, *The Territory*, Angus & Robertson, Sydney, 1951.

Lewis, Darrell, *The Murranji Track, Ghost Road of the Drovers*, Central Queensland University Press, Rockhampton, 2007.

Lunney, Bob, *1500 Down The Murranji*, Crawford House, Adelaide, 1998.

Stuart, John McDouall, *Explorations In Australia*, Saunders, Otley & Co., London, 1864.

Chapter 9 – Canning's Folly

Canning, Alfred, *Report to WA Mines Department*, 10 January 1907.

Gard, Ronele and Eric, *Canning Stock Route: A Traveller's Guide* (3rd edition), Western Desert Guides, Wembley Downs, 2009.

Hewitt, David (ed.), *Australian Geographic Book of the Canning Stock Route*, Australian Geographic, Sydney, 1998.

Smith, Eleanor, *The Beckoning West: The Story of H. S. Trotman and the Canning Stock Route*, St George Books, Perth, 1966.

Chapter 10 – She was a Good Man

Barker, Hector, *Droving Days*, Hesperian Press, Carlisle, 1994.

Buchanan, Gordon, *Packhorse and Waterhole*, Angus & Robertson, Sydney, 1933.

Farwell, George, *Land of Mirage*, Cassell, Sydney, 1950.

Idriess, Ion, *Flynn of the Inland*, Angus & Robertson, Sydney, 1932.

Mahood, Marie, *Legends of the Outback*, Central Queensland University Press, Rockhampton, 2002.

Troughton, Elwyn, *Red Jack*, self-published, Mareeba, 1995.

Williams, R. M., *Beneath Whose Hand*, Macmillan, Melbourne, 1984.

———, *I Once Met a Man*, Angus & Robertson, Sydney, 1989.

Epilogue

Gilfoyle, John, *Bloody Agents!*, self-published, Roma, 2005.

Phillips, Amy, *Droving Backwards*, ABC Rural, broadcast 10 June 2009.

BIRDSVILLE: MY YEAR IN THE BACK OF BEYOND

Evan McHugh

For a town with seventy residents (on a good day), Birdsville is remarkably well known – the Birdsville Track, the rodeo, the pub, the infamous races. With its ruggedness, inaccessibility and larrikin charm, this small town on the edge of the Simpson Desert has become a symbol of the great Australian outback.

What is it about Birdsville that has made it stand so large in our legends? And what's it like to live there amongst the floods and the heat and the dust storms?

To find out, Evan McHugh packed up his Sydney home, bought a four-wheel-drive and headed off with his wife for a year in the back of beyond. Here, he tells us of the large adventures – midnight desert rescues, aerial mustering on vast cattle stations, relentless heat and massive floods – but also the small details of life in one of Australia's most isolated towns, like driving 700 kilometres to go shopping. As the months fly by, Evan learns about an ancient culture, sees dunes carpeted in millions of tiny wildflowers and meets the members of an outback community facing extraordinary challenges with quiet determination and buckets of good humour.

Birdsville is about the breathtaking beauty and harshness of this country, the generosity of its salt-of-the-earth people and one man's discovery of his own reserves of courage and resilience.

'McHugh is a clever mixture of curious outsider and eager participant . . . Written in a simple but elegant style where honesty and thoughtfulness build an accurate picture of the richness of life in one of Australia's most famous outback towns.' THE AGE

OUTBACK PIONEERS

Evan McHugh

In *Outback Pioneers*, Evan McHugh gathers the enthralling stories of the men and women who opened up the Australian outback and in the process discovered the beauty and terror of this extraordinary country.

We meet the little-known convict explorer John Wilson, the first European to cross the Blue Mountains (though history favours the proper English gentlemen Blaxland, Wentworth and Lawson); we follow Australia's greatest drover, Nat Buchanan, as he blazes stock routes from one side of the country to another; and we marvel at the genius and grit of the men who overcome political treachery to build the Coolgardie Pipeline and the Trans-Australian Railway.

There are some delightful inclusions: a gentle Pakistani cameleer who saves foolhardy expeditioners, a nerdy ham radio operator who invents the pedal radio and paves the way for John Flynn's Flying Doctor, two bush nurses who toil in the ruins of a pub while saving outback lives and the modern-day pioneers who battle apathy to save endangered wildlife.

'A fascinating collection of stories about our lesser-known achievers.'
SYDNEY MORNING HERALD

Red Centre, Dark Heart

Evan McHugh

Journey into Australia's heart of darkness, where life is lived by a different set of rules and it is easy for criminals to disappear into the vast landscape – and yet it can be difficult to remain anonymous. The worst aspects of human nature reveal themselves in the red centre.

Beginning with the chilling tale of convict and cannibal Alexander Pearce, *Red Centre, Dark Heart* explores historic and recent true-crime in the outback, including the Belango State Forest murders and the disappearance of Peter Falconio. Read these stories and you'll discover that Australia's dark heart is frighteningly close to home.

'It's enough to make you run for the beach.'
Sunday Herald Sun